Serve and Protect

Serve and **Protect**

Selected Essays on Just Policing

Tobias Winright

FOREWORD BY
Todd Whitmore

CASCADE *Books* • Eugene, Oregon

SERVE AND PROTECT
Selected Essays on Just Policing

Copyright © 2020 Tobias Winright. All rights reserved. Except for brief quotations in critical publications or reviews, no part of this book may be reproduced in any manner without prior written permission from the publisher. Write: Permissions, Wipf and Stock Publishers, 199 W. 8th Ave., Suite 3, Eugene, OR 97401.

Cascade Books
An Imprint of Wipf and Stock Publishers
199 W. 8th Ave., Suite 3
Eugene, OR 97401

www.wipfandstock.com

PAPERBACK ISBN: 978-1-7252-5391-9
HARDCOVER ISBN: 978-1-7252-5392-6
EBOOK ISBN: 978-1-7252-5393-3

Cataloguing-in-Publication data:

Names: Winright, Tobias L., author. | Whitmore, Todd, 1957–, foreword.

Title: Serve and protect : selected essays on just policing / by Tobias Winright ; foreword by Todd Whitmore.

Description: Eugene, OR : Cascade Books, 2020 | Includes bibliographical references and index.

Identifiers: ISBN 978-1-7252-5391-9 (paperback) | ISBN 978-1-7252-5392-6 (hardcover) | ISBN 978-1-7252-5393-3 (ebook)

Subjects: LCSH: Peace—Religious aspects—Christianity. | War—Religious aspects—Christianity. | Pacifism—Religious aspects—Christianity. | Just war doctrine.

Classification: BT736.4 .W56 2020 (print) | BT736.4 .W56 (ebook)

"Militarized Policing: The History of the Warrior Cop" from *Christian Century* 131, no. 19 (September 17, 2014) 10–12, is reprinted by permission from the *Christian Century.*

"Demilitarize the Police!" from *Sojourners* 43, no. 11 (December 2014) 10–11, is reprinted with permission from *Sojourners*, (800) 714-7474, www.sojo.net.

Manufactured in the U.S.A.   11/11/20

Dedicated to my mother, Patricia A. Juhl, who became a police officer during the 1970s and retired as a deputy sheriff and homicide detective after a distinguished career, including being awarded in 1991 as Finalist for the Florida Sheriffs Association's Deputy Sheriff of the Year. If it weren't for her, these pages probably would never have been written in the first place.

The basic mission for which police exist is to prevent crime and disorder as an alternative to the repression of crime and disorder by military force . . . .

—Sir Robert Peel

Contents

Foreword

No Christian ethicist in the last twenty-five years has thought and written more about the ethics of policing than Tobias Winright. Until now, this treasure trove of insight and analysis has been scattered as articles within a wide array of journals and periodicals, from *Criminal Justice Ethics* and the *FBI Law Enforcement Bulletin* to the *Journal of the Society of Christian Ethics* and *Christian Century* magazine, and as chapters in various anthologies and books. While many Christian ethicists write about questions of ethics in various professions, Professor Winright also has written *to* those professionals in their own professional journals. It should come as no surprise, then, that before he was a scholar, Professor Winright was a law enforcement officer, in both corrections and patrol. In other words, well before the current interest in ethnographic fieldwork as a method for doing Christian ethics took off, Professor Winright was doing his own "participant observation," and doing so very much as an insider. Therefore, what he puts forward is not just an exercise in academic theorizing, but is also, as stated in the first essay in this volume, a "helpful tool to which law enforcement agencies may refer during the hiring and screening process, as well as during academy training." This is not mere posturing. Professor Winright has taught ethics courses at two police academies.

It gets even more personal: in his law enforcement training, Professor Winright qualified as a shotgun sharpshooter. He also received training in riot control. Noteworthy, too, then, is that, other than in target practice, Professor/Officer Winright never fired his weapon. This is a person who knows from the inside both the demands of the job and the requirement of restraint. His writings display a deep concern about the over-militarization of the police force. While, as the first essay in the volume argues, there are analogues between the "just war theory" designed for the military and the restraints necessary for good policing, there is also a strong disanalogy: citizens should not be viewed as enemies. As Professor Winright puts it in the last essay, the "military or crime fighter model alienates the police from the public, often leading to the dehumanization of the very people that police are pledged to serve and protect." It should neither be a surprise, then, that he has taught a university course, "Black Theology and Social Change," for over twenty years, most recently at Saint Louis University, where one of his students was a leader in the Black Lives Matter movement. A number of Professor Winright's friends in the clergy were among the Ferguson protesters.

The lacuna in Christian writing on the ethics of policing, once noted, can be baffling. There has been significant attention to issues in the criminal justice system such as capital punishment and prison reform/abolition, but, other than in the writings of Professor Winright (who has also been published on these other criminal justice issues), there has been almost no work on the question of policing, particularly as it pertains to the use of force. Professor Winright is the perfect person to have stepped into this gap. His treatment of police ethics demonstrates a deep knowledge both of the history of policing and of current practices. Historically he points out how industrialization and urbanization led to modern conceptions of policing that stress crime fighting in a manner closely associated with the military. With regard to contemporary practices, he highlights an alternative model, that of "social peacekeeping," also known as "community policing," which has included (and continues to do so in various ways) "traffic control, the prevention of cruelty to children and animals, finding missing persons, the care of the poor and destitute, extinguishing fires, the inspection of weights, bridges and buildings, and even waking people up for work." Such passages highlight the fact that in addition to having firsthand experience of being an officer of the law, Professor Winright brings a scholar's breadth of historical and theoretical knowledge to the question of policing.

Professor Winright, both in person and in writing, is at once vigilant and patient, deeply moral and aware of the ambiguities that can arise in charged situations in life. There is no better person to write this book.

Todd Whitmore

Acknowledgments

B ecause this book contains essays I wrote and published as peer-reviewed journal articles, book chapters, and popular opinion pieces spanning nearly twenty-five years, there are many persons and publishers I should acknowledge. I am indebted to my professors who challenged me to think about ethics and, specifically, the ethics of the use of force in law enforcement. Of course, this does not mean that we always have agreed, but my thinking over the years owes much to them. Any remaining faults and errors on my part (I'm still learning) are mine and should not be attributed to anyone else. I am especially grateful to my undergraduate advisor at the University of South Florida St. Petersburg, Regis A. Factor (1937–99); my Duke Divinity School ethics professors, Harmon L. Smith and Stanley Hauerwas; and my University of Notre Dame ethics professors, Todd Whitmore, Jean Porter, Maura Ryan, M. Cathleen Kaveny, Richard A. McCormick, SJ (1922–2000), and John Howard Yoder (1927–97). Catholic ethicist Edward A. Malloy, CSC, who was president of the University of Notre Dame at that time, also warrants mention for his own preliminary work on law enforcement ethics and for his encouragement to me for pursuing the subject. Classmates and peers at Duke and Notre Dame who read early drafts of some of these essays, or who were conversation partners—and who, as true friends, offered honest, helpful feedback back then and over the years—include H. David Baer, James Ball, Michael Baxter, Daniel M. Bell, Jr., Rebekkah Brodhacker, Lee Camp, Joseph Capizzi, William T. Cavanaugh, Neve Gordon, Laurie Jordan, D. Stephen Long, Maria (Malkiewicz) Pitt (1972–2019), William C. Mattison III, Margaret Pfeil, Tom Poundstone, Gerald W. Schlabach, Michael S. Sherwin, OP, and David Weiss. I thank God for putting me in such good company.

I would add that Todd Whitmore deserves extra appreciation for his supervision of my PhD dissertation and for his generous foreword to this present volume of selected essays. He is a mentor who has never let me down. My gratitude, too, goes to Wipf & Stock's staff and editors, including Charlie Collier and Rodney Clapp, who for a long time have expressed interest in my work and helped to bring it to fruition with this collection.

The chapters of this book first appeared elsewhere. In the first footnote on the first page of each chapter, the original citation is provided, both to acknowledge the publisher and to remind the reader when it was initially published, giving it context. Although permission was not needed to re-print these essays, since this present volume is an assemblage of my own works, I am nonetheless thankful to the following journals and periodicals: *Criminal Justice Ethics*, the *Journal of the Society of Christian Ethics*, *Ecumenical Review*, the *Journal of Military Ethics*, the *Christian Century*, *Sojourners*, and *Religious Education*.

In addition, my graduate assistant, Addison Tenorio, diligently and promptly formatted these chapters. Thank you, Addison! Finally, as always, I owe so much to my wife, Liz, and my daughters Clare and Lydia, who put up with my work and all that it entails.

Introduction

On August 9th, 2014, in Ferguson, a town on the outskirts of the city where I live, St. Louis, Missouri, eighteen-year-old Michael Brown and a friend were walking in the middle of a two-lane street when police officer Darren Wilson drove by and told them to use the sidewalk. Heated words were exchanged and then the situation spiraled out of control between the white officer and the black young man. In the end, Wilson shot and killed Brown, who was unarmed, leading to months of protests and demonstrations as well as a heavily militarized police response—not only in Ferguson but also in my neighborhood and others in the city of St. Louis, including on the campus of Saint Louis University, where I teach theological and health-care ethics.

I felt compelled to write about what I saw happening, and many of my friends and colleagues locally and elsewhere were asking what I thought, given my previous experience in law enforcement—mainly in corrections but also later in patrol—and my scholarly research and publications on policing and the use of force. So I wrote a short piece that I sent to my friend Richard Kauffman, who at the time was an editor for the *Christian Century* magazine, and it appeared soon online and subsequently as the cover story for the September 17th print edition as "Militarized Policing: The History of the Warrior Cop." On the front page of that issue there was an eye-catching portrait of a police officer armed and garbed much more like a military soldier. It garnered a lot of attention, including from the White House and the US Department of Justice, which invited me to participate in conference calls with US Attorney General Eric Holder, Valerie Jarrett, who was senior advisor to President Barack Obama, and other experts, community and religious leaders. That article is chapter 7 of this present book.

Since Ferguson there have been many—far too many—more such shootings by police officers around the country, not only ending the lives of fellow citizens—a disproportionate number being persons of color—but also ruining the careers and, I suspect, scarring the psychological, moral, and spiritual health of those who swore an oath once upon a time to "serve and protect" and who pulled the trigger. When I wore a uniform and a badge, I wrestled with questions about the use of force. As a Christian, I felt that there was a tension between the use of force, especially lethal force, and my identity as a follower of Jesus Christ. When I began to search for explicit treatments of this subject by theological ethicists, however, I found that very few had attempted to address policing. To be sure, during the past two millennia, many theologians, bishops, and ethicists wrote about violence and nonviolence, war and peace, but mostly connected with either personal, one-on-one altercations or to large-scale military conflicts. And in relation to criminal-justice issues, their attention focused predominantly on prisons, restorative justice, and the death penalty. The lack of a serious—other than brief and incidental—treatment of police use of force led me to write a research paper on it, in which I argued that the ethical framework, criteria, and mode of reasoning of traditional just-war theory is applicable and helpful as an analogue. The course for which I wrote that paper during the spring of 1994 was on moral methods and just war, and it was taught by John Howard Yoder. The next year it became my first peer-reviewed scholarly article, appearing as "The Perpetrator as Person: Theological Reflections on the Just War Tradition and the Use of Force by Police" in the journal *Criminal Justice Ethics*, which at the time was edited by philosopher and criminal justice ethicist John Kleinig, whose work appears prominently in my own to this day. That article is chapter 1 of this book.

My PhD dissertation, "The Challenge of Policing: A Christian Social Analysis," which was the first that Todd Whitmore graciously agreed to supervise at Notre Dame, was successfully defended in 2002, but I never published it in its entirety—only portions as articles and book chapters over the years, usually in academic journals and texts. When Ferguson happened, I realized that many of my colleagues and peers in theological ethics, who were now deeply concerned about police shootings that seemed unjustified, and about police brutality and excessive force, were bereft of the moral resources to apply to these matters. Although I had written extensively about this topic since 1995, much of it can be difficult to find or obtain. Plus my thinking on the subject, although it has been evidently constant, has continued to develop, especially in recent years. As will be evident in the essays I selected to be included in this volume, I consistently rely on the contributions of Edward Malloy, John Kleinig, Ralph Potter, Paul Ramsey, and James Childress for the ethical evaluation of the use of force by police in a way that is analogous to the moral approach we employ for the use of force by nations and their militaries in war. In either case, such use of force must be morally justified and morally conducted. In other words, just as there are just and unjust wars, there is just and unjust policing. The use of the adverb *just* before the verb policing in this book's subtitle is thus an invocation of the virtue of justice.

Of course, a lot hinges on which version of just-war theory we have in mind, since there are more than one circulating in recent decades (see chapter 2). Moreover, having studied with two of the most influential pacifist theologians in recent history—Yoder and Hauerwas—I have also taken nonviolence seriously, been challenged by it, and have even considered it, not only personally but also vis-à-vis policing (chapter 3).

This core thesis about the relevance of just-war ethics to just-policing ethics runs throughout these essays. It yields, I have argued, fruitful application to other related questions, including: whether a military preemptive strike, rather than preventive war, is ever justified (chapter 4); whether the responsibility to protect (R2P) norm espoused by the United Nations this century is a stricter application of just-war theory that is akin to just policing (chapter 5); and whether the police should play a role, and if so, how, in post-war settings (chapter 6). Thus the subtitle's adverb *just* does not mean the book deals *only* with policing.

Because some of the fundamental groundwork appears more than once in some of these chapters, readers do not have to begin with the first one and read them in chronological order. They should feel free to begin reading whichever chapter seems most relevant to their interests. On the other hand, I believe that astute readers who read this book from front cover to back will detect some developments in my thinking over the last twenty-five years (as well as in my writing style; I'm now a bit embarrassed about its "graduate student" tone in the earliest essays). Chapters 7 and 8, of course, were written for a wider, more popular audience, and they were more recently done in the aftermath of Ferguson. Chapter 9, which concludes the collection, represents my most recent take on the subject, reflecting both continuities with my previous efforts and initial connections to other areas of concern regarding policing. Speaking of audience, these essays sometimes sought to address a wider, more public audience, or a criminal justice audience, or a more theological and Christian audience—or sometimes, all the above.

Indeed, I am working on a new book on *Just and Unjust Policing* that will plow fresh ground, not only on the use of force, but also on issues such as racial profiling and deception. I regard the present volume, *Serve and Protect*, as setting the stage for this next project. I should note, too, that my use of the word "selected" in this book's subtitle implies that there are more extant articles and book chapters. If interested, these are included in the bibliography towards the end of the book. Also, if anyone is curious about my writings on other criminal-justice issues, such as prisons and the death penalty, they remain as articles and book chapters, and as such have yet to be pulled together as these on policing now are. I will add this to my "to do" list.[1]

Before closing this introduction, I should follow the example of my friend Gerald Schlabach, who in his recently published book *A Pilgrim People: Becoming a Catholic Peace Church* refers to the need to "turn to that more freighted acknowledgment of my debt to the late John Howard Yoder, one of my teachers . . . [whose] legacy is rightly suspect—as in, subject to trenchant hermeneutics of suspicion—due to his now-well-documented sexual abuse, which he used his brilliant theological mind to rationalize."[2] Like Schlabach, I have really struggled with what to do with our teacher's work and how it has informed my own; and like Schlabach, I have written about this scandal elsewhere.[3] In the chapters that follow, I felt that I must retain all of the references to Yoder's work. It's been painful, although nowhere close to the suffering of the women whom he violated sexually. Still, readers should be able to discern less, if any, mention of Yoder in the more recent essays appearing towards the latter part of this volume. His stamp on my thinking is undeniable, and I acknowledge it. Its presence continues, too, but more beneath the surface.

---

1. In the meantime, two recent articles are Winright, "Matter of Degrees," which is about an associate's degree program that Saint Louis University offers in a state prison and that is offered both to inmates and—my idea, given my own background—to officers and staff, all of whom tend to come from socioeconomic backgrounds lacking access to higher education, and Winright, "Pope Francis on Capital Punishment: A Closer Look," which examines the pope's contribution to the development of Catholic teaching on the death penalty.

2. Schlabach, *Pilgrim People*, xiv.

3. Winright, "I Was John Howard Yoder's Graduate Assistant: Should I Still Use His Work?"

These earlier essays are a record of it, and the more recent ones reflect the direction I am headed at this time.

In short, I have left these essays pretty much untouched. I felt that they should be read in the form they were originally published. Readers should be able to get a sense of the concerns I was attempting to address at the time. In a few places, I added something to a footnote, for instance, an update on the latest data on police shootings, or I corrected some erroneous grammar that somehow slipped by an editor earlier. I also deleted some material that seemed superfluous, but did so sparingly since some readers might not read the book from beginning to end. Otherwise, these essays are almost exactly as they were when originally published elsewhere. It is my hope especially that Christians and others who are—or who are considering becoming—police officers find them useful, that clergy and chaplains who provide pastoral care and counseling to such Christians also benefit from them as a resource, and that my colleagues and peers in the field of theological ethics will join me in continuing this important conversation.

Chapter One

The Perpetrator as Person

Theological Reflections on the Just-War Tradition
and the Use of Force by Police[1]

S ince the end of the Cold War, much of the attention of citizens and
politicians in the United States has swiveled inward upon other issues
of life and death, in particular the crime and violence on their own streets.
Cries for action in this domestic arena appear to be growing, as evidenced
by the past decade's call to arms in a so-called war against drugs and by
Washington's recent, torrid advocacy for a crime bill and for more police officers in the "war" against crime. Indeed, such trends have led one observer
to remark, "We are a nation at war with ourselves: a civil war. The war of law
enforcement against the forces of crime."[2] At the same time, however, several highly publicized incidents have provoked public alarm and scrutiny;
therefore, reflection and assessment are called for to consider whether and
how this kind of "war" ought to be waged.

One notorious incident involved an African-American male named
Rodney King. While driving on the evening of March 3, 1991, King was
pulled over by, and had a confrontation with, Los Angeles police officers,
who proceeded to arrest him on a number of charges. On the surface this
sort of incident occurs frequently and could have been reported as a routine
traffic arrest, except for the additional fact that it was filmed by a bystander
with a video camera. Indeed, the video showed all who watched the replays
on the news media how several of fifteen uniformed officers repeatedly
beat, bruised, and lacerated King. Although shocking to many Americans,
one criminal-justice expert notes, "That beating was not unique in the

1. Originally published in *Criminal Justice Ethics* 14.2 (1995) 37–56.
2. Elias, "Taking Crime Seriously," 131.

1

history of policing. It probably has kin in every state in the Union, in every country, and indeed in every significant police force as far back as we can trace the police function."[3]

To be sure, considering the prevalence of violence in our culture, and given the rote adoption of the "war" model or paradigm for law enforcement by the government, such incidents are likely to be less rare. In fact, researchers estimate that police officers kill about 600 criminal suspects yearly, shoot and wound an additional 1,200, and fire at and miss another 1,800.[4] This being the case, the issue of the use of force, especially deadly force, by law enforcement officials in the performance of their duties deserves vigilant scrutiny. How are such uses of force justified and restrained? Is there a uniform approach? What model for restraint would be most appropriate for law enforcement in the United States? If police forces are in a "war" against crime, how do they determine when to use force and when it is excessive? What can prevent another Rodney King incident from happening? Is there a way to restrain the use of force among our police, and if so, what is the ethical basis?

Such questions are certainly formidable and are attracting, in the light of incidents like King's, burgeoning attention from social scientists, criminologists, and increasingly, philosophers. For example, criminal-justice ethicist Lawrence Sherman proposes that, on the one hand, many issues in police ethics are "in fact clear-cut, and hold little room for serious political analysis," while on the other hand, the use of force deserves such attention since it is "very complex, with many shades of gray."[5] Furthermore, Sherman asserts, "The most basic question of all criminal justice ethics, of course, is whether and under what conditions one can reconcile doing harm to others with our widespread norms against harm."[6] At this juncture, he muses that the literature on pacifism, nonviolence, and conscientious objection may be relevant, but adds that he has unfortunately not seen such an approach applied to the domestic use of force by police. Moreover, he queries, "Can a pacifist be a police officer or a judge? Can

3. Davis, "Do Cops Really Need a Code of Ethics?" 14.

4. Loftus et al., "'Reasonable' Approach to Excessive Force Cases," 136. *The Washington Post* now has a database showing how many persons are shot and killed annually by police in the United States, and the numbers are higher than what I found when I originally wrote this article in the early 1990s: 994 in 2015, 962 in 2016, 986 in 2017, and 992 in 2018 (see "Fatal Force").

5. Sherman, "Learning Police Ethics," 19.

6. Sherman, *Ethics in Criminal Justice Education*, 38.

THE PERPETRATOR AS PERSON

a Christian? Can a Rawlsian? What is the ethical defense for saying that killing is wrong and then urging killing in response to killing?"[7] These are profound questions, deserving of sober reflection.

In fact, these are the sort of considerations that usually fall within the purview of ethicists, including moral theologians, except that the latter group has failed to broach seriously this particular topic in relation to law enforcement. Indeed, the history of Christian thought is replete with theological wrestlings with such life-shaking issues as war and peace, abortion and euthanasia; and yet, oddly, the dilemma of the use of force by police officers appears to have been a theological blindspot, which is all the more intriguing given that probably as many persons in recent years have found themselves struggling over precisely this issue, for surely there are many police officers who are also Christians.

Indeed, vividly etched in my memory is a question posed by a panelist during my own oral board interview within the application process for a position with a local law enforcement agency: "Would your Christian faith hinder or prevent you from a performance of duty, such as shooting to kill an alleged perpetrator?" I cannot recall what provoked this query, but I do remember that I was at a loss as to how to respond. Indeed, I had struggled with this question, but the Bible and the official church statements—the usual authoritative sources for Christian ethical guidance—were silent about this concrete issue, although the Bible does discuss the one-on-one situation of turning the other cheek, and the church's tradition includes just-war theory. What I did, therefore, was to build a bridge from church teaching concerning just-war principles to the context of law enforcement, and I was thereby enabled to respond "no" to the panelist's question, given that I believed that the agency's policies were in line with the attitude of restraint which undergirds just-war thinking.

Hence, in view of both the present, general need for further, sustained ethical reflection concerning the use of force in our society, and the surprising dearth of serious attention to this in theological circles, my aim in this essay is to provide a three-pronged theological contribution to the present discussion. First, attention will be given to the age-old wealth of ethical reflection concerning the use of force—putatively oriented toward restraint in the use of force—known as the just-war tradition, as a background against which the use of force in law enforcement may be scrutinized and evaluated. In other words, the objective here will be to amplify current

---

7. Sherman, *Ethics in Criminal Justice Education*, 38.

reflection on such use of force and the adequacy of present normative judgments about it by bringing to bear the rich resources offered in the history of Christian thought. Critical efforts to restrain violence are not recent developments, but have antecedents in history, especially among theologians. This is not to say that this venue is richer or clearer than Kantian, Rawlsian, or other approaches being tapped today, but it does add a deeper historical and intellectual dimension, which may even underlie, at least implicitly, the more modern perspectives. Moreover, I do not intend some kind of "institutionalizing" of Christian belief. Rather, since most Christian proponents of just-war theory have held that it involves general, essential moral norms which are regarded as applicable to all human persons *as human persons* (instead of viewing just-war theory as an essentially Christian ethic, whereby a Christian makes decisions precisely because he or she belongs to a community which makes moral demands upon the Christian *as Christian*), the following reflections ought to inform the general discussion in the same way that moral theologians have been able to contribute to the public debate concerning war or bioethics.[8]

Secondly, since the just-war tradition itself has been adopted, advanced, and advocated by most Christians throughout the history of Christianity, I intend for this essay to furnish needed Christian theological input concerning the use of force in law enforcement. Indeed, it is precisely because of the fact that law enforcement may provide a better context for legitimate application of central tenets or core concepts of just-war thinking, especially concerning the basic underlying presumption against harm, that I hope to provide Christians involved in law enforcement a basis for reflection on how they might perceive their vocation and justify their possible resort to force which is, to some degree, inherent in that profession. Closely connected with that, what follows will, thirdly, possibly serve as a helpful tool to which law enforcement agencies may refer during the hiring and screening process, as well as during academy training. It may also be a resource for police chaplains who are called upon to counsel officers struggling with the issue. In this way, I hope at least to take a step toward responding to Sherman's important question, "Can a Christian be a police officer?"

---

8. For a more clearly articulated account of why and how theology should have a voice in public policy debates, see McCormick, "Theology and Bioethics," 5–10.

Common Foci of Theological Reflections on Violence

Sherman appears to be accurate in his observation that scant attention has been devoted to the subject of police use of force by Christian thinkers and ethicists, and this is striking given the wealth of theological reflection on other life-and-death issues such as war, abortion, and euthanasia. For example, one prolific Christian writer who has recently voiced concerns that are similar to Sherman's nonetheless overlooks the issue of the use of force by police:

> The key moral question to my mind is whether there can ever be justifiable homicides, apart from the most exceptional of unavoidable emergencies or the rarest of medical abortions to save a life. Arguments for other morally permissible killings, such as those put forth in defense of capital punishment, just war, euthanasia, or suicide, appear inadequate. "Thou Shalt Not Kill" can hardly be a command limited to the innocent, the good, our compatriots, our allies, or mature fellow citizens. Christians, for their part, have been given a stricter injunction: to forgive and love your enemies and persecutors, and to do good to those who harm you (or harm your children).[9]

Several knotty issues of life-and-death gravity are listed in this provocative paragraph, but no explicit reference to law enforcement's use of force is made. Similarly, the American Catholic bishops, in their major pastoral letter on war in 1983, focus solely on the Catholic presumption against war and the principle of legitimate self-defense by a person or by a nation, thereby neglecting the momentous issue of police officers and force.[10] Because it is likely that just as many police officers as soldiers are Catholics, what does the church have to say to them? Moreover, since over 85 percent of Americans consider themselves to be Christian,[11] and it is likely that just as many police officers as soldiers are Catholic or Christian, what does the church have to say to them, especially given that it claims to address two audiences—adherents of the faith and society at large—in such official documents concerning war, peace, and even

---

9. Callahan, "Killing Kills the Spirit," 7.

10. National Conference of Catholic Bishops, *Challenge of Peace*, 22.

11. Benne, "Paradoxical Vision," 213. Pew Research, through their 2018–19 telephone surveys, have assessed that the percentage of adults to claim Christianity has dropped to 65 percent (Smith et al., "In US, Decline of Christianity Continues at Rapid Pace").

economic issues? Yet, there is a conspicuous void concerning this topic within Christian moral theology.

Indeed, most Christian theological reflection on the use of force seems concentrated on two ends of a spectrum, with personal self-defense at one extremity and war at the other. Meanwhile, any significant Christian attention to criminal justice focuses primarily on prison conditions and reform, or grapples with the quandary of capital punishment, passing over the issue of the use of force by police on the beat. David A. Hoekema, for example, while acknowledging that Christianity has profoundly influenced Western philosophical and political theory and the formation of social institutions which define and enforce laws, nevertheless recognizes the diversity of thought within the Christian tradition and its major theologians on such issues, including anything pertaining to criminal justice. This is why he adds: "The topic has seldom been a focal point of theology or Christian social ethics."[12] Indeed, he suggests that the development of the modern police force was not due to any input or participation by churches. Instead, according to Hoekema, Christianity played a role in criminal justice primarily by advocating mercy and justice, and by promoting the rehabilitation of criminals.[13] Hoekema attempts to initiate a dialogue between criminal justice, philosophy, and theology, but he confines his treatment to the topic of punishment without any consideration of the legitimacy of the use of force before punishment—that is, during apprehension. In sum, then, it appears to be the case that most thoughtful Christians relegate theological reflection on the issue of police use of force to the realm of "possibilities worth considering," without pursuing the topic any further.[14]

.

12. Hoekema, "Punishment, the Criminal Law, and Christian Social Ethics," 31.

13. Hoekema, "Punishment, the Criminal Law, and Christian Social Ethics," 47.

14. See Sider, *Non-violence*, 4. Sider, a Mennonite, fleetingly alludes to the possibility of nonviolent alternatives that might replace lethal violence in police work. An earlier statement of the dilemma of being a Christian police officer troubled by the use of force can be found in the anonymous essay, "In This World: By a Policeman," 247–53. Other sparse references to the literature linking law enforcement and a Christian perspective include Forster, *"To Live Good"—The Police and the Community*, and Holdaway, "Policing and Consent," 30–39.

The Bridge Is Raised: The Analogy Between Military and Police Force

There is one noteworthy exception, however, and it is Edward A. Malloy's treatment of ethics and the use of force by police in chapter 1 of his *The Ethics of Law Enforcement and Criminal Punishment*. He writes:

> At the theoretical level, most ethical reflection about the problem of violence has centered on difficulties in personal relations or on the horror of warfare. In between these two extremes stands the role of the police in a contemporary setting.[15]

To fill this vacuum, Malloy advocates an application of the historical tradition commonly called just-war theory, "which has Christian roots but has also been incorporated into codes of International Law."[16] He is convinced that such an adaptation of this tradition of "justified violence" will provide a beneficial ethical framework for police in the context of the United States today.

Malloy bases his contribution to the development of a professional ethic for law enforcement, in its endeavor to understand and limit the use of force, on "an exercise of analogical interpretation" which, he hopes, "has not stretched the just war tradition too far."[17] Indeed, it is his view that the classic criteria for the justified use of force are easier to observe and conform to in the domestic context of police work than they are in the international setting of military conflict. His concern that the just-war criteria may be overextended is probably a consequence of his self-description as a "strict constructionist" just-war theorist.[18] In other words, he requires that each criterion be met before justifying war, or in this case, the use of force by police. If any of the five criteria cannot be satisfied, a "no" to the use of force must be the result.[19] This approach to the use of force in law enforcement

---

15. Malloy, *Ethics of Law Enforcement*, 10.

16. Malloy, *Ethics of Law Enforcement*, vii.

17. Malloy, *Ethics of Law Enforcement*, 24. Of course, analogies are neither univocal nor equivocal; rather, they involve attributes which are neither precisely the same nor yet simply different. In this way, analogies possess limitations, and thus the similarities between nations defending themselves through resort to warfare and human persons being defended by police officers are not exact. For example, nations are not individuals but are made up of individuals. For an investigation of the use of analogy in moral argument, see Cahill, "Abortion and Argument by Analogy," 271–87.

18. Malloy, *Ethics of Law Enforcement*, 28.

19. Malloy, *Ethics of Law Enforcement*, 11. The lists of criteria often vary among

is oriented toward restraint and possesses "teeth" by allowing for a "no" to the use of force. Accordingly, Malloy hopes that his "modest venture in a field which is ripe for interdisciplinary cooperation might encourage other Christian ethicists to grapple with this problem of the control of, and response to, domestic violence."[20]

Malloy is not entirely alone in observing the similarity between the use of force in war and the use of force in law enforcement. The analogy is advanced sporadically by a few recent just-war thinkers, both theologians and political scientists, and this is at least one point at which they touch indirectly upon the context of law enforcement. James Turner Johnson, for example, who is one of the major contemporary contributors to just-war thinking, often illustrates principles or points about just war by reference to analogous situations in law enforcement. Thus, while venturing to explain the principle of double effect and its utility in thinking about collateral damage, or the harming of innocent noncombatants in war, Johnson refers to a police force's response to a hostage situation in which the officers attempt to shoot the perpetrator without harming hostages or bystanders. Elsewhere, Johnson uses a similar analogy—"A sniper is barricaded in his house with his family and some neighbors"[21]—to argue that just as it is justifiable for a police sniper to shoot at the perpetrator, but not blow up the whole house to get at him, so too it is justifiable to bomb a military target such as a convoy, but not to obliterate with a nuclear bomb the whole province in which it is traveling.

In spite of his use of such analogies, Johnson adds the following, unexplained qualification: "There is, nonetheless, a considerable difference between the example of the policeman who shoots a terrorist and 'collaterally' kills a hostage and a typical wartime case."[22] Perhaps he is simply alluding to the basic fact that there is a difference between war and the law enforcement incident that is essentially one of degree and not of kind. In other words, and this is in line with Malloy's and my own thesis, there are many factors, variables, and persons to take into consideration at the level of war that make the whole situation more complex and thus make the facile

---

writers on just war, and in this essay Malloy's list will be analyzed against the backdrop of John Howard Yoder's more detailed and extensive list. See Yoder, *When War Is Unjust*, 18.

20. Malloy, *Ethics of Law Enforcement*, ix.

21. Johnson, *Just War Tradition and the Restraint of War*, 363.

22. Johnson, *Just War Tradition and the Restraint of War*, 222.

application of just-war thinking less plausible. In the case of police, on the other hand, the application of just-war type thinking, and its principle of double of effect, is more easily accomplished.

Johnson concludes his book by suggesting that police use of force is the ideal context for the ameliorated application of the sort of thinking exhibited in the just-war tradition: "The problem, for military planners who would try to anticipate how to make war morally yet effectively, is how to approach the case of the police marksman shooting to disable the sniper."[23] He thus assumes that law enforcement can resort to and use force more morally and effectively than the military.

The Lutheran, Charles P. Lutz, in his brief introduction to Mennonite John Howard Yoder's *When War Is Unjust*, also contends:

> An analogy [to just-war thinking in warfare] would be that of the police function within our communities. Because of an evident need to protect the innocent and to thwart the destructive impulses of a few, we legitimate the use of force by police officers. We arm them with lethal weapons. We justify their use of such weapons under certain circumstances.
>
> But we do *not* authorize police to use the force at their disposal indiscriminately, arbitrarily, or wantonly. There are rules by which police must abide. And those rules bear a certain resemblance to the rules of the just war ethic.[24]

Lutz, like Malloy and Johnson, employs an analogy between law enforcement and the military, and hopes that Christians who use force—and here he is primarily concerned with soldiers but is implying police officers as well—will do so with reserve.

It is noteworthy that one of the pivotal figures in Christian ethics during the twentieth century—Paul Ramsey, a thinker who often concentrates on war issues as well as medical ethics—mentions the police when illustrating just-war principles. Ramsey argues that the just use of political violence in warfare must include two principal elements: 1) a specific justification for sometimes killing another human being; and 2) severe and specific restrictions upon anyone who is under the hard necessity of doing so. "Both are exhibited," says Ramsey, "in the use of force proper to the domestic police power."[25] Accordingly, police officers distinguish between aggressor,

---

23. Johnson, *Just War Tradition and the Restraint of War*, 222.

24. Lutz, in Yoder, *When War Is Unjust*, 7–8.

25. Ramsey, *Just War*, 144.

victim, and bystanders; and though an officer may harm some innocent party accidentally, it would never be right for him or her to "enlarge the target" and deliberately, or directly, kill any number "in the crowd on Times Square *as a means* of preventing some criminal from injurious action."[26] Ramsey grounds this justification of such limited use of force upon what he identifies as "social charity," in which the Christian, or anyone else for that matter, is called to love the neighbor by protecting him or her from the other aggressive neighbor who has chosen to become an enemy. Although Christians are called to love the enemy as well, Ramsey asserts that when a "choice *must* be made between the perpetrator of injustice and the many victims of it, the latter may and should be preferred—even if effectively to do so would require the use of armed force against some evil power."[27] In this way, Ramsey maintains that restraint in the use of force is still necessary to respect and, indeed, love the alleged perpetrator. While this is the only point at which Ramsey devotes any attention to the context of law enforcement, it is noteworthy that it is a pivotal illustration upon which he bases the rest of his work concerning the justification of war.

Another respected scholar in just-war circles, although a political scientist rather than a moral theologian, is Michael Walzer, who also connects the military and the law enforcement contexts with regard to their use of force. As he puts it: "Every reference to aggression as the international equivalent of armed robbery or murder, and every comparison of home and country or of personal liberty and political independence, relies on what is called the *domestic analogy*."[28] He notes that the international structure provides an imperfect, shaky context for the surest application of just-war principles, since there are no internationally authorized "police officers." Nations self-assume status as police officers in order to defend themselves or other victims of aggression. In Walzer's view, humanitarian intervention "comes much closer than any other kind of intervention to what we commonly regard, in domestic society, as law enforcement and police work."[29] In making such assertions,

26. Ramsey, *Just War*, 144, 187.

27. Ramsey, *Just War*, 143. I am adapting Ramsey's love-based presumption toward restraint in the use of force against the enemy, and his advocacy of respect for the patient by doctors in his *The Patient as Person*, to argue that law enforcement's presumption in favor of restraint in the use of force also be based on a view that sees the alleged perpetrator as person.

28. Walzer, *Just and Unjust Wars*, 58, original italics.

29. Walzer, *Just and Unjust Wars*, 106.

he seems to imply that the restraining principles of just-war thinking can be better applied in the context of law enforcement.

Scholars are not the only persons who have noted or assumed some kind of connection between military action and law enforcement. At the everyday, popular level, making a connection between soldiers and police officers is not at all outlandish, especially considering how military jargon shows up in virtually any discussion of the police.[30] Spend some time around the halls of a police department or riding as a passenger in a police car, and words like "chain of command," "division," "squad," "trooper," "sergeant," and "lieutenant" will soon be audible. Or recall how the politicians in Washington are implementing a "war on crime" through their crime bills. A recently published book, readily available wherever popular books are sold, provides numerous narratives of police officers who have killed someone in the line of duty. One such account posits: "Even if an officer never fires his weapon in anger, he still perceives his environment as hostile and threatening. The next trouble call, the next moment, could erupt in violence. While it may not be war in a classical sense, it is nonetheless *war*. More important, the policeman sees it as war."[31] Such word associations lead one sociologist to assert that an "implicit *combat and warfare* model is also a feature . . . among police."[32]

It is precisely because of this oft-made association that I believe, with Malloy, that the wealth of Christian reflection on restraint in war can be of service to the present soul-searching occurring within law enforcement circles on the use of force. Yet, in contrast to Malloy, I also believe that an explicit use of each and every principle of just-war theory to justify police uses of force may reinforce the old crimefighter model of policing from which, as will be noted later, more recent models of policing are striving to distance themselves. Although just-war principles aim to limit unnecessary violence, the military connotation may unfortunately undermine the presumption of restraint in police work, elevating force from a last resort to a first option or standard procedure status. I still think that law enforcement can learn from the just-war tradition, but maintain that its incorporation and elaboration of the core presumption of restraint should be accomplished in a way that

---

30. Skolnick and Fyfe, *Above the Law*, 113.

31. Sasser, *Shoot to Kill*, 233, italics in original. Sasser's concluding remarks are just as frank: "The streets are a combat zone to the American police officer. The war against crime is a *real* shooting war" (266).

32. Toch, *Peacekeeping: Police, Prisons, and Violence*, 7, italics in original.

reinforces that presumption as strongly as possible in officers and is also explicated as clearly as possible for them.

Christian Attitudes toward War

The just-war tradition is the dominant—though not the only—current within the stream of Christianity. It has competed with four other approaches—the pacifist, the "crusade," the "realist," and the "Rambo."[33] Though its historical antecedents lie in the classical pagan world, from the early Middle Ages the just-war tradition developed primarily within Christian theology along with other confluences toward restraint, such as medieval chivalry, the modern evolution of international law, and efforts to deal with the mushrooming production of destructive weaponry through smarter technology.

The history of the tradition's development is more complex than usually depicted. Studies of early Christian attitudes toward military service and action have uncovered practically no evidence that Christians served in the military before approximately 170 or 180 CE.[34] But by the late fourth century, following the reign of the Roman emperor Constantine, when the status of Christianity shifted from that of a persecuted minority to that of the official religion of the empire, Christians assumed responsibility for the good of the overall society, and Christian participation in the military increased. Associated with this was the elaboration of theological moral norms prescribing limits to legitimate warfare, and these have developed into what we now know as the just-war tradition. Just-war principles were affirmed implicitly by Ambrose (d. 397) and Augustine (d. 430), integrated systematically into Christian moral theology by Thomas Aquinas (d. 1274), and developed into a system or theory by Francisco de Vitoria (d. 1546) and Francisco Suárez (d. 1617). Although such principles have been advocated by most of the manuals of Catholic moral theology, they have nonetheless

33. Here my overview is in line with Yoder's typology. Yoder goes beyond most other thinkers about war, who usually identify only two positions: just war and pacifism. See Yoder, *When War Is Unjust*, 17–18. For further reading about the just-war tradition, see Bainton, *Christian Attitudes Toward War and Peace*; Walzer, *Just and Unjust Wars*; Holmes, *War and Christian Ethics*; Ramsey, *Just War*; Johnson, *Just War Tradition and the Restraint of War*; Johnson, *Ideology, Reason, and the Limitation of War*; Childress, "Just War Theories," 427–45.

34. Bainton, *Christian Attitudes Toward War and Peace*, 67–68; Ryan, "Rejection of Military Service," 9; Hollenbach, *Nuclear Ethics*, 8.

not been proclaimed as official doctrine, in contrast to the confessional statements of Lutherans, Anglicans, and Presbyterians.

Put simply, the just-war tradition considers war an evil, but claims that under specific circumstances it is justifiable as a lesser evil than the execution of some threat which it counters or the continuation of some system which it changes. It recognizes a set of criteria calculated to measure with some clarity and objectivity when it may be deemed that the evil of war is justifiable because the evil it is expected to prevent is greater. There are two categories of criteria, one governing the choice to go to war, *jus ad bellum*, and the other governing proper conduct within the midst of hostilities, *jus in bello*.

A simple listing of the criteria can be sketched as follows, with the first six criteria grouped under the first category of *jus ad bellum*, and the remainder under *jus in bello*:

1. The authority to wage the war must be legitimate.

2. The cause being fought for must be just.

3. The ultimate goal or objective intention must be peace.

4. The subjective intention or motivation must not be hatred or vengeance.

5. War must be the last resort.

6. Success must be probable.

7. Finally, the means used must be discriminating, both

8. quantitatively, in order not to do more harm than the harm hoped to be prevented (proportionality), and

9. qualitatively, in order to avoid harming innocent persons (immunity).

The US Catholic bishops ground just-war doctrine on the "presumption which binds all Christians: we should do no harm to our neighbors; how we treat our enemy is the key test of whether we love our neighbor; and the possibility of taking even one life is a prospect we should consider in fear and trembling."[35] Pope John Paul II's *Evangelium Vitae* underlines this foundational orientation: "*Not even a murderer loses his personal dignity.*"[36] Others, though not basing just-war theory on this Christian foundation of neighbor love, nonetheless identify an underlying

---

35. National Conference of Catholic Bishops, *Challenge of Peace*, 26.

36. John Paul II, *Evangelium Vitae*, §9.

presumption against doing harm that is based on the human dignity of the aggressor. Childress and Johnson, for example, both acknowledge a presumption against hostilities, based on the view that war is evil and never to be approved *prima facie*.[37] It is this foundational presumption, moreover, that the Catholic bishops, as well as the United Methodist bishops in their own pastoral letter, identify as a common presumption shared with the pacifist undercurrent within Christianity.[38]

In other words, both the just-war tradition and the tradition of pacifism began with the foundational imperative of nonviolence, which is basically equivalent to saying that it is wrong to harm one's fellow human. The just-war tradition, however, parts from pacifism when it comes to dealing with circumstances in which, in relation to a particular adversary, the duty not to harm may legitimately be overridden, because of a greater value which is at stake, such as that of an innocent human life. In this way, the just-war criteria can be considered as rules that manage the claim that there is an exception that overrides the basic rule or presumption.

The pacifist thread, by contrast, was predominant in the church of the first four centuries. This position opposed all killing, military service, and warfare. In the middle of the second century, Justin Martyr announced that Jesus Christ was the fulfillment of Isaiah's promise of peace, and that Christians, therefore, have "through the whole earth changed our warlike weapons—our swords into ploughshares, and our spears into implements of tillage."[39] Some of the early Christian opposition to military service was a response to the idolatrous practices which prevailed in the Roman army. Another critical factor was that fighting and killing were involved. In the fourth century, for example, Saint Martin of Tours renounced his own soldierly profession by affirming: "Hitherto I have served you as a soldier. Allow me now to become a soldier of God . . . I am a soldier of Christ. It is not lawful for me to fight."[40] Early Christians were therefore opposed

---

37. Childress, "Just War Theories"; Johnson, *Ideology, Reason, and the Limitation of War*. Childress and Johnson come to disagree in a debate about this presumption elsewhere, as will be seen in chapter 2 of this volume.

38. National Conference of Catholic Bishops, *Challenge of Peace*, 37; The United Methodist Council of Bishops, *In Defense of Creation*, 33, 37.

39. Long, *Christian Peace and Nonviolence*, 16.

40. Long, *Christian Peace and Nonviolence*, 47–48; see Bainton, *Christian Attitudes Toward War and Peace*, 81, 88. It should be noted that pacifism is not a univocal term and that as many as twenty-five different sub-groupings of pacifists have been identified by Yoder in his *Nevertheless: The Varieties and Shortcomings of Religious Pacifism*.

to participation in warfare either because of its intrinsic wrongness or because of its accompanying factors.

Although the just-war tradition would become dominant with the Constantinian establishment in the fourth century, the pacifist tradition persisted as one of the Christian moral postures toward warfare. It was transmitted by the monks in the post-Constantinian period, echoed in the twelfth century by Saint Francis, and passed on into the Protestant communities by the "historic peace churches," including the Mennonites, the Church of the Brethren, and the Society of Friends (Quakers). Today, pacifism is a growing tradition within Christian circles and, since it shares and can reinforce the presumption against harm discernible within the just-war tradition, that is why the Catholic and Methodist bishops now acknowledge it as a legitimate option for Christians. In this way, these two official church statements have forged new territory by explicitly asserting that the just-war tradition and pacifism are complementary, both in the sense that each is grounded in the prior presumption against killing or harming, and in the sense that they both reject unjust warfare.[41]

The three other approaches to thinking morally about war do not depend upon this presumption against harm. The "holy war" or "crusade" option is an approach to war that is transcendent in cause, often religious as to authority, dismissive of the restraining criteria of probable success and last resort, and disparaging of the rights of the enemy. This option was advocated by the ancient Israelites against their Canaanite neighbors in the Hebrew scriptures, by Catholics against the Turks at the end of the eleventh century, and also between Christians themselves during the sixteenth century's wars of religion. The churches no longer advocate it, although its terminology is occasionally heard—in the propaganda of some recent ultra-right militia groups, and when the former President Reagan called the Soviet Union an "evil empire."

The "realist" position also denies that other party's rights can be fully respected, and claims national interests as the overarching concern. Though there are various nuances, it is concerned primarily with success. It denies, in short, that one should think morally about war. All that matters is winning, even if the rules must be broken. The "Rambo" position has

41. Hollenbach, *Nuclear Ethics*, 15. A few writers have questioned this complementarity, arguing instead that the two traditions are in opposition and not just in some kind of reinforcing tension. See James Finn, "Pacifism and Just War," in Murnion, *Catholics and Nuclear War*, 132–45. Nevertheless, I find the bishops' and Hollenbach's reflections to be accurate and helpful.

the fewest constraints. Its self-ascribed "virtues" are honor, manliness, and heroism. It is not concerned with rights or even success. Walzer does not refer to this stance as "Rambo" but as "frenzy" or "hysteria."[42] It is prevalent in the media and football locker rooms.

In each of these last three positions, the line of restraint breaks down.[43] They provide no assistance for law enforcement in its attempts to discover resources for eliminating excessive force. Officers who exhibit such attitudes are precisely the ones that coherent use of force procedures should check or weed out.

The History of the Police
Authorization to Use Force

The affinity of the fundamental concepts of just-war thinking with law enforcement procedures concerning force should not be too surprising. The view that police are similar to soldiers in war has its origins in the initial establishment of the police themselves.[44] Modern police departments are a relatively new invention, beginning with the "New Police" organized in 1829 in London, at the urging of Sir Robert Peel, who originally intended to distinguish police officers from soldiers, but ended up appropriating heavily from the military organizational model in order to convince critics that his New Police would perform as impeccably as the British military's perceived discharge of its duties.[45] To be sure, opposition existed, but this was based on the anxiety that the New Police would be a political puppet and tool.[46] Peel attempted to distinguish the New Police from the military by refraining from arming the police. More profoundly, he sought to abide by the prohibition on

42. Walzer, *Just and Unjust Wars*, 305.

43. See Yoder, *When War Is Unjust*, 21–31, 56. It would seem more likely that law enforcement needs to be aware of the temptation to the realist or Rambo position, as popularly depicted in the actions of the leading police characters in movies such as *Dirty Harry*, *Deathwish*, and *Lethal Weapon*. Other shows, such as *Kojak*, *Hill Street Blues*, *NYPD Blue*, and *Law and Order*, more accurately portray officers who wrestle with ethical issues in law enforcement while striving for what is right.

44. Skolnick and Fyfe, *Above the Law*, 116.

45. Skolnick and Fyfe, *Above the Law*, 116–17.

46. Reiner, *Politics of the Police*, 16–17. See Berkley, *Democratic Policeman*, 5. Interestingly, no mention is ever made of any church or theological reaction, except for a brief hint by Steve Uglow that Quakers and working classes opposed police forces at first. He doesn't delve into the Quaker criticism, however (Uglow, *Policing Liberal Society*, 15).

the arbitrary use of physical force by the state, a core concept within classical political liberalism, with its view that the rights of the human person are inalienable over and against state coercion.[47]

The transplanting of the police force onto American soil began in a similar way. In 1834, Boston drafted citizens to take turns in maintaining order. Initially policemen were unarmed and were "restrained from committing brutal acts by the prior warning of their superiors, by their own good judgment, and by fear of physical retaliation."[48] But even at this stage, as an unarmed force, police departments in the United States aroused misgivings among the populace, many of whom labeled these departments as "un-American."[49]

The supposedly "un-American" police in the United States would soon diverge from the unarmed British police, however, and become distinctively American with their recourse to firearms in enforcing the law. Even more debate surrounded the arming of the police in America: "Our police first patrolled the streets unarmed but—after great debate both inside and outside their ranks—began wearing guns in the middle of the nineteenth century only when it became unavoidably clear that it was not safe to do otherwise."[50] Police officers in American cities began to carry revolvers in the 1850s as a response to the increasing use of firearms by criminals. Furthermore, the availability of thousands of army revolvers on the surplus market after the Civil War hastened the general armament of an increasingly violent urban society and resulted in official acceptance of police use of revolvers.[51] The Boston police, for example, first acquired firearms in the aftermath of the Draft Riot of 1863, though it was not until 1884 that they were fully armed at public expense. In view of this, Lane suggests that "the fact that most policemen carried their revolvers tipped the physical balance in their favor, making them more formidable but also

---

47. Uglow, *Policing Liberal Society*, 53. Indeed, it is this secularized version of the Christian view of the fundamental dignity of the human person as *imago Dei* that provides the basis for the modern liberal state's presumption against the use of force upon its citizens.

48. Lane, *Policing the City*, 187.

49. Berkley, *Democratic Policeman*, 5. One wonders if, as well, any theological arguments were mustered to claim that police departments were "un-Christian."

50. Skolnick and Fyfe, *Above the Law*, 128. Still there is no mention of any Christian contribution to this debate.

51. Sherman, "Execution without Trial," 190.

increasing the danger of brutality on their part."[52] Obviously, the American variant of Peel's English vision has experienced more violence and controversy, which is probably due to "some combination of American social and historical forces [which have] blended with the military model to produce a volatile mix."[53]

The Quest for an Appropriate Model

Further consideration of the chronicle of American municipal police discloses a history of struggles to define their role in society. Law enforcement is most often understood as crimefighting, enforcing the law, capturing criminals, and maintaining order—all of which requires an ethic of restraint such as that provided by an adaptation of just-war thought. At the same time, police perform a variety of functions, and a chorus of criminologists now emphasize alternative social service or social-peacekeeper models of law enforcement.[54] Other critical thinkers who advocate this move do so because they assume that any war connotations in law enforcement entail brutality and excessive force. For example, Virginia Mackey writes, "An analysis of the current war model of crime control shows that it exhibits the same characteristics and suffers the same flaws as the war models that nations use to protect their 'national interests.'"[55]

Other writers also advocate a move toward alternative models of law enforcement which will, it is hoped, diminish the need for violence. Most radically, Robert Elias recommends a shift of paradigms for the police: "We must reconstitute police work as community service rather than community control.... State power should be reduced, not enhanced; police forces should be demilitarized (if not eventually disarmed), and bans on police violence must be strictly enforced."[56] Another champion for the professionalization of police in ways that will inhibit the use of force, or at least mitigate excessive use of force, is Edwin Delattre, who encourages training that focuses on character and virtue development which will enable officers to actually live

52. Lane, *Policing the City*, 187–88.

53. Skolnick and Fyfe, *Above the Law*, 128.

54. Betz, "Police Violence"; also see Reiman, "Social Contract and the Police Use of Deadly Force."

55. Mackey, "Mixed Motives, Mixed Messages," 183.

56. Elias, "Peace Movement Against Crime," 211.

up to their codes and procedures.[57] Unlike Elias, Delattre assumes that the use of force will remain an element of the police officer's job description, and therefore he encourages better training to enable the officer to discern limits and to abide by the "principle of lesser means."[58]

Finally, Malloy, too, recommends more college-educated and less military-oriented recruits who are better trained in "a body of knowledge with a clear assertion of the priority of certain values and the presentation of workable principles and rules which protect these values in practice."[59] Because Malloy's answer to the crucial question of whether it is possible to disarm the police today in the United States is "no"—notwithstanding his advocacy of a professional, less military-oriented police officer—he maintains that the just-war tradition, with its presumption toward restraint, is most fitting for approaching the ethics of the use of force in law enforcement.[60]

Despite Elias's aim to gradually disarm the police in his new model of policing, all other alternative models, even if they are community-oriented, still allow room for some degree of force to be used by police. Although such alternative models may rightly place emphasis on service rather than crimefighting, they nonetheless do not obviate the need for restrained force as a final resort and therefore require some stipulation for its use. This being the case, Malloy's recommended tactic remains relevant; indeed, the strict application of Malloy's just-war thinking solely to the use of force in police work aims to bridle such usage and to avert the excessiveness and brutality about which Elias, Mackey, and others express concern.

The Place of Force in Policing

Some writers do posit that the use of force is essential and central in policing. Skolnick and Fyfe frankly contend: "No matter how many warnings may be issued by superiors about limitations on the use of force, no matter how much talk about policing as a profession, police training continually reminds recruits that coercive power is a central feature of police life."[61] They claim that such force will remain an inevitable component of

---

57. Delattre, *Character and Cops*, 5.

58. Delattre, *Character and Cops*, 55, 208; see Hansen, *Police Ethics*, 56–57.

59. Malloy, *Ethics of Law Enforcement*, 6.

60. Malloy, *Ethics of Law Enforcement*, 11.

61. Skolnick and Fyfe, *Above the Law*, 95.

policing.[62] Vance McLaughlin similarly asserts that although the use of force by police is not as frequent as the public may imagine, police officers routinely use force to carry out their role as enforcers. His view is that the use of force is "inherent in the profession" just as legitimate force is an "essential ingredient in maintaining an ordered society."[63] Accordingly, in every nation today, law enforcement officers possess the right to use force.[64] Lawrence Sherman maintains a comparable perspective in saying: "Force is the essence of criminal justice, just as the monopoly on the legitimate use of force is the essence of the nation-state."[65]

For these criminal-justice experts, this observation apparently holds true regardless of the form of government of the nation-state and would also apply to democratic nations—although there are those who argue that liberal democracies, at least, confine the use of force to a minimum and keep it at the margins of the instruments of government. The British thinker, Steve Uglow, for example, suggests, "The guiding principle developed within liberal societies has been that such force must be *essential* and *minimum*."[66] Likewise, Robert Reiner, another Englishman, puts forward his view that in a democratic state "successful policing is to be able to minimize the use of force."[67]

Unfortunately, democratic societies are not immune to excessive uses of force by police officers. Such societies display, moreover, significant variations. The United States provides a "startling contrast" to Europe—notably,

---

62. Skolnick and Fyfe, *Above the Law*, 37.

63. McLaughlin, *Police and the Use of Force*, 1.

64. McLaughlin, *Police and the Use of Force*, 7.

65. Sherman, *Ethics in Criminal Justice Education*, 37.

66. Uglow, *Policing Liberal Society*, 12, italics in original. It is important to consider the place for "the sword" in government. Although many writers, including Christian theologians such as Saint Augustine, view the state's capacity to use force, or "the sword," to be the essence of the state, others, including Aristotle and modern neo-Thomists like Yves Simon, define the state in terms of completeness and self-sufficiency. Simon, for example, favors democratic governments that rely on *persuasion* primarily and most of the time, and less often use *coercion* (justified externally imposed force, e.g., police arrests). Violence, however, is the unjust use of force and is abusive, never to be used as an instrument of the state. Each of these—persuasion and coercion—is considered by Simon to be an *instrument* of a state rather than the *essence* of the state. This being the case, there would be a *prima facie* orientation toward restraint (Simon, *Philosophy of Democratic Government*, 69, 112–13, 118–19).

67. Reiner, *Politics of the Police*, 2.

Great Britain—on justified use of force by police.[68] A clear statement of principles is urgently needed.

Current Statutes and Guidelines

As McLaughlin rightly points out, many elements currently affect the situational context in which police work.[69] The tendency to respond to violence with violence, the presence of different and frequently antagonistic cultures, and the gap between rich and poor are all variables that factor into the uniquely American situation. Within this setting, federal and state laws strive to delineate the parameters of appropriate police conduct, especially when force is to be used. In addition, the various local law enforcement agencies set out departmental standard operating procedures that provide guidance and restrictions.

The use of force often reflects an on-the-spot decision made by the police officer on the scene. The officer must quickly assess the situation and take proper action. So many factors may come into play that guidelines, restrictions, and laws may seem too vague to be of practical use to the officer; the use of force is thus difficult to control.[70] Yet, with more precision and uniformity, most recent guidelines and laws attempt to check excessive force and provide assistance to police by admonishing them that they should use no more force than is "necessary" or "reasonable" or that such force should be used only as a "last resort." In this way, they echo the language of just-war thinking, with its fundamental posture of restraint.

A brief glimpse at statements that are intended to function as guidelines for the use of force corroborate this trend, and as well provide an entry point from which the more detailed discussion of the similarities of just-war thinking to police work may proceed. The International Association of Chiefs of Police's 1989 Code, renamed the "Police Code of Conduct" in 1991, offers two terse paragraphs on the use of force:

> A police officer will never employ *unnecessary* force or violence and will use only such force in the discharge of duty as is *reasonable* in all circumstances.
>
> The use of force should be used only with the *greatest restraint* and only after discussion, negotiation and persuasion have been

68. Berkley, *Democratic Policeman*, 111.

69. McLaughlin, *Police and the Use of Force*, 2–3.

70. Skolnick and Fyfe, *Above the Law*, 38.

found to be inappropriate or ineffective. While the use of force is occasionally unavoidable, every police officer will refrain from unnecessary infliction of pain or suffering and will never engage in cruel, degrading or inhuman treatment of any person.[71]

As will be shown, the words "unnecessary" and "reasonable" echo the fundamental perspective of the just-war tradition. Such language is intended to assist the officer in deciding when to escalate her response to a violent criminal from discussion, negotiation, and persuasion to some degree of physical force—assuming, of course, that there will be general and universal agreement about what "unnecessary" and "reasonable" denote.

Many departmental guidelines attempt to provide similar direction.[72] One Indiana agency describes a use of force continuum in which control "may be achieved through advice, warnings, and persuasion, or by the use of physical force." Such force should be "necessary" and should not be employed "unless other reasonable alternatives have been exhausted." Force is to be used only to protect the officers or others from imminent physical danger. A North Carolina departmental directive that also advocates a use of force continuum notes that the "prohibition against the use of unnecessary force shall not be construed as requiring the officer to meet an assaulting or resisting subject with strictly equal force. Rather, the officer is allowed to use that degree of force which would appear reasonably necessary to bring the subject under the officer's control." Officers are authorized to "use whatever degree of force as reasonably appears necessary, under the circumstances then known to them, to defend themselves or others from the use or immediate use of force." Another department in Florida claims that its members "are justified in the use of deadly force as a last resort when there is reasonable belief that such force is necessary" to prevent death or great bodily harm to the officer or another person, and to apprehend the perpetrator of a felony which involved the use or threatened use of deadly force and who poses an immediate threat to the life and safety of the officer or other persons.

In each of these departmental guidelines, it is assumed that most persons understand what is meant by such statements, just as the principles of

71. Italics added. This document can be found, along with many other interesting documents throughout the history of policing, in Kleinig and Zhang, *Professional Law Enforcement Codes*.

72. The three departmental guidelines in this paragraph are from the South Bend Police Department (Indiana), the Guilford County Sheriff's Department (North Carolina), and the Pinellas County Sheriff's Department (Florida).

just-war thinking are assumed to be commonsensical or "naturally" accessible to most normal persons. Obviously, there is a reverberation of just-war language, which is a minimum point of contact between law enforcement and the military. If criminal-justice ethicists and lawmakers continue to take the restrained use of force as seriously as ethicists traditionally have for the setting of war, and in this way adapt the core principles of just-war thinking to the law enforcement context, then maybe future Rodney King incidents will be prevented.

The Just-War Criteria Adapted
to Law Enforcement

Beyond identifying the similarities of the core restraining principles in law enforcement guidelines and just-war theory, Malloy thinks that the just-war criteria are much easier to adopt and satisfy in the domestic context of police work than in the military, and he walks through each criterion to demonstrate this. The first six criteria in just-war thinking are generally grouped under the heading *jus ad bellum* and have to do with going to war. Until these criteria have been met, a nation cannot enter war. Adapting this to the domestic situation of police forces, the criteria must be met prior to any use of force whatsoever. Hence, the first criterion is legitimate authority, that is, war may be waged only by a legitimate authority. This may be the monarch, the president, the legislature, or the United Nations, to name a few. Adapting this to the police context, the police officer may use coercive force only when he or she truly represents the body politic.[73] Though sworn to uphold the law, police possess an enormous amount of discretion and cannot always consult with a superior or make a decision in advance; in many cases, therefore, they are authorized under oath to determine on the spot when to use force. A comment by Skolnick and Fyfe has similar import. They write: "[W]here police derive their authority from law and take an oath to support the Constitution they are obliged to acknowledge the law's moral force and to be constrained by it"; furthermore, if an officer uses force in an inappropriate way, "he or she undermines the very source of police authority."[74]

73. Malloy, *Ethics of Law Enforcement*, 12.

74. Skolnick and Fyfe, *Above the Law*, xvi. This understanding of the legitimate authority of the police officer corresponds to the official position of the United States' federal criminal law, which states that persons who act in their official capacity shall not

In other words, if the criteria for using force are violated, their authority is vitiated and dissipated. This would seem to echo Malloy's "strict constructionist" stance, namely, that every criterion must be satisfied, and if one is not, then the whole act of force is unjustified.

The second criterion is that war may be fought only for a just cause.[75] Thus, war is never to be entered into for trivial reasons. The offense must be actual, not only possible, and intentional, not an inadvertent, unintended, or honest error. Examples of just causes include national self-defense and the protection of beleaguered allies. Adapting this criterion to the context of policing would require the existence of an operative legal code from which could be derived any situation in which police use of force would be warranted. This, of course, would presuppose the justice of the code as a whole. Police in the United States may use force only if the cause is just as described by these codes. Thus, along the lines of the just causes to which reference was made in regard to warfare, most police agencies have limited the right to shoot a firearm, for example, to two categories: 1) the officer may shoot to defend herself or himself from grievous bodily injury, and 2) the officer may shoot to save another person from grievous bodily injury.[76] Departments no longer allow their officers to shoot fleeing felons under any circumstances, especially in situations in which the perpetrator no longer poses an immediate threat to anyone's life. Provisions for the investigation and review of incidents involving force should accompany such policies and statutes. These might be conducted by internal affairs units, civilian review boards, and recourse to legal action by any possible victims. An indication that such principles actually have "teeth" would be the disciplining and prosecution of cases in which the use of force is determined to be excessive.

The third criterion comes under the heading of "right intention" in an objective sense (*finis operis*), which is the goal or end that is sought. This is usually justified in terms of the global common good. It ordinarily consists in bringing about a lasting peace, and also includes consideration of the enemy's real best interests. In the case of police, Malloy maintains that they "may use the full force available to them only when they are

---

violate the civil rights of persons through, for example, excessive force (18 US Code 242; the same holds of federal civil law in 42 USC 1983); see McLaughlin, *Police and the Use of Force*, 12–13.

75. Malloy, *Ethics of Law Enforcement*, 12.

76. McLaughlin, *Police and the Use of Force*, 85.

convinced that the common good is being served."[77] Therefore, the most objective "goal of any officer in a physical confrontation is to have an opponent cease and desist from further resistance."[78] The test of such a stance is taking someone as prisoner or, in other words, arresting him rather than using more force than is necessary. The best interests of all, including the alleged perpetrator's, are to be kept in view, thereby maintaining the overall common good of society.

The fourth criterion also comes under the heading of "right intention," but involves a subjective sense (*finis operantis*) that deals with motivation or attitude.[79] It hearkens back to Saint Augustine's condemnation of intentions such as hatred, vengefulness, cruelty, love of violence, desire for power or fame, and material gain.[80] The cause may be justified, but the soldier's participation is vitiated by the wrong intention. Appropriate intentions include humility and regret at the necessity for force in the evil of warfare. Adapting this criterion to the police role would entail officer attitudes which would control "emotional reactions to the insults and threats of the moment," thereby making it more likely that the performance of their representational function will be effective.[81] As Delattre remarks along similar lines: "We allow police to use force because we prefer a disinterested party to have this authority, rather than allow those impassioned by involvement to use force against each other."[82] If an officer happens to use more force than is necessary when someone explicitly expresses his or her will to capitulate, or if the officer shoots the offender anyway (as "Dirty Harry" did in the movie), perhaps out of anger, hate, or revenge, then the right intention in this sense is lacking.

A fifth criterion, known as "last resort," involves due process or procedural integrity that qualifies both *ad bellum* and *in bello* criteria. On this criterion, sufficient time should be allowed for processes of negotiation and the exercise of diplomacy. Applying this notion to the police predicament, officers "should exhaust all other possible methods for controlling a

---

77. Malloy, *Ethics of Law Enforcement*, 14.

78. McLaughlin, *Police and the Use of Force*, 15.

79. This is not explicit in Malloy's treatment, but is included under "right intention" in the objective sense; see Malloy, *Ethics of Law Enforcement*, 14–15.

80. Augustine, "Reply to Faustus the Manichean," 64.

81. Malloy, *Ethics of Law Enforcement*, 15.

82. Delattre, *Character and Cops*, 27.

conflictive situation before resorting to the more severe levels of force."[83] Only when all else fails should a police officer resort to a higher degree of force. Admittedly, this is an onerous call for the police officer to make in a tense situation, such as a domestic conflict. Yet, this is precisely why there is a need for clearer principles and rules, as well as prior training to clarify and instill them.

The issue of last resort has recently provided an impetus for developing and utilizing alternative methods of dealing with crime and violence. David Friedrichs, for example, recommends a "peacemaking criminology" which offers a nonviolent response to crime.[84] Ronald Sider briefly mentions the success of the Philadelphia Quakers' nonviolent "police force" at the Black Panthers' Convention in 1970.[85] Another indication that last resort is being taken seriously is the current research into nonlethal weapons that are to be used before lethal force in the so-called use of force continuum.[86] One example of this latter option is the employment of Pressure Point Control Tactics (PPCT) by law enforcement in Savannah, Georgia—a system of less-than-lethal tactics based on legal, tactical, and medical research.[87] Francis Burke also makes a parallel last-resort argument when considering lying during crisis negotiations. He argues that lying should almost never be utilized as a means of resolving a hostage situation "unless all other reasonable options have been exhausted."[88] He traces the grounds for this position back to the "preservation of life, that of both innocent hostages and wrongdoers."[89]

As a further consideration under the "due process" category, and as the sixth criterion overall, the war must be "winnable." This is closely linked to a further criterion, namely, that the war must cause less harm than the harm it seeks to prevent. In the police context, the use of force may be called into question in relation to the fact that the US government and the police "declare wars repeatedly on crime and drugs, even though

---

83. Malloy, *Ethics of Law Enforcement*, 13.

84. Friedrichs, "Crime Wars and Peacemaking Criminology," 159–60; also Pepinsky and Quinney, *Criminology as Peacemaking*.

85. Sider, *Non-violence*, 34.

86. McLaughlin, *Police and the Use of Force*, 16–17.

87. McLaughlin, *Police and the Use of Force*, 31.

88. Burke, "Lying During Crisis Negotiations," 57.

89. Burke, "Lying During Crisis Negotiations," 51.

these wars are never won."[90] In their book, Skolnick and Fyfe assert that a crime war cannot be won, and for them this casts doubt on the whole war analogy.[91] Others, perhaps, would counter by pointing out that all that is necessary to justify the "war" on drugs or crime is that the problem be prevented from getting worse.

Still, the basic principle here may apply more directly to individual police behavior, such as an arrest attempt. Consider a document from the Boston Police Department in 1865, entitled "Advice to a Young Policeman," which focuses the principle on the decision to arrest: "Whenever it is necessary to make an arrest, and you attempt to do it, *don't fail*; but use no more force than is necessary to protect yourself and secure your man."[92] Thus, although crime may not be eradicated with a single arrest or even a multitude of arrests, any individual use of force to effect an arrest ought to have a good probability of success before it is attempted. It almost goes without saying that an arrest ought not to be attempted if the officer is outnumbered or outgunned.

The remaining criteria to be assessed and adapted from the setting of just-war thought fall under the rubric of *jus in bello*, which maintains that a war may be fought only by the use of legitimate means. Simply put, these principles govern *how* a just war might be fought.[93] Traditionally, the *jus ad bellum* criteria received primary emphasis, but more recently the *jus in bello* has been given greater attention. In law enforcement, too, the means covered by this category have attracted additional scrutiny. Thus, the third article of the United Nations' *Code of Conduct for Law Enforcement Officials* reads: "Law enforcement officials may use force only when strictly *necessary* and to the extent required for the performance of their duty." The commentary that follows this statement proposes that the use of force "should be exceptional" as well as "*reasonably necessary* under the circumstances" and "in accordance with a principle of proportionality."[94]

Until recently, two different standards were applied in federal proceedings: a "reasonableness" standard and a "shock the conscience"

90. Elias, "Taking Crime Seriously," 132.

91. Skolnick and Fyfe, *Above the Law*, 114.

92. Kleinig and Zhang, *Professional Law Enforcement Codes*, 48.

93. Malloy, *Ethics of Law Enforcement*, 15.

94. United Nations General Assembly, *United Nations: Code of Conduct for Law Enforcement Officials*; italics added.

standard.[95] For many years, the circuit courts remained inconsistent in deciding which constitutional standard to apply to excessive force cases under section 1983 of the Civil Rights Act, which provides for a cause of action against public officials when constitutional rights have been infringed. Some circuits applied the "reasonableness" test of *Tennessee v. Garner*,[96] in which the Supreme Court determined excessive force during an arrest to be a violation of the arrestee's Fourth-Amendment right to be secure against unreasonable searches and seizures.

Other courts, however, treated excessive force by police as a violation of the arrestee's Fourteenth-Amendment right to substantive due process of the law, using a "shock the conscience" test that originated in the 1952 case of *Rochin v. California*.[97] The "shock the conscience" standard considers subjective factors, such as malice displayed by the officer, as well as the seriousness, or disproportionateness, of the injury.[98] However, in the 1989 Supreme Court decision of *Graham v. Connor*,[99] the Court said that any excessive force claim against the police must be assessed under the Fourth-Amendment reasonableness standard.[100] Never far behind discussions of the "reasonable" use of force are considerations of proportionality and the least restrictive alternative, while the need for an appropriate motive is still maintained.

As pointed out earlier, words such as "reasonable" and "necessary" appear repeatedly in key sentences within the proposed guidelines of law enforcement agencies at all levels. Thus, while the above *ad bellum* criteria may perhaps be understood as being implicit in law enforcement thinking about force, the *in bello* considerations seem much more explicitly present. In line with this, one of the major assumptions underlying the whole just-war tradition, as well as guidelines for law enforcement, is that those authorized to use force are rational and reasonable human beings who can understand and agree on these issues. This, indeed, is a principal assumption about human beings in general—that all people putatively know what is reasonable or unreasonable, right or wrong, justified or excessive. As

95. Loftus et al., "'Reasonable' Approach to Excessive Force Cases," 136.

96. *Tennessee v. Garner*, 471 US 1 (1985).

97. *Rochin v. California*, 342 US 165 (1952).

98. Loftus et al., "'Reasonable' Approach to Excessive Force Cases," 140, 143.

99. Loftus et al., "'Reasonable' Approach to Excessive Force Cases," 144.

100. Loftus et al., "'Reasonable' Approach to Excessive Force Cases," 155; see McLaughlin, *Police and the Use of Force*, 13.

Skolnick and Fyfe so poignantly express it: "Like hardcore pornography, we may not be able to define it [police brutality or excessive force] but we know it when we see it. And when most of us saw the beating of Rodney King on the widely disseminated videotape, we knew that we were witnessing a significant incident of police brutality."[101]

The first criterion under *jus in bello*, and the seventh criterion overall, is that the means must be discriminating, indispensable, the only way, or, as usually rendered, "necessary." In the context of justified war, unnecessary combat is to be eschewed even when there is just cause. Furthermore, during such combat no unnecessary death or wanton destruction ought to be inflicted. The question still arises, however: What is "necessary" and what qualifies as "unnecessary"? How can we ascertain whether the means are indispensable? McLaughlin identifies the source of difficulty: "The problem, of course, lies in defining *reasonableness*."[102] This is why clearly-stated guidelines are desirable. As Roger Wertheimer puts it, "A policeman wants to know *beforehand* just what is meant here by 'necessary' and 'proper.' . . . He commonly operates alone, making choices in crisis situations under extreme uncertainty where the risks and stakes are very high, the circumstances largely unique, and the need for action immediate. And he knows he will be held accountable."[103] Lucid, concise principles indicating when force is necessary may provide the rational officer with tools for making such life-and-death decisions. Such fleshed-out principles are even more urgent given how "necessity" is often used in "realistic" arguments to justify instead *breaking* the rules. When a person expresses that he or she will do whatever is "necessary," that person is sometimes laying the groundwork for going all-out, so to speak. Such a person might become the next Dirty Harry. Therefore, guidelines concerning what is considered to be "necessary" should be as precise and thorough as possible.

This requires that the means be proportional. For example, the damage inflicted must not be greater than the damage prevented or the offense being avenged. Proportion must be constantly tested on every level:

101. Skolnick and Fyfe, *Above the Law*, xvi. See Delattre, *Character and Cops*, 63. Here he also mentions how rationality is presupposed on the part of the general citizenry in contradistinction to the police: "When authority, power, and discretion are granted to police officials . . . rational people presume that they will not use more than they need for their legitimate purposes, because rational people would never grant more authority or discretion to abridge liberty or use force than they believed necessary."

102. McLaughlin, *Police and the Use of Force*, 14.

103. Wertheimer, "Regulating Police Use of Deadly Force," 96.

a given tactic, a weapon, a strategy, or a battle. Both short- and long-range effects must be taken into account, and this will include physical damage as well as the subtler dimensions of social and political life—"the impact on children, public confidence in government, precedents for terror as a solution to problems, and the general breakdown of civility."[104] The response must always be proportionate to the offense. Malloy is convinced that this principle is readily applicable to police work, and he illustrates this by referring to the use of lethal force. He submits that the police officer may use a firearm only to protect his or her life or someone else's. The rationale for this is that, on the basis of the proportionality principle, a life may be taken only when a life is at stake.[105] In any other instance, some lesser measure of force must be used. As seen earlier, the guidelines for force currently in place do presuppose this principle, especially those that prohibit the shooting of a fleeing suspect or felon.

Another implication that Malloy draws from the criterion of proportionality is that the prime intention of a police officer who uses a firearm should be to incapacitate the criminal agent. This, of course, also derives from the criterion of objective intent. Malloy thinks that it is "possible to shoot in such a way that wounding is all that will result."[106] *Contra* Malloy, however, most police would argue that since they are justified in shooting only in life-threatening situations, the movie-style "shooting to disable/disarm" option is untenable. Of course, police officers are usually trained to shoot at the most central spot of the target since the likelihood of actually hitting is higher, and the probability of harming an innocent bystander is lower. In order to increase the likelihood of hitting the target, police shoot dead center. Perhaps it could be said that incapacitating the subject is the primary intent, though killing happens to be the consequence.

A further implication that Malloy draws from the criterion of proportionality relates to the type of weapon and ammunition that officers should be allowed to carry. Weapons or bullets that inflict more harm than is necessary are not to be given a place within police work. Yet, since departments today are upgrading more and more from .38 caliber pistols to 9 mm semiautomatic handguns, Malloy says: "The argument for more powerful weapons is that in those few situations where a gun might be required, the police are often at a disadvantage in terms of the accuracy, range and fire-power

104. Malloy, *Ethics of Law Enforcement*, 16.
105. Malloy, *Ethics of Law Enforcement*, 17–18.
106. Malloy, *Ethics of Law Enforcement*, 18.

of their weapons. Since the goal is incapacitating the opponent, whatever would achieve that end most effectively is deemed acceptable."[107] A relevant example of how this type of approach is being wrestled with today is provided by James B. Brady's discussion of the justifiability of using lethal and destructive hollow-point bullets by police, which includes a consideration of their accuracy, their "stopping power," the harm they cause to their intended targets, and the danger they pose to innocent bystanders.[108]

A further area in which the principle of proportionality appears to figure, though Malloy ignores it, relates to the sub-point made above that proportionality must be tested at every level. This is the impetus behind current calls to elaborate on use of force continuums in law enforcement.[109] Recommended continuums seek to delineate when an officer may escalate or de-escalate force based on (in proportion to) a subject's resistance. Of course, where to start in the continuum depends on the situation, but the officer is supposed to begin at the lowest possible point. These continuums usually begin at the low end of the scale with the officer's mere presence, which is a sort of psychological force. Verbalization is the next step, leading to another level of verbal communication, namely, command. This is followed by empty-hand techniques (soft or hard), grips, and come-along holds. The next place on the continuum involves intermediate weapons or techniques, such as mace or electrical devices. The final and highest level on the use of force continuum is deadly force, which usually involves firearms, though not always, since some techniques mentioned earlier if applied improperly or excessively can be lethal.

These considerations, which counsel constraint, seem to corroborate Malloy's optimistic judgment that proportionality is most easily applied to law enforcement. Wertheimer concurs: "We wanted to make clear to officers that they could err on the side of restraint and caution with impunity. Our principle here is an analogue of another famous principle in the design of the criminal-justice system: better that ten guilty men go free than that one innocent be convicted."[110]

107. Malloy, *Ethics of Law Enforcement*, 19.

108. Brady, "Justifiability of Hollow-Point Bullets," 9.

109. McLaughlin, *Police and the Use of Force*, 21, 65–66; Skolnick and Fyfe, *Above the Law*, 38–41.

110. Wertheimer, "Regulating Police Use of Deadly Force," 109. One wonders from whence this deontological principle came in the first place, especially since the other considerations under proportionality involve consequentialist reasoning. Of course, some may argue that the principle Wertheimer puts forward can also be understood

The eighth overall principle, which is also discriminating, upholds the immunity of the innocent. The innocent comprise those who pose no threat to the officer or anyone else. In the police context, this would include bystanders and hostages. Police need to remember vigilantly that they are serving the public. Serious danger arises if an officer begins to exhibit a "siege mentality" which divides the world into "us" and "them."[111] Delattre reminds police officers that in the United States "we have chosen the presumption of innocence out of regard for justice and for the importance of the individual. For all its deficiencies, our system exhibits greater respect for the dignity of humanity than any other ever devised."[112] The presumption of innocence, along with its correlative respect for the dignity of the human person as rational and social, seeks to prevent harm to noncombatants as well as cruelty to the alleged criminal. The criterion of innocence is especially important where the lives of noncombatants are indirectly jeopardized. In war, innocents may be holding out in a besieged city or may simply happen to be close to a military target.[113]

Thus, such methods of thinking about justifying force also fall under the *in bello* umbrella criterion, namely, the principle of discrimination. Obviously, there is some overlap between each of these criteria, the existence of which would seem to buttress Malloy's stance as a strict-constructionist concerning just war and justified force in law enforcement. In other words, with this degree of interconnectedness and overlap, each criterion should be observed, and if one is not satisfied, then it is also likely that the rest of the criteria cannot be fully satisfied. The criterion of discrimination calls for the means of force to be subjected to measured control. As noted above, this overarching criterion is satisfied when noncombatant immunity and proportionality are respected.

---

consequentially, i.e., by taking into consideration how the killing of one innocent person may have detrimental repercussions in society or may irreparably vitiate the public trust in and credibility of the police. For a discussion of some of the intricacies involved in determining a proportionality in ethical reasoning, see McCormick and Ramsey, *Doing Evil to Achieve Good.*

111. Skolnick and Fyfe, *Above the Law*, 106; see Sherman, "Learning Police Ethics," 13. Even the criminal is not really to be understood as an "enemy," since he or she is also another citizen in the society rather than a foreign invader.

112. Delattre, *Character and Cops*, 23.

113. For a law enforcement application, see Johnson, *Just War Tradition and the Restraint of War*, 21.

Conclusion

It is Malloy's view that the fundamental principles of just-war thinking are "much easier to satisfy in the domestic context of police work than they are in the international setting of war."[114] To be sure, the type of thinking that underlies the just-war tradition is not alien to present endeavors to justify and limit force in the police context. The thinking and methodology are in fact quite similar. One might even conjecture that the essential ingredients that now suffuse use of force guidelines in law enforcement have their historical and philosophical roots in the tradition of thinking about just war. For the central, underlying thrust of each of them is the presumption against harm and for restraint. Perhaps, therefore, the just-war criteria could serve as a backdrop for law enforcement thinking about using force, for although departments probably will not (and will not want to) provide such an extensive checklist as the one that Malloy advocates, the core principles ought to be articulated and promoted with just as much ardor.

Before closing, two pressing, but not insurmountable, obstacles must be acknowledged. First, there is the problem of "realism." It was said previously that realism may lead to attitudes and actions of a Dirty Harry. Robert Elias expresses his suspicions about this approach: "The prevailing thinking about crime in the United States assumes that crime is inevitable, that it is committed by irretrievably evil people, and that nothing much can be done short of get-tough measures to hold the line against society's worst violence."[115] And David Friedrichs also admits: "No serious student of the history of crime and criminal justice will likely imagine that we can dramatically eliminate crime in the twenty-first century."[116] Such gloomy observations can discourage law enforcement officials and lead them to escalate action in ways that seek to eliminate crime. Indeed, Skolnick and Fyfe believe that the Dirty Harry temptation, in which officers come to believe that the end justifies the means, is one that every officer confronts.[117]

Lawrence Sherman suggests that this mindset begins in the police academies, which convey "folklore" and war stories that show "the

---

114. Malloy, *Ethics of Law Enforcement*, 24.

115. Elias, "Peace Movement against Crime," 218.

116. Friedrichs, "Crime Wars and Peacemaking Criminology," 164.

117. Skolnick and Fyfe, *Above the Law*, 107; see Delattre, *Character and Cops*, 207, where he refers to the *Dirty Harry* problem as being connected with the stretching of the notion of "necessity," in which "a multitude of inexcusable moral wrongs has sought, and found, refuge under the slippery argument that it was 'necessary.'"

impossibility of doing things 'by the book' and the frequent necessity of 'bending the rules.'"[118] Such "realism" is compounded when the rookie officer begins patrol with his or her field training officer who says, "Forget everything they taught you in the academy, kid; I'll show you how police work is really done."[119] Let it be clearly noted that this "realist" approach is contrary to the just-war tradition, and by extension, it is in stark opposition to present departmental and legal guidelines concerning police use of force. "Realism" does not recognize restraint; just-war criteria and most present law enforcement guidelines do.

Yet, secondly, it must be admitted that simply possessing a clear set of ethical criteria concerning the use of force will not necessarily produce police officers who will always conform their behavior to those principles. Many thinkers have pointed out how codes of ethics fall short, on the one hand, because they are too simple and vague or too elaborate and complex, or, on the other hand, because they fail to motivate the officers to act rightly.[120] In this regard, Delattre's proposals for ethical training appear promising.[121] Such training would promote the intellectual, psychological, and moral requisites—in other words, concrete knowledge of the principles as well as character formation, including the virtue of restraint—for recruits to become police officers who are ready to make such critical moral judgments, as well as prepared to say "no" to certain actions such as excessive force.

These obstacles are not insuperable, and the continued refinement and promotion of these underlying principles which law enforcement happens to share with the tradition of just-war thinking seems timely in the light of the approach being taken today by law enforcement in the United States in its so-called "war" against crime. Until this military attitude and framework is done away with in law enforcement—and this is certainly desirable for many reasons—many resources are being mined in order to limit the use of force as much as possible. In this quest, attention should be given to every possible resource, including study and perhaps some adaptation of just-war thinking to the police context.

---

118. Sherman, "Learning Police Ethics," 12.

119. Sherman, "Learning Police Ethics," 13.

120. See Wertheimer, "Regulating Police Use of Deadly Force," 96; Davis, "Do Cops Really Need a Code of Ethics?" 25; Skolnick and Fyfe, *Above the Law*, 120; Kleinig and Zhang, *Professional Law Enforcement Codes*, xi; and Delattre, *Character and Cops*, 33.

121. Delattre's welcome book, *Character and Cops*, focuses on academy training based on virtue theory and deserves attention by police academy instructors.

This essay was stimulated by two primary concerns and intended to serve as a response on both fronts: one, on behalf of society in general and its police agencies, as a contribution to the current heightened efforts to prevent further Rodney King-type incidents; the other, on behalf of all police officers who are also Christians, as a reply to Sherman's earlier leading question, "Can a Christian be a police officer and potentially use lethal force?" The former issue has just been addressed in that I have attempted to demonstrate a congruence between the basic, underlying principles of restraint and limitation within just-war theory and current guidelines for the use of force in law enforcement. It is to be hoped that, with this tradition as an added dialogue partner, the efforts of criminal-justice experts will be enhanced and buttressed in their endeavors to provide ethical guidelines for the use of force for officers on the streets.

Concomitantly, in regard to those Christian police officers who may be critically reflecting on whether or not, and how, they should resort to force, this essay has demonstrated two things. First, the answer to Sherman's question is "no," if the Christian belongs to a church or denomination that is part of the pacifist tradition (unless that person chooses to deviate from his or her church teaching). If there were positions in a department in which an officer never had to possibly resort to force (perhaps as a D.A.R.E. officer), then the answer would possibly be a qualified "yes." However, force is endemic to the job for the foreseeable future, and so pacifist Christians will have to hold police officers accountable to their principles of restraint. Secondly, the answer is affirmative for those Christians who belong to the majority of denominations that adhere to the just-war tradition. They may use force as long as it is a last resort, necessary, proportionate, and limited. Some Christians may belong to denominations that accept both of these stances (for example, Roman Catholic or United Methodist), and these individuals must make an informed decision concerning where they stand on the use of force.

Chapter Two

Two Rival Versions of Just-War Theory and the Presumption against Harm in Policing[1]

" I t was right in front of me the whole time!" In embarrassment I have uttered these words on several shopping occasions during which, in exasperation at failing to find the object of my desire, I finally succumb to requesting assistance from a clerk, who simply points to where it sits practically under my nose. Instead of an illusion, or perceiving what is *not* there, I have experienced visual agnosia, or not perceiving what *is* there. A similar problem exists, I think, among Christian ethicists in a debate that is currently rekindling.

Some years ago, J. Bryan Hehir predicted that during the 1990s "another review of the ethical premise of the just war theory" would occur.[2] And recent articles by James F. Childress and James Turner Johnson, about whether or not the just-war tradition rests upon a presumption against harm and violence, have proven Hehir correct.[3] In his piece, Childress recounts his espousal, over the past two decades, of what I will call *the presumption-against-harm version* of just-war theory, which holds

1. Originally published in *Annual of the Society of Christian Ethics* 18 (1998) 221–42.

2. Hehir, "Just War Theory in a Post-Cold War World," 248.

3. Childress, "Nonviolent Resistance," 213–20; Johnson, "Broken Tradition," 27–36. My teacher, John Howard Yoder, expressed a keen interest in this particular debate, writing, for example, unpublished letters to both Childress and Hehir in 1994 and 1996, respectively, inquiring about the history of the discussion and proposing to consider it at an upcoming conference or Society of Christian Ethics meeting. Yoder's enthusiasm was reflected, also, in his encouragement of another student, Joseph A. Capizzi, and me as we participated in a round-table discussion on this debate at a conference. See my "Complementarity of Just War Theory and Pacifism" and Capizzi's "Against."

that "war is at least *prima facie* wrong and thus requires justification." It is upon this "shared starting point" that pacifists and proponents of justified violence putatively converge. "This has been," Childress reflects, "one of the most important moves in my work and also one of the most controversial."[4] *Important,* I suppose, in that an affirmative response has been developed and advanced in parallel ways by other ethicists and, moreover, officially recognized in various denominational documents, including the US Catholic bishops' pastoral letter *The Challenge of Peace* (1983) and the United Methodist bishops' *In Defense of Creation* (1986). *Controversial,* I gather, in that critics of this understanding of a mutual presumption against violence contend that it represents an abandonment of the classic just-war heritage. Thus Johnson, in his essay, counters that the tradition has been "broken" and that the real "font" and "core" of the just-war tradition is based on the *jus ad bellum* criterion of "just cause as a response to injustice." In other words, Johnson advocates what I will call *the presumption-against-injustice version* of just-war theory, in which the starting point (which is not shared with pacifism) is the duty "to prevent, punish, and remedy injustice," or, to "police injustice."[5]

It is not my aim in this essay to adjudicate the historical debate between Childress and Johnson. Rather, what I will attempt to do is draw upon a limited case (just alluded to above by Johnson's metaphor, namely, domestic policing) to begin to establish an empirical base for a normative argument about which way the just-war tradition ought to go. Indeed, proponents of *both* the presumption-against-harm and the presumption-against-injustice versions of just-war theory occasionally mention policing but, like the experience of visual agnosia, fail to perceive it as meriting a closer look. Perhaps this should not be surprising, however, given that policing, as a subject itself, is a lacuna in Christian ethics. Yet, I wish to focus on domestic policing precisely because it is a limited case with fewer variables. To be sure, my argument is not determinative or conclusive, but only a first step in the empirical part of a normative argument. For the argument to be more conclusive, the range of cases would need to be expanded. Nevertheless, it is my view that

---

4. Childress, "Nonviolent Resistance," 216.

5. Johnson, "Broken Tradition," 27–28, 35. Moreover, Johnson describes this "recent metathesis" based on a "presumption against war," which has become generally accepted in the last three decades, as an "intellectual deterioration" of just-war theory. In contrast, Hehir lauds how the "last thirty years have been a time of substantial development in the just war tradition" (Hehir, "Just War Theory in a Post-Cold War World," 239).

investigation of domestic policing in the United States can make a contribution to the empirical investigation.

This essay will develop in three sections. First, I will sketch the state of the question concerning the supposed presumption against harm in the just-war tradition, while noting any references to policing on either side. Second, I will turn to the preliminary work of Edward Malloy, a Christian ethicist who *has* dealt with policing, in order to consider more closely the analogous logic of the use of force justifications in policing and in the just-war tradition. And third, I will draw upon recent literature in the field of criminal-justice ethics, especially the work of philosopher John Kleinig, in order to help clarify which understanding of the just-war tradition is preferable.

Two Rival Versions of Just-War Theory

Proponents of the Presumption

The publication of the Catholic and Methodist bishops' respective pastoral letters on war and peace initially kindled the debate concerning a supposed presumption against harm and violence shared by the just-war tradition and pacifism.[6] In their document, for example, the Catholic bishops claim that both just-war teaching and pacifism share a "complementary

6. National Conference of Catholic Bishops, *Challenge of Peace*; United Methodist Council of Bishops, *In Defense of Creation*. Hehir writes that the response to the Catholic bishops' position "ran from an indictment that it amounted to a confusion of tongues to an endorsement of the pastoral as a development in Catholic theology" (Hehir, *Catholic Teaching on War and Peace the Decade 1979–1989*, 370). Commemorating the tenth anniversary of *Challenge of Peace*, the US Catholic bishops reiterate that both traditions share "the strong presumption against the use of force" (United States Conference of Catholic Bishops, *Harvest of Peace*, 4–5). It should be noted that these statements do not place just-war teaching and pacifism on an equal par, in that just war is advocated for most Christians and nations, and pacifism is an option only for individuals. In addition to the shared presumption against harm, which is the subject of this essay, other areas of convergence include the following: 1) just war and pacifism both reject the "realist" and "crusade" approaches, 2) they both oppose total and nuclear warfare, and 3) they interlock concerning nonviolent resistance as a legitimate and effective option for fostering or defending peace and the common good. Interestingly, Yoder suggested to me that, just as the threat of nuclear war brought together serious just-war and pacifist thinkers, so too might the development of low intensity conflict (that is, police actions). Policing, itself, has sometimes been an area of convergence between just-war thinkers and pacifists; see chapter 3 of this present volume.

relationship."[7] In a "new moment" in the Catholic Church's evaluation of war and peace, the bishops view "just-war teaching and non-violence as distinct but interdependent methods of evaluating warfare."[8] Admittedly, the two stances "diverge on some specific conclusions," but they at least "share a common presumption against the use of force"[9] or a "presumption *in favor of peace* and *against* war."[10] According to the bishops, all Christians alike are called to defend peace against aggression, but it is the question of "the *how* of defending peace which offers moral options."[11] Hence, the just-war tradition begins with the pacifist presumption against harm and violence, but it sometimes considers it necessary, in defense of the common good, to override that presumption while still restricting and reducing the horrors of war.[12] Especially when confronted with modern warfare, both pacifists and just war advocates "agree in their opposition" to unjust and total warfare.[13] Similarly, in their own statement on war and peace, the United Methodist bishops "invite pacifists and nonpacifists among our people . . . to recapture their common ground," their shared "moral presumption against all war and violence."[14]

In actuality, however, the presumption-against-harm thesis did not originate with these church statements. Rather, it was initially articulated by ethicists James Childress and Ralph Potter. Moreover, this thesis has been assumed, accepted, defended, or developed variously by Bryan Hehir (who is credited for incorporating it into the Catholic bishops' letter), David Hollenbach, Charles Curran, Richard Miller, and Lisa Sowle

7. United Methodist Council of Bishops, *In Defense of Creation*, 24; National Conference of Catholic Bishops, *Challenge of Peace*, para. 74.

8. United Methodist Council of Bishops, *In Defense of Creation*, 37; National Conference of Catholic Bishops, *The Challenge of Peace*, para. 120.

9. United Methodist Council of Bishops, *In Defense of Creation*, 37; National Conference of Catholic Bishops, *The Challenge of Peace*, para. 120.

10. United Methodist Council of Bishops, *In Defense of Creation*, 27; National Conference of Catholic Bishops, *The Challenge of Peace*, para. 83.

11. United Methodist Council of Bishops, *In Defense of Creation*, 23; National Conference of Catholic Bishops, *The Challenge of Peace*, para. 73.

12. United Methodist Council of Bishops, *In Defense of Creation*, 27; National Conference of Catholic Bishops, *The Challenge of Peace*, para. 83.

13. United Methodist Council of Bishops, *In Defense of Creation*, 37; National Conference of Catholic Bishops, *The Challenge of Peace*, para. 121.

14. United Methodist Council of Bishops, *In Defense of Creation*, 13.

Cahill.[15] Because some of these scholars presuppose the work of Childress and Potter, the positions of only these two presumption-against-harm authors will be examined.[16]

Building upon philosopher W. D. Ross's ethical framework of *prima facie* duties, which is utilized "whenever we face conflicting obligations or duties, whenever it is impossible to fulfill all the claims upon us, to respect all the rights involved, or to avoid doing evil to everyone," Childress claims that occasionally "we confront two or more *prima facie* duties or obligations, one of which we cannot fulfill without sacrificing the other(s)."[17] Two *prima facie* duties that flow from the principle of love are the duty to do justice by protecting the innocent and the duty to do no harm. Because of this latter duty of nonmaleficence, pacifism and just war share the same starting point, namely, that "war is at least *prima facie* wrong and thus requires justification."[18] According to Childress, "The moral tension arises when these two *prima facie* obligations conflict."[19] For pacifism, nonmaleficence is an absolute stance

15. See Hehir, "Just-War Ethic and Catholic Theology," 15–39; Hollenbach, *Nuclear Ethics*, 1–33; Charles E. Curran, "Roman Catholic Teaching on Peace and War," in *Critical Concerns in Moral Theology*, 144–70; Miller, *Interpretations of Conflict*; and Cahill, *Love Your Enemies*. To be sure, the views of each of these authors are not identical, but they all at least regard pacifism and just war as sharing significant points of contact.

16. As far as I can determine, no one pinpoints when this way of understanding and articulating the logic of the just-war tradition began. Potter was one of the first to present it this way, and Childress at a roughly contemporary point in time did the same. Hehir presumably inherited it from Potter, with whom he did his PhD at Harvard. Hollenbach cites Childress's work; Miller and Cahill mention all of the above. According to my classmate H. David Baer, Potter first suggested this idea in 1970 (Baer, *Recovering Christian Realism*, 10).

17. Childress, "Just-War Theories: The Bases, Interrelations, Priorities, and Functions of Their Criteria," 429; see Ross, *Foundation of Ethics*, and *The Right and the Good*. Elsewhere, Childress draws upon another philosopher, William Frankena, in order to delineate four levels of beneficence, which is part of but not equivalent to "the very principle that supported pacifism: the principle of love": 1) one ought not to inflict evil or harm; 2) one ought to prevent evil or harm; 3) one ought to remove evil; and 4) one ought to do or promote good. Childress maintains that many Christians have held that "1 has priority over 2 through 4" (Childress, "Moral Discourse about War," 119).

18. Childress, "Nonviolent Resistance," 216. Elsewhere, Childress portrays how the early Christians opposed war and/or participation in war for a number of reasons, including an aversion to bloodshed, and that this "aversion to bloodshed was important and required attention even after the other reasons for opposing military service became obsolete because of Christianity's dominant role" (Childress, "Moral Discourse about War," 118).

19. Childress, "Nonviolent Resistance," 217; "Just-War Theories," 433, 435.

admitting no exceptions; whereas, for the just-war advocate, the presumption against harm is *prima facie* and may be overridden for the sake of other *prima facie* duties, such as protecting the innocent. In this way, there exists no *prima facie* duty to go to war, "but because some other *prima facie* duties (for example, to protect the innocent) may override the *prima facie* duty not to injure or kill, there may be an *actual* duty to fight."[20] The proponent of just war, therefore, "bears a heavy burden of proof" for justifying the overriding of the *prima facie* presumption against harm. In addition, Childress points out that throughout the remaining, assorted just-war criteria, the *prima facie* presumption retains a "trace" or "residual" effect, in which the conduct that follows the overriding of the *prima facie* presumption of nonmaleficence continues to be affected by it.[21]

As an example, Childress tersely posits, "Even a policeman who has a duty to try to stop an escaped criminal who has taken hostages still must respect certain moral and legal limits."[22] The *duty* to use force, according to Childress, arises when the *prima facie* duty of nonmaleficence (vis-à-vis anyone) is overridden (in this case, vis-à-vis the criminal) by the *prima facie* duty to protect the innocent (e.g., the hostages). For Childress, this duty follows from the overall framework of *prima facie* duties, but the presumption against harm and violence remains central, as is evident in the leaning toward restraint in the other criteria of the just-war tradition. Thus, I suspect that Childress would rule out shooting the criminal as a first rather than as a last resort, rule out shooting the criminal with hollow point bullets when a standard bullet would suffice, and rule out blowing away the criminal with an inaccurate shotgun blast (which would probably harm the hostages).

Similar to Childress, Potter proposes the relevance of just-war theory "to all situations in which the use of force must be contemplated," and he holds that it is especially appropriate as "a mode of thinking for assessing the use of domestic police power."[23] Beginning with a "debt of love that Christians owe to their neighbors," Potter identifies two moral claims that are at "opposite poles of the continuum of Christian attitudes toward war and violence."[24] At

20. Childress, "Just-War Theories," 444.

21. Childress, "Just-War Theories," 431–33. Regarding "trace" or "residual" effect, Childress draws upon Nozick, "Moral Complications and Moral Structures," 1–50.

22. Childress, "Just-War Theories," 444.

23. Potter, *War and Moral Discourse*, 49–50. In addition to domestic police power, Potter mentions revolution and international peacekeeping.

24. Potter, *War and Moral Discourse*, 53–54.

one end is the claim to "contend for justice" or "protect the innocent," and at the other end is the claim "that we should not harm any neighbor." Both claims, Potter insists, must be held in tandem through the "framework" of the just-war tradition. Accordingly, the first claim establishes a burden of proof upon those, including pacifists, who reject resorting to force in certain instances. That is, if they refuse to take up arms to protect the innocent, they must nevertheless resort to other nonviolent methods of defense or promoting justice. Conversely, the second claim places a burden of proof upon those, including just warriors, who justify the use of force. That is, there exists a "strong presumption against the use of violence, a presumption established for the Christian by the non-resistant example of Jesus and for the rational non-Christian by prudent concern for order and mutual security."[25] And this presumption may be overridden only by the other strong claim, to do justice and protect the innocent against unjust aggressors.

As an example of the latter, Potter appeals to the role of the police, "as servant[s] of the community," who "promise to risk [their] own [lives] in defense of . . . any who need protection from unjust attack."[26] Indeed, Potter is one of the few Christian ethicists who specifically addresses the role of the police, and he calls on other Christian ethicists to help police officers, who "deserve counsel and instruction," to carefully "reflect upon the mode of reasoning appropriate to their office that would guide them in determining when they should act, how they should act, and why."[27] Employing the just-war "mode of reasoning" to the context of policing, therefore, Potter proposes that if a Memphis police officer had seen the rifle aimed at Martin Luther King Jr., the claim to protect the innocent would have overridden the claim to do no harm, thereby obligating the officer to fire upon the assailant.

This basic lexical structure of presumption and exception proposed by Childress and Potter has become conventional wisdom among a number of ethicists and has been incorporated into the statements of various churches.[28] Proponents of this version of just-war theory offer a generally

25. Potter, *War and Moral Discourse*, 61; see also 32.

26. Potter, *War and Moral Discourse*, 55–56.

27. Potter, *War and Moral Discourse*, 60. Anecdotal evidence of the need for a resource dealing with the intersection *of* policing and Christian faith is provided in a book targeted at a popular audience and edited by Kowalski and Collins, *To Serve and Protect*.

28. For example, Hehir accepts "the point that the moral tradition which legitimizes war as the *ultima ratio* must begin at the point where the nonviolent tradition stands, with a presumption against taking life" (Hehir, "Catholic Teaching on War and Peace,"

accepted framework that purports to boil down the just-war criteria into a single, coherent logic of presumptive duties, claims, and rules which, when they conflict with each other, are permitted to be overridden conditionally for the sake of the stronger duty or claim. In this way, the presumption-against-harm proponents maintain that their approach reinforces a posture of restraint, placing a strong burden of proof on those who find it necessary to resort to force. And the brief references made by Childress and Potter to policing seem to give support to the actual application of this version of just-war theory in at least that domestic context.

Opponents of the Presumption-Against-Harm

James Turner Johnson, however, takes issue with the "idea that the just-war tradition is rooted in a 'presumption against war,'" a version of just-war theory that he critically characterizes as being "clearly an innovation."[29] In contrast to the presumption-against-harm version, Johnson retorts that a survey of the classic just-war tradition (for example, Ambrose, Augustine, Aquinas, Vitoria, and Grotius) "suggests that, above all, the first requirement of *jus ad bellum*—that it have a just cause as a response to injustice—is the font of the entire tradition."[30] If anything, therefore, there is a presumption against injustice. Ambrose and Augustine, for example, began with "the duty of love to protect the innocent, not with a presumption against doing harm, even to an enemy." It is only subsequent to the duty to use force to protect the neighbor that restraint comes into consideration, and it, too, follows from the duty to love. In Johnson's view, then, the use of force *per se* never constitutes a moral problem in itself, although he, for some reason, uses the language of "permission" in his discussion, which seems curious if the use of force is a duty of love and justice.[31] The

---

372). He adds, however, that the just-war ethic "must be able to *legitimate* force as well as to limit it." Similarly, Cahill thinks that Hehir and Childress correctly note "that both pacifism and just-war theory share a presumption against violence . . ." (Cahill, "Theological Contexts of Just War Theory and Pacifism," 260).

29. Johnson, "Broken Tradition," 33. Similarly, George Weigel believes that *The Challenge of Peace* represents the "abandonment of the classic Catholic heritage" on war and peace (Weigel, *Tranquillitas Ordinis*, 280–84). Indeed, Weigel calls for "an abandonment of the 'dual tradition' concept promoted by" the Catholic bishops (Weigel, "Back to Basics," 68).

30. Johnson, "Broken Tradition," 28.

31. Johnson, "Broken Tradition," 30. Similarly, James E. Dougherty thinks that the

presumption-against-harm proponents, on the other hand, appear to perceive force, itself, to be problematic, and their strong presumption against it, Johnson warns, pushes "just-war theory close to outright rejection of any resort to force."[32] For Johnson, the right question is not "*whether* the political community should exercise power but what kind of power it should exercise, when, and for what reasons."[33]

Johnson believes that the mistaken emphasis on the presumption against harm is to blame for the narrowing down of just cause in the twentieth century—in, for example, international law and Catholic social teaching—only to defense against wrongful aggression. He advocates, instead, a renewed emphasis on the presumption against injustice, which would reclaim two other instances of classic just cause in addition to defense: namely, "retaking something wrongly taken, or punishment of evil." In this way, the classic just-war calls for the use of force to prevent, remedy, or punish injustice—in other words, to "police injustice." Johnson believes that his version helpfully applies to today's conflicts such as humanitarian interventions, which are also sometimes referred to as "police actions."[34]

Much of Johnson's critique of the presumption-against-harm position echoes and updates the work of Paul Ramsey on this issue. Ramsey's alternative account holds that just war is a positive service of love to the victim of wrongful aggression and to the community as a whole. For him, there are no *prima facie* duties or goods that are commensurable, so that any one could override another. Rather than being an exception to an *a priori* rule, just war, for him, is a rule of its own, not a lesser evil but a positive duty of

---

just-war tradition with its "coercive power was a divinely appointed remedy for human sinfulness, but the coercive power itself was deemed good, not sinful" (Dougherty, *Bishops and Nuclear Weapons*, 33).

32. Johnson, "Broken Tradition," 33. See also Johnson, review of *Love Your Enemies*, 284; and Johnson, "Just War Tradition and the American Military," 6.

33. Johnson, *Just War Idea*, 5.

34. Johnson, "Broken Tradition," 35; also, *Just War Idea*, 11, 15. Russell Sizemore similarly suggests that just cause "arguably has logical priority and is the most illuminating of tensions in the post-cold war world" (Sizemore, "Just Cause and New World Order," 173). Interestingly, Hehir acknowledges that, with regard to interventionary wars, "we need to follow Johnson's lead in giving renewed attention to *jus ad bellum* issues" (Hehir, "Just War Theory in a Post-Cold War World," 247). Similarly, Hollenbach recognizes the importance of this stress on just cause, in that it helps consideration of "the full range of human values that are at stake in international affairs: human rights, freedom, justice, security, and peace itself." He adds that just cause still "depends on whether the other criteria of the tradition are met" (Hollenbach, "War and Peace in American Catholic Thought," 722–23).

love. It is not surprising, then, that Ramsey inveighs against the Methodist bishops' document: "I am bewildered overall, puzzled in detail, as to what to make of the Bishops' statements about pacifism and just-war traditions," especially their claim about a "common ground" and a "moral presumption against all war and violence."[35] According to Ramsey, "justified-war Christians *do not believe that killing is intrinsically wrong*."[36] Only after a just cause has been identified is there, with the secondary principle of last resort, a presumption against harm similar to that of pacifism. With the duty to protect against injustice as the overarching principle and lexically prior to other considerations, including any presumption against violence associated with last resort, Ramsey also calls for a return to a broader, three-pronged understanding of just cause, rather than only defense against aggression.[37] Thus Ramsey, himself, allows for "aggressive just war."[38]

Undergirding his version of just-war theory, Ramsey often asserts, is an "Augustinian insight" about "the *logic*, the heart and soul, of such protective love."[39] As an example of such charity or love of the neighbor, Ramsey mentions the Good Samaritan who assisted the man victimized by thieves on the Jericho road. Suppose, however, that one encounters an enemy-neighbor. Ramsey insists, with Augustine and Ambrose, that love requires nonresistance in one-to-one neighbor relations, but if there is more than one neighbor involved, love requires shifting to a tactic of resistance on behalf of the victim-neighbor against the enemy-neighbor. Augustine, according to Ramsey, shows how, "in a world of conflicting neighbor relations," it is "possible to move from the presumption of

35. Ramsey, *Speak Up for Just War or Pacifism*, 51. With regard to this mistake, Ramsey also prolixically and polemically engages the Catholic bishops' letter, Hehir, Hollenbach, Potter and Childress, inquiring how all of them could have gotten just war wrong.

36. Ramsey, *Speak Up for Just War or Pacifism*, 104. This is because Ramsey incorporates the just war into a theory of statecraft which claims that the "use of power, and possibly the use of force, is the *esse* of politics" (Ramsey, *Just War*, 4–5, 7, 142). Thus, the criteria governing use of force apply to any use of power, armed or not. George Weigel attempts to preserve this "theory of statecraft implicit in the just war tradition" which seeks an ordered peace, with freedom, justice, security and order (Weigel, "War, Peace, and the Christian Conscience," 71, 85).

37. Ramsey, *Speak Up for Just War or Pacifism*, 53–54, 81–86, 109.

38. Ramsey, *Speak Up for Just War or Pacifism*, 88.

39. Ramsey, *Speak Up for Just War or Pacifism*, 72.

universal love for all to preference for some neighbors, and to the idea of a justifiable use of lethal force."[40]

So, returning to the story of the Good Samaritan, Ramsey suggests, "By another step it would have been a work of charity, and not of justice alone, to maintain and serve in a police patrol on the Jericho road to prevent such things from happening." After all, what would Jesus have made the Samaritan do "if he had come upon the scene while the robbers were still at their fell work?"[41] Answer: act like a police officer. Whenever a choice must be made between "the perpetrator of injustice and the many victims of it," the latter are to be preferred. Therefore, the just use of force is not an exception to but an expression of Christian love.[42] This duty of Christian love, moreover, requires that the application of force must also be limited, but Ramsey appears to restrict his concern here solely to safeguarding the innocent neighbor, that is, noncombatant immunity. In this way, Ramsey thinks that the two elements—"(1) a specific justification for sometimes killing another human being; and (2) severe and specific restrictions upon anyone who is under the hard necessity of doing so"—are both "exhibited in the use of force proper to the domestic police power."[43] Indeed, he warns that the police officer should never forget this distinction between the victim-neighbor, the enemy-neighbor, and bystander-neighbors. But Ramsey's version of just-war theory applied to policing seems to ignore ethical considerations vis-à-vis the perpetrator.

By now it should be apparent that the disagreement runs deep between these two versions of just-war theory concerning whether or not there is a presumption against harm at the tradition's core. However, a point of contact exists, though it is often not noticed—namely, references to policing. In the version of just-war theory offered by Childress and Potter, the emphasis is on a presumption against harm, which is overridden if someone's life is threatened by an attacker. This is a tighter, more restrained version of just-war theory that seems consonant with police practice. It advocates protection from harm for innocent persons, but through methods that attempt to do as little harm as possible to the attacker. In contrast, the version of just-war

---

40. Ramsey, *Speak Up for Just War or Pacifism*, 82. See his *Just War*, 142–43; *Basic Christian Ethics*, 165, 169–71; *War and the Christian Conscience*, xvi–xvii.

41. Ramsey, *Just War*, 142–43.

42. Ramsey, *Just War*, 151.

43. Ramsey, *Just War*, 144. Indeed, the rules for the "laws of war are the same as the rules governing any use of force," including "the laws governing the use of force domestically" (468, 475).

theory proposed by Johnson and Ramsey seems to focus so much on just cause that it is in danger of underemphasizing other criteria. By stressing the criterion of just cause, and by expanding this criterion to include punishment, the presumption-against-injustice version certainly calls for police to protect the innocent, but concern for the perpetrator may drop out of the picture. Indeed, Childress fears that this position may lead to the "use of force without any reservation or any hesitation about that use of force, so long as it remains within the limits of justice that require the protection of noncombatants against direct attack."[44] The language of duty associated with this concentration on just cause, moreover, may lead to or support crusades and holy wars. Hence, the presumption-against-injustice version seems more consonant with the general public demands in the United States for a "war on crime" in which law enforcement gets tough, rather than consonant with the actual guidelines and practices currently being advocated in policing to avert or at least mitigate the use of force. Attention to ethical treatments of the use of force in contemporary US policing, I think, will substantiate these reflections about the difference it makes to emphasize either a presumption against harm or a presumption against injustice.

Speak Up for Policing

I have noted how an analogy with policing has frequently been postulated in the just-war debate, but there has been a conspicuous absence of critical reflection by Christian ethicists on policing, itself. This state of affairs is especially surprising given the long and rich history of Christian theological reflection on violence. As Lisa Cahill observes, "The challenge to decide about violence, especially state-supported and institutionally perpetuated violence, has been with Christians from the beginning."[45] Likewise, Stanley Hauerwas claims that the "the question of violence is the central issue for any Christian social ethic."[46] To be sure, the question of police violence

---

44. Childress, "Nonviolent Resistance," 217; and "Just-War Theories," 444. Also, see Cahill, *Love Your Enemies*, 94, 202; Miller, "Pacifism and Just War Tenets," 469. As Yoder put it, "In sum: the 'just war tradition' is not a position but a broad stream of traditions. At one side of the stream it shades off into the crusade, in that a single criterion will suffice to justify a war; at the other bank it agrees with pacifism that war always has the burden of proof, and honorably faces this burden by respecting all the criteria . . ." (Yoder, review of *Tranquillitas Ordinis*, 505).

45. Cahill, *Love Your Enemies*, ix.

46. Hauerwas, *Peaceable Kingdom*, 114.

has commanded the attention of the US public in recent years with incidents like the Rodney King beating in 1991 by Los Angeles police.[47] And yet, while much theological attention has been given to whether or how Christians should participate in war, Edward Malloy accurately perceives "a noticeable deficiency in applying such analysis to the domestic context of crime" and police use of force in response to it.[48]

Indeed, Malloy is the only Christian ethicist, to my knowledge, who offers a fairly substantial treatment of police use of force. The first chapter of his *The Ethics of Law Enforcement and Criminal Punishment* stands as one of the few theological treatments of the topic of police use of force that, although preliminary and brief, deals with this issue as a subject worthy of attention. He writes:

> At the theoretical level, most ethical reflection about the problem of violence has centered on difficulties in personal relations or on the horror of warfare. In between these two extremes stands the role of the police in a contemporary setting.[49]

In response to this lack of attention to policing, Malloy recommends the just-war tradition as a "helpful ethical framework for analysis." With it he conducts "an exercise of analogical interpretation" that, he hopes, "has not stretched the just-war tradition too far," in which each criterion of the just-war tradition is analyzed vis-à-vis guidelines for the use of force in policing, yielding a coherent, restrained ethical grid for application in the latter context.[50] Malloy also intends that his "modest venture in

47. Other examples include the 1985 bombing of the radical group MOVE's house by Philadelphia police, which destroyed sixty-one homes and killed six adults and five children, and the 1996 beating of two immigrants pulled out of their truck by Riverside County Sheriff's deputies in California. Examples at the level of federal law enforcement include the burning of the Branch Davidian compound in Waco and the shooting of Vicki Weaver at Ruby Ridge.

48. Malloy, *Ethics of Law Enforcement*, 2.

49. Malloy, *Ethics of Law Enforcement*, 10.

50. Malloy, *Ethics of Law Enforcement*, 24. Of course, analogies are neither univocal nor equivocal, rather they involve attributes which are neither precisely the same nor yet simply different. The similarities and dissimilarities between policing and war have been noted by various writers, including Bainton, *Christian Attitudes Toward War and Peace*, 240–41; Cady, *From Warism to Pacifism*, 36; Teichman, *Pacifism and the Just War*, 38–46; Yoder, *Politics of Jesus*, 204. Most of the differences noted by these writers are that of degree rather than kind. Even if the analogy between war and policing has both strengths and weaknesses, the use of force in either context requires justification, hence, the ethical logic or framework used to evaluate the justifiability of the use of force in either case does seem to be analogous.

a field which is ripe for interdisciplinary cooperation might encourage other Christian ethicists to grapple with this problem of the control of, and response to, domestic violence."[51]

It will be helpful to discern the ways in which the logic of the ethical framework is analogous between the use of force in policing and the use of force in the just-war tradition by giving attention to Malloy's list of criteria particularly pertinent for this essay. The first criterion with which he deals is "legitimate authority," that is, war may be waged only by a recognized government. Adapting this to the police context, the police officer may only use coercive force when he or she truly represents the body politic.[52] Sworn to uphold the law, police possess an enormous amount of discretion and cannot always consult with a superior or make a decision in advance; in many cases, therefore, they are required to determine on the spot when and how to use force. Yet, such authority is derivative and is thereby withdrawn when other criteria for justifiable use of force are not satisfied. Criminologists Jerome Skolnick and James Fyfe corroborate this view: "[W]here police derive their authority from law and take an oath to support the Constitution they are obliged to acknowledge the law's moral force and to be constrained by it"; furthermore, if an officer uses excessive force, "he or she undermines the very source of police authority."[53]

The second criterion, according to Malloy's reckoning, is that war may be fought only for a "just cause."[54] Because the legitimate goals of war in the just-war tradition, in Malloy's account, include both vindicating justice and restoring peace, traditional examples that he mentions are national defense and protecting allies. Importantly, Malloy does not include punishment in this category. So, adapting this criterion of just cause to the context of policing requires the existence of an operative legal code from which can be derived any situation where police use of force may be warranted. This, of course, presupposes the justice of the code as a whole. Therefore, when a just law is broken, intervention by police is justified. But Malloy immediately introduces consideration of the criteria of "proportionality" and "last resort," which together determine, in the first place,

---

51. Malloy, *Ethics of Law Enforcement*, ix. Malloy initially considered the problem of police use of force in a paper, "Ethics and Police Intervention in Domestic Violence," which he presented at the 1979 annual meeting of the Society of Christian Ethics (Long, *Academic Bonding and Social Concern*, 117).

52. Malloy, *Ethics of Law Enforcement*, 12.

53. Skolnick and Fyfe, *Above the Law*, xvi.

54. Malloy, *Ethics of Law Enforcement*, 12–13.

whether intervention is really necessary and, in the second place, what level of intervention (that is, force) is appropriate.

Since the response must be proportionate to the offense, police officers possess the discretionary ability to perhaps issue a warning for many infractions, or to help persons in a conflict to talk and work things out, rather than make a forceful arrest. The pivotal role of proportionality and last resort especially comes into view by considering the use of lethal force. According to Malloy, a police officer may fire a weapon only to protect life (one's own or someone else's), for a "life may be taken only when a life is at stake."[55] Killing someone is equivalent to imposing "an irrevocable" sentence or punishment, which may be the reason that Malloy does not include punishment as an example of just cause. For him, the role of the police is not to punish but to apprehend or incapacitate the perpetrator. Thus, it should be a "reluctant decision to employ" force, especially lethal force, which is why it is a last resort.[56] The police should exhaust all other possible methods, in other words, for handling a situation before resorting to force. Again, Malloy's view finds corroboration in a process of tightening the restraints on use of force during the past few decades in the law and in departmental standard operating procedure guidelines. Most police agencies have limited the right to shoot a firearm to two categories: 1) the officer may shoot to defend herself or himself from grievous bodily injury, and 2) the officer may shoot to save another person from grievous bodily injury.[57] Departments no longer allow their officers to shoot fleeing felons in situations in which the perpetrator no longer poses an immediate threat to anyone's life.[58]

It should be readily apparent that, for Malloy, the criteria coalesce tightly as an interlocking framework. He does not make any claims about a primary starting point for his version of just-war theory. It is based neither upon only a presumption against harm nor only a presumption against injustice. Both, though, seem to be implicit within it. Yet, Malloy's application of just-war thinking to police use of force seems more consonant with

55. Malloy, *Ethics of Law Enforcement*, 17–18.

56. Malloy, *Ethics of Law Enforcement*, 13, 18, 22.

57. Geller, "Police and Deadly Force," 218. Geller calls this a "defense-of-life" shooting policy that has been adopted in recent years.

58. Whereas, in the eighteenth century the English jurist, William Blackstone, justified deadly force in stopping a felon who was fleeing, in recent years "the rationale for the rule is gone, that while all felonies were capital crimes in the 18th century, relatively few are in the 20th" (Hall, "Deadly Force, the Common Law and the Constitution," 27).

the presumption-against-harm version in that it exhibits a strong leaning toward restraint. I attribute this to the fact that Malloy identifies himself as a "strict constructionist" just-war theorist.[59] That is, he requires that each and every criterion be met before justifying war, or in this case, the use of force by police. If any of the criteria cannot be satisfied, a "no" to the use of force must be the result.[60] This differs from Ramsey, who says the "supravalent" presumption of just war is against injustice and that the presumption against harm is "infravalent."[61] Malloy's version might be understood as holding that all the criteria are *polyvalent*. In this way, it may stand closer to Childress's version which bonds each criterion closely together through the residual or trace effects of the presumption against harm. Like Childress's version, the result of Malloy's strict constructionist approach is that there is strong burden of proof to justify force, and this framework seems to find empirical support within the context of policing. Attention to more recent treatments of the topic of the police use of force, from the perspective of the nascent field of police ethics itself, will help to see if this is the case.

To Serve and Protect

In the wake of the Rodney King incident, one criminal-justice expert observed: "That beating was not unique in the history of policing. It probably has kin in every state in the Union, in every country, and indeed in every significant police force as far back as we can trace the police function."[62] With regard to the use of lethal force, researchers estimate that police officers kill nearly 600 suspects annually, shoot and wound an additional 1,200, and fire at and miss another 1,800.[63] All of this has provoked philosophers and criminal-justice scholars in recent years to give attention to the ethics of police use of force. Philosopher John Kleinig provides the most comprehensive book on the subject, *The Ethics of Policing*. In it he examines both the moral foundations of policing and the specific problem of the use of force, identifying models of policing currently advocated, along with their respective understandings of the use of force. The two main models in tension

59. Malloy, *Ethics of Law Enforcement*, 28.

60. Malloy, *Ethics of Law Enforcement*, 11.

61. Ramsey, *Speak Up for Just War or Pacifism*, 92.

62. Davis, "Do Cops Really Need a Code of Ethics?" 14.

63. Loftus et al., "'Reasonable' Approach to Excessive Force Cases," 136. As noted in the previous chapter, these numbers are higher now.

with each other are the "crimefighter" model and the "social peacekeeper" model, with the former striving to continue in the United States as the primary paradigm, and the latter gradually gaining acceptance instead.[64] Consideration of his treatment of police use of force should help clarify which understanding of the just-war tradition is appropriate.

With regard to the moral foundations of policing, Kleinig begins with social contract theory, since it undergirds most liberal democratic thinking and seems to offer "good prospects for accountable policing."[65] Given that policing as we know it developed in Western liberal democracies, most philosophers and criminologists who address the subject—and in particular the use of force—turn to social contract theory. Jeffrey Reiman, for example, draws from classical social contract thinkers, who emphasize individual rights, personal freedom, and government through consent, in order to construct an ethical approach to police use of force.[66] According to this view, since the problem of some hypothetical "state of nature" is that "everyone's freedom to use force at his own discretion undermines everyone else's freedom to work and live as he wishes, it becomes rational for freedom-loving people to renounce their freedom to use force at their own discretion . . . if (and only to the extent that) the sacrifice of this freedom results in a gain in real and secure freedom to live as one wants."[67] Instead of the insecurity of some "state of nature," in which each person protects his or her own interests, and in which there is a danger of escalating, unlimited coercion, citizens in the social contract consent to an exchange of some of their freedoms to a civil government authorized to have the power to protect their fundamental rights. The institution of law enforcement is a manifestation of this government authority and power. At the same time, however, the right to use force that is deposited in the police, according to this social contract perspective, is not without limits.

Indeed, for liberalism there remains a normative cutting edge that hinges on "whether renouncing a private use of force and allowing a public

64. Kleinig, *Ethics of Policing*, 24–29. Two additional models identified—the "emergency operator" and the "social enforcer"—continue to focus "too directly on the coercive dimension of police authority" as their "distinguishing feature," although they each claim to downplay the "crimefighting" character of policing.

65. Kleinig, *Ethics of Policing*, 11.

66. See Reiman, "Social Contract and the Police Use of Deadly Force." Reiman relies on Locke's *Second Treatise of Government*, Hobbes's *Leviathan*, Rousseau's *The Social Contract*, and Rawls's *A Theory of Justice*.

67. Reiman, "Social Contract and the Police Use of Deadly Force," 239.

agency to enforce this renunciation results in greater concrete freedom for everyone."[68] The liberal emphasis on freedom thus provides a general guide with which to distinguish between legitimate and illegitimate exercises of power. That is, coercive action by police that restricts or endangers citizen freedom, instead of securing and broadening it, undermines the authority of the police by reproducing the conditions of the state of nature that the police are supposed to remedy. Social contractarians, therefore, usually limit police use of force, first, to self-defense (private citizens retain this right in the absence of a police officer) and, second, to protect the lives of private citizens. Until recently, this approach justified police use of force, including lethal force, to protect property or to stop a fleeing felon who may or may not have posed a physical threat, but these are now unjustifiable causes for the use of lethal force.

To be sure, this philosophical perspective regards coercive power as the *raison d'être* of policing. As Vance McLaughlin puts it, "[Police] routinely use force to carry out their role as enforcers—the use of force is inherent in the profession."[69] Similarly, police are characterized by Robert Reiner as "specialists in coercion."[70] This is why Kleinig observes—I think rightly—that the predominant paradigm for policing associated with a liberal contractarian approach is the "crimefighter" or "war" model. As he puts it, "Classical social contract theory perceives such a role for police. Just as an army is needed to protect us from the barbarian without, a police force is required to protect us from the barbarian within."[71] Yet, although Kleinig acknowledges that "any model of policing that fails to take into account their authority to employ force will be inadequate," he correctly argues that there are "serious practical and moral problems" with the crimefighter model.[72] Quite simply, it encourages an "us" versus "them" mentality, in which the police view their role as a punitive one, so that they are inclined to be cynical in their attitudes toward the public and treat suspects as though they are guilty criminals. More problematic, most police officers *like* to see themselves as crimefighters (some of my fellow officers and I often enjoyed *Dirty Harry*-type movies), even though their actual work is diversified, with such activities as helping injured accident victims,

68. Reiman, "Social Contract and the Police Use of Deadly Force," 240.

69. McLaughlin, *Police and the Use of Force*, 1.

70. Reiner, *Politics of the Police*, 2, 59–60.

71. Kleinig, *Ethics of Policing*, 24–25.

72. Kleinig, *Ethics of Policing*, 24–25.

searching for lost children, calming quarreling spouses, or coaching youth basketball teams. Kleinig, therefore, believes that the crimefighter model "runs a risk of excess."[73] And ethical perspectives on the use of force that are based on social contract theory, he suggests, are too minimalistic and attenuated to rein in this model.

As an alternative approach, Kleinig recommends the "social peacekeeper" model, which seems to be gaining adherence currently with the implementation of community-oriented policing. He believes that this model is historically rooted in the Anglo-Saxon tradition of the king's peace, in which the "role of the police is to ensure or restore peaceful order."[74] This model does not obviate the logic of restraint that social contractarians describe; rather, it reinforces restraint through couching it within a wider framework of community and social practices of service. This would counter the tendency toward excess. As Kleinig puts it, "So understood, the peacekeeper model is broad enough to encompass most of the work that police do, whether it is crimefighting, crime control, or interventions in crisis situations. But what is more important is the irenic cast that it gives to police work."[75] Accordingly, police use of force "becomes a last (albeit sometimes necessary) resort rather than their dominant *modus operandi.*"[76]

Such a perspective *does* perceive the use of force to be a problem. Indeed, Kleinig suggests that it is a "*prima facie* evil" or "the lesser of two evils" to use force in policing. He maintains that there is a *prima facie* "presumption against the use of force," which is why force requires justification, even in police use of force.[77] This is especially the case for lethal force, because its use is irrevocable, with "no room for mistake, for changes of mind, for remission or pardon, no room for compensating the person who is killed." Indeed, lethal use of force risks judging and punishing a person to death, which undercuts the principle "innocent until proven guilty." Upon this basis, Kleinig delineates some key principles of current moral and legal assessments of police use of force. With regard to the current moral assessments of intermediate and lethal force, Kleinig identifies the primary criteria currently employed, including right intention (which rules out

73. Kleinig, *Ethics of Policing*, 24.

74. Kleinig, *Ethics of Policing*, 27–28.

75. Kleinig, *Ethics of Policing*, 29.

76. Kleinig, *Ethics of Policing*, 29.

77. Kleinig, *Ethics of Policing*, 96–98, 101. Kleinig does not indicate from where he gets this language, but it is strikingly similar to Childress's.

punishment and instead calls for restraint and apprehension), reasonableness (that is, it should not "shock the conscience"), proportionality (that is, force used to achieve legitimate ends ought not to be disproportionate to the seriousness of the alleged offense), and minimization (that is, employing a use of force continuum with lethal force as last resort).

In line with this ethical perspective, Kleinig observes that, on the legal front in the past decade or so, there has been "a tightening up of state legislative permissions or, in many cases, departmental policies and practices."[78] For example, a monumental Supreme Court decision in 1985 ruled out the use of deadly force in instances of a non-life-threatening fleeing felon.[79] In other words, "we have arrived at a situation," says Kleinig, "in which the police use of deadly force has been significantly limited—one in which the fleeing felon privilege has been all but subsumed under the defense-of-life privilege."[80] The more a social-peacekeeper model is implemented, with police officers trained to see themselves as serving the community in which they are integrally involved, the stronger the presumption against force is reinforced.

Conclusion

At this point, it should be evident that the experience (in theory and, increasingly, in practice) of police in the United States indicates an empirical basis for favoring the presumption-against-harm version of the just-war tradition. Indeed, Kleinig's social-peacekeeper model, with its use of force guidelines based on a strong presumption against harm, seems quite consonant with the "mode of reasoning" offered by Potter and Childress. Moreover, Malloy's earlier attempt at providing a "strict constructionist" treatment of the use of force in policing seems to share more affinity with the presumption-against-harm proponents. Each of these perspectives aim at justifying force in a way that takes into consideration all the agents involved in a possible conflict situation: the victim, the police officer, and the perpetrator. In this way, the presumption-against-harm version attempts to rein in excessive force by police. In contrast, the presumption-against-injustice version, by focusing primarily upon the criterion of just cause, and by including punishment as a just cause, may reinforce a crimefighter model that runs the risk of excess through calls for "crusades against crime"

---

78. Kleinig, *Ethics of Policing*, 112, 114–18.

79. *Tennessee v. Garner*, 471 US 1 (1985).

80. Kleinig, *Ethics of Policing*, 116.

or the like. In this version, the rights of the perpetrator are in danger of dropping out of the equation. In my view, the trajectory over the past few decades—in police law and ethics, and in the just-war teachings of the churches—has been strikingly parallel, with the restraints tightened in each through a strong presumption against harm.

Childress points out that his own position on this debate "can be assessed on several grounds, including its fidelity to tradition, broadly understood, its consistency and coherence, and its congruence with contemporary experience."[81] I have endeavored to investigate the "contemporary experience" of policing in the United States in order to begin to establish an empirical base for a normative argument about which way the just-war tradition ought to proceed. The above attention to the justification of the use of force in policing, I think, is congruent with that version of the just-war tradition calling for a coherent, restrained approach to the use of force, with a strong presumption against harm. Of course, a conclusive argument would require more case studies, especially those that cross national borders (e.g., international police actions and humanitarian interventions), but if the domestic US case is analogous, then the initial evidence suggests that whatever the historical understanding of the just-war tradition, normatively for now and in the foreseeable future, the presumption-against-harm version of just-war theory should be followed.

81. Childress, "Nonviolent Resistance," 217.

Chapter Three

From Police Officers
to Peace Officers[1]

Quis custodiet ipsos custodies . . . ?—Juvenal[2]

I n his biography of the pacifist Leo Tolstoy, Ernest J. Simmons relates a humorous story about a response that Tolstoy gave to a question regarding the possible inconsistency of those Russian Revolutionists and Social Democrats who, on the one hand, detested violence, but, on the other hand, advocated its use against opponents to the revolution. Because the inquirer's sympathies lay with the revolutionists rather than the Russian secret police, he asked, "Is there not a difference between the killing that a revolutionist does and that which a policeman does?" In reply, however, Tolstoy tersely opined, "There is as much difference as between cat-shit and dog-shit. But I don't like the smell of either one or the other."[3]

I can imagine Tolstoy, were he living in the United States today, giving a similarly critical evaluation of police violence. Indeed, several highly publicized cases involving excessive force by police in recent years promptly come to mind. The well-known Rodney King case is one example. While driving on the evening of March 3, 1991, this African-American male was pulled over and confronted by Los Angeles police officers, who proceeded to arrest him on a number of charges. On the surface this sort of incident occurs frequently and could have been reported as a routine traffic arrest, except for the additional fact that it was

1. Originally published in Hauerwas et al., *Wisdom of the Cross: Essays in Honor of John Howard Yoder*, 84–114.

2. Juvenal, *Sixteen Satires*, satire 6, ll. 347–48: "But who will keep guard on the guardians . . . ?"

3. Simmons, *Leo Tolstoy*, 651. I am grateful to my classmate Lee Camp for bringing this story to my attention.

filmed by a bystander with a video camera. All who saw the replays on the network news watched fifteen uniformed officers repeatedly bludgeon, bruise, and lacerate King. Although shocking to the consciences of the American public, one criminal-justice expert has observed: "That beating was not unique in the history of policing. It probably has kin in every state in the Union, in every country, and indeed in every significant police force as far back as we can trace the police function."[4]

Another example is the bombing of the radical African-American group MOVE by Philadelphia police in 1985. Founded in the early 1970s, members of MOVE adopted the surname "Africa," advocated animal rights, opposed technology, and communally lived together, usually in friction with neighbors and police. When a shoot-out occurred in 1978 with the Philadelphia police, the result was one officer's death and the imprisonment of several MOVE members. Relocating to another house, the remaining members installed loudspeakers outside that they used to demand the re-opening of their fellow members' legal cases. When neighbors complained about the noise, trash, and evidence of weapons, the Philadelphia police decided to take action. On May 13, 1985, five hundred heavily armed police officers surrounded the house, demanding the surrender of four members on charges including harassment, rioting, and possessing explosives. A ninety-minute gun battle ensued that ended in stalemate. Thereupon, the police resorted to dropping a bomb on MOVE's house. It ignited a tremendous fire, however, that quickly consumed the building. The blaze, which the police allowed to burn, ultimately engulfed and destroyed sixty-one other houses in the neighborhood and killed eleven MOVE members, including six adults and five children.[5]

Other examples of excessive use of force by law enforcement include the beating of undocumented Mexican aliens by deputies in California (videotaped by a news helicopter), the ATF and FBI assault on the Branch Davidians at Waco, and the 1992 FBI shooting of Vicki Weaver, using rewritten rules of engagement, deviating from standard operating procedure, ordering "shoot to kill" at Ruby Ridge. Considering the prevalence of violence in American culture, and given the rote adoption of the "war" or "crimefighting" paradigm for law enforcement, similar incidents have continued to be likely.

---

4. Davis, "Do Cops Really Need a Code of Ethics?," 14.

5. Wagner-Pacifici, *Discourse and Destruction*, 29, 66.

One need not be a Tolstoyan pacifist, however, to criticize such instances of police violence. Most of the scholarly literature pertaining to the topic of police use of force addresses the matter from a variety of disciplines: criminology, political science, sociology, or philosophy. One of the first scholars to philosophically scrutinize police use of force, criminal-justice expert Lawrence Sherman, suggests that, on the one hand, many issues in police ethics are "in fact clear-cut, and hold little room for serious philosophical analysis," while on the other hand, the use of force deserves sober study since it is "very complex, with many shades of gray."[6] Getting to the crux of the matter, Sherman claims, "The most basic question of all criminal-justice ethics, of course, is whether and under what conditions one can reconcile doing harm to others with our widespread norms against harm."[7] In passing, he muses that the literature on pacifism, nonviolence, and conscientious objection may be relevant, but adds that he has unfortunately not seen such an approach applied to the domestic use of force by police. So, sincerely curious, he forthrightly asks: "Can a pacifist be a police officer or a judge? Can a Christian? Can a Rawlsian? What is the ethical defense for saying that killing is wrong and then urging killing in response to killing?"[8]

In what follows, I shall treat Sherman's question about "the ethical defense for saying that killing is wrong and then urging killing in response to killing," which he addresses specifically to the three groups (i.e., pacifists, Christians, Rawlsians), though my investigation will proceed in reverse order. Most of my attention, however, will focus on the question about whether a pacifist can be a police officer, for as Lisa Cahill has observed with a hint of curiosity: "Pacifists generally are opposed not only to war, but to any form of direct physical violence, although they may make exceptions to this bias by permitting police action."[9] In view of this, J. Philip Wogaman suggests that pacifists' mere acceptance of—in addition to the issue of possible participation in—police actions, including violence, in order to maintain

6. Sherman, "Learning Police Ethics," 19.

7. Sherman, *Ethics in Criminal Justice Education*, 38.

8. Sherman, *Ethics in Criminal Justice Education*, 38. See Geller, "Officer Restraint in the Use of Deadly Force," where he similarly asks, "What is the bearing of an officer's personal moral code concerning when and whom it is proper to shoot on his or her actual use of deadly force? Insight into this question . . . will be useful in anticipating the extent to which administrative policy and training can effectively override—or harness—individual officer predilections" (160).

9. Cahill, *Love Your Enemies: Discipleship, Pacifism, and Just War Theory*, 2.

the state may "in one sense ... be equivocation."[10] Therefore, in the pacifist section I shall survey the various pacifist responses that might lead Wogaman to draw such a conclusion. Finally, because the subject of policing was of much interest to my teacher, John Howard Yoder, I shall attempt to offer a Christian pacifist perspective on police use of force, drawing and building on the few, brief reflections he wrote on the subject.[11]

Can a Rawlsian Be a Police Officer?

The so-called Rawlsians, for their part, have not been reluctant to offer their views, in response to Sherman's question, on this issue. Indeed, almost every contribution in the public debate, although not always self-identified as "Rawlsian," arises from a social contractarian perspective. This is probably the case due to the fact that policing, as we know it, is a modern institution that coincided with the rise of the liberal democratic nation-state.

Though its functional origins may be traced to ancient communal self-policing, modern policing began institutionally at the urging of Sir Robert Peel in 1829 with the "New Police" of Metropolitan London. Due to increasing crime and riots, against which the earlier, decentralized constables were ineffective and the military was excessively forceful, Peel organized the first modern police department, in which policing came to be under stood as "a distinctive career, with a specific ideology of service, professional identity and craft skills."[12] Indeed, Peel intended to distinguish police officers from soldiers, but ended up appropriating heavily from the military organizational model in order to convince critics that his New Police would perform

10. Wogaman, *Christian Ethics: A Historical Introduction*, 280.

11. As for Yoder's interest in this subject, the last memo that I received from him, dated December 24, 1997, was a three-page critique of a local police department for a coerced confession that it conducted, which was videotaped and later featured on the NBC news program *Dateline*. Yoder suggested that I give "further visibility" to this in a "police ethics periodical ... for some moral pressure on local police." One of the reasons why he directed this memo, and others like it, to me is that some members of my family—including my mother—and I have previous experience in the field of law enforcement, with personal stories that Yoder often enjoyed discussing. As for why I say "attempt to offer a Christian pacifist perspective," I must confess that I, myself, am not currently a pacifist, although Yoder's life and work has influenced me tremendously. See my caveat in the introduction about my reliance on Yoder's work.

12. Reiner, *Politics of the Police*, 45. This historical sketch draws from Reiner, who provides a balanced account of both "orthodox" and "revisionist" interpretations of the rise and development of modern policing; see especially 9–51.

its duties as impeccably as the British military. Nevertheless, the New Police differed from the military in that the police did not carry swords and fire-arms, though they did sometimes have truncheons. To be sure, opposition to an established police department existed, but it was based on the anxiety that the New Police would serve as a political puppet and tool of the upper class.[13] Over the span of the next century, however, the Metropolitan Police gradually gained widespread acceptance.

The transplanting of the police onto American soil began similarly. In 1834, Boston policemen were also unarmed and "restrained from commit-ting brutal acts by the prior warning of their superiors, by their own good judgment, and by fear of physical retaliation."[14] But even at this stage, as an unarmed force, police in the United States aroused misgivings among the people, many of whom labeled these departments as "un-American," "un-democratic," and "militaristic."[15] Such accusations were aggravated as the police began wearing uniforms and often obtained their jobs through a spoils systems for supporting certain politicians. For these reasons, the American people perceived police as a threat to their personal liberties.

The supposedly "un-American" police soon diverged from the British model, however, and became distinctively American with the use of firearms to enforce the law. Police in increasingly violent American cities began car-rying revolvers in the 1850s for their own protection after criminals began using firearms. And after the Civil War, the availability of thousands of army revolvers on the surplus market hastened the widespread rearmament of the general society, resulting in official acceptance of police use of revolvers.[16] The Boston police, for instance, acquired firearms in the aftermath of the Draft Riot of 1863. Roger Lane suggests that, as a result, "the fact that most policemen carried their revolvers tipped the physical balance in their favor, making them more formidable but also increasing the danger of brutality on their part."[17] Obviously, the American version of Peel's vision has experienced more police violence over the years, probably due to "some combination of

13. Reiner, *Politics of the Police*, 16–17. Cf. Berkley, *Democratic Policeman*, 5. Interest-ingly, no reference is made of any church or theological reaction, except for a brief men-tion by Steve Uglow that Quakers and working classes initially opposed police forces. He does not delve into the Quaker criticism however (Uglow, *Policing Liberal Society*, 15).

14. Lane, *Policing the City*, 187.

15. Berkley, *Democratic Policeman*, 5. Cf. Fosdick, *American Police Systems*, 70–71.

16. Sherman, "Execution Without Trial," 190.

17. Lane, *Policing the City*, 187–88.

American social and historical forces [which have] blended with the military model to produce a volatile mix."[18]

Given that policing as we know it developed in Western liberal democracies, I suspect it should be no surprise that most philosophers and criminologists who address the subject—and in particular the use of force—turn to social contract theory. Jeffrey Reiman, for example, draws from classical social contract thinkers in order to construct an ethical approach to police use of force which emphasizes individual rights, personal freedom, and government through consent.[19] According to this view, since the problem of some hypothetical "state of nature" is that "everyone's freedom to use force at his [or her] own discretion undermines everyone else's freedom to work and live as he [or she] wishes, it becomes rational for freedom-loving people to renounce their freedom to use force at their own discretion . . . if (and only to the extent that) the sacrifice of this freedom results in a gain in real and secure freedom to live as one wants."[20] In other words, instead of the insecurity of some "state of nature," in which each person must protect his or her own interests, and in which there is a danger of unlimited coercion, citizens in the social contract consent to an exchange of some of their freedoms to a civil government authorized to have the power to protect their fundamental rights. The institution of law enforcement is a manifestation of government authority and power, functioning as an executor of the legislative will. At the same time, however, the right to use force, which is deposited in the police, according to this social contract perspective, is not without limits.

Indeed, for liberalism there remains a normative cutting edge that hinges on "whether renouncing a private use of force and allowing a public agency to enforce this renunciation results in greater concrete freedom for everyone."[21] The liberal emphasis on freedom thus provides a general guide with which to distinguish between legitimate and illegitimate exercises of power. That is, coercive action by police that restricts or endangers citizen freedom, instead of securing and broadening it, undermines the authority of the police by reproducing the conditions of the state of

18. Skolnick and Fyfe, *Above the Law*, 128.

19. Reiman, "Social Contract and the Police Use of Deadly Force"; Reiman relies on John Locke's *Second Treatise of Government*, Thomas Hobbes's *Leviathan*, Jean-Jacques Rousseau's *The Social Contract*, and John Rawls's *A Theory of Justice*.

20. Reiman, "Social Contract and the Police Use of Deadly Force," 239.

21. Reiman, "Social Contract and the Police Use of Deadly Force," 240.

nature that the police are supposed to remedy. Accordingly, Steve Uglow interprets Peel's careful organization of the police in contradistinction from the military as seeking to abide by the prohibition on the arbitrary use of physical force by the state, a core concept within liberalism with its view that the rights of the person are inalienable over and against state coercion. In addition, Uglow writes:

> The capacity to use force crystallizes the relationship between individual and state, defining the measure of control that citizens are granted over their own lives. . . . The guiding principle developed within liberal societies has been that such force must be essential and minimum. The former implies that state violence is a tactic of last resort, the latter that the violence must be no more than is needed to prevent the anticipated harm.[22]

Social contractarians, therefore, usually limit police use of force, first, to self-defense (private citizens retain this right in the absence of a police officer) and, second, to protect the lives of private citizens. Until recently, this approach justified police use of force, including lethal force, to protect property or to stop a fleeing felon who may or may not have posed a physical threat. It seems to me, however, that the social contract approach does not necessarily rule out these latter possibilities.

To be sure, this philosophical perspective regards coercive power as the *raison d'être* of policing. As Vance McLaughlin puts it, "[Police] routinely use force to carry out their role as enforcers—the use of force is inherent in the profession."[23] Although they are supposed to minimize the use of force, police nevertheless are referred to by Reiner as "specialists in coercion."[24] This is why philosopher John Kleinig observes—I think rightly—that the predominant paradigm for policing associated with a liberal contractarian approach is the "crimefighter" or "war" model. As he puts it, "Classical social contract theory perceives such a role for police. Just as an army is needed to protect us from the barbarian without, a police force is required to protect us from the barbarian within."[25] Yet, although Kleinig acknowledges that "any model of policing that fails to take into account their authority to employ force will be inadequate," he correctly argues that there are "serious

---

22. Uglow, *Policing Liberal Society*, 53, 12; cf. Reiman, "Social Contract and the Police Use of Deadly Force," 237–38, 240–43; Berkley, *Democratic Policeman*, 2–4, 107–9.

23. McLaughlin, *Police and the Use of Force*, 1.

24. Reiner, *Politics of the Police*, 2, 59–60.

25. Kleinig, *Ethics of Policing*, 24–25.

practical and moral problems" with the crime-fighter model.[26] Quite simply, it encourages an "us" versus "them" mentality, in which the police view their role punitively, so that they are inclined to be cynical in their attitudes toward the public and treat suspects as though they are guilty criminals. More problematic, most police officers like to see themselves as crimefighters, even though their actual work is diversified, with such activities as helping injured accident victims, searching for lost children, calming quarreling spouses, or coaching a youth basketball team. Kleinig, therefore, believes that the crimefighter model "runs a risk of excess."[27] And ethical perspectives on the use of force that are based on social contract theory, he suggests, are too minimalistic and attenuated to rein in this model.

Can a Christian Be a Police Officer?

Despite Sherman's query to Christians, their voice is conspicuously absent in the public discussion regarding police use of force.[28] To be sure, this omission may be attributed to the fact that the question of the use of force by law enforcement officers has basically been a lacuna in the literature of Christian social ethics. This state of affairs is curious given the long and rich history of Christian theological reflection on violence. As Lisa Cahill observes, "The challenge to decide about violence, especially state-supported and institutionally perpetuated violence, has been with Christians from the beginning."[29] Similarly, Stanley Hauerwas claims that "the question of violence is the central issue for any Christian social ethic."[30] And yet, while much theological attention has been given to whether or how Christians should participate in international conflicts and warfare, Edward Malloy

---

26. Kleinig, *Ethics of Policing*, 24–25.

27. Kleinig, *Ethics of Policing*, 24.

28. The lack of a Christian or theological contribution to the debate is evident in a recent collection of essays edited by Geller and Toch, who observe that the book's contributors all share a common concern about this controversial subject even while representing "many diverse perspectives" (Geller and Toch, *Police Violence*, viii). That volume contains mostly social science contributions which—although representing a variety of disciplines and genuinely aiming to help police avert or at least mitigate their use of force—continue to presuppose, philosophically and politically, a liberal democratic or social contractarian perspective. See the essays by Bayley, "Police Brutality Abroad," 273–91; Geller and Toch, "Understanding and Controlling Police Abuse of Force," 292–328.

29. Cahill, *Love Your Enemies*, ix.

30. Hauerwas, *Peaceable Kingdom*, 114.

accurately perceives "a noticeable deficiency in applying such analysis to the domestic context of crime" and police use of force in response to it.[31] Again, this is interesting given that many law enforcement officers are also Christians, who presumably struggle on a regular basis with the issue of violence or force.[32] Of course, Sherman's questions about whether a Christian and whether a pacifist can be a police officer are not necessarily the same question. For not all Christians are pacifists.

One nonpacifist Christian ethicist who mentions at least in passing the use of force by police is Ralph Potter. In his book, *War and Moral Discourse*, Potter writes that the "mode of thinking" associated with the just-war tradition pertains "to all situations in which the use of force must be contemplated."[33] Beginning with a "debt of love that Christians owe to their neighbors," he identifies two claims that are at "opposite poles of the continuum of Christian attitudes toward war and violence."[34] At one end is the claim to "contend for justice" or "protect the innocent," and at the other end rests the claim "that we should not harm any neighbor."[35] Both claims, Potter insists, must be held in tandem through the framework of the just-war tradition. Because of the latter claim of nonmaleficence, there exists a burden of proof upon those who attempt to justify the use of force. In other words, there is a "strong presumption against the use of violence, a presumption established for the Christian by the nonresistant example of Jesus and for the rational non-Christian by prudent concern for order and mutual

---

31. Malloy, *Ethics of Law Enforcement*, 2.

32. Anecdotal evidence of this daily struggle concerning violence and faith is provided in a book aimed at a popular audience: Kowalski and Collins, *To Serve and Protect*.

33. Potter, *War and Moral Discourse*, 49–50. Paul Ramsey also touches on the subject of policing when he grounds his version of just-war theory in the duty to love. As an illustration of this, he embellishes the story of the Good Samaritan from Luke 10:25–37, suggesting that it would have been better to prevent the violent robbery by having a police force on the road to Jericho. Indeed, Ramsey asks what would Jesus have made the Samaritan do "if he had come upon the scene while the robbers were still at their fell work?" Answer: act like a police officer. Whenever a choice must be made between "the perpetrator of injustice and the many victims of it," the latter are to be preferred out of Christian charity (see Ramsey, *Just War*, 165, 169–71; *War and the Christian*, xvi–xvii). In contrast to Ramsey, Kaufman suggests that, whenever Cain is threatening to kill Abel, perhaps Cain is in greater need of redemptive love, which may be more important for Christians than protection of the innocent (Kaufman, *Context of Decision*, 98, 105).

34. Potter, *War and Moral Discourse*, 53–54.

35. Potter, *War and Moral Discourse*, 53–54.

security."[36] This presumption may be overridden only by the other strong claim, namely, to do justice and protect the innocent against unjust aggressors. As an example, Potter appeals to the role of the police, "as servant[s] of the community," who "promise to risk [their] own life in defense of . . . any who need protection from unjust attack."[37] Thus, according to Potter, if a Memphis police officer had seen the rifle aimed at Martin Luther King Jr., the claim to protect the innocent would have overridden the claim to do no harm, thereby obligating the officer to fire upon the assailant. Indeed, Potter is one of the few Christian ethicists who specifically addresses the role of police, calling on other Christian scholars to help officers, who "deserve counsel and instruction," to carefully "reflect upon the mode of reasoning appropriate to their office that would guide them in determining when they should act, how they should act, and why."[38]

The only other Christian ethicist, to my knowledge, who offers a fairly substantial treatment of police use of force is Edward Malloy, who, like Potter, writes from a just-war perspective. The first chapter of his *The Ethics of Law Enforcement and Criminal Punishment* stands as one of the few theological treatments of the topic of police use of force that, although preliminary and brief, deals with this issue as a subject worthy of attention itself. Malloy writes:

> At the theoretical level, most ethical reflection about the problem
> of violence has centered on difficulties in personal relations or on
> the horror of warfare. In between these two extremes stands the
> role of the policeman in a contemporary setting.[39]

Thus homing in on the neglected role of police, Malloy recommends the just-war tradition as a "helpful ethical framework for analysis." With it he conducts "an exercise of analogical interpretation" that he trusts "has not stretched the just war tradition too far," in which each criterion of the just-war tradition is analyzed vis-à-vis guidelines for the use of force in policing, resulting in a coherent, restrained ethical grid for application in the latter context.[40] Malloy hopes that his "modest venture in a field which is ripe for interdisciplinary

---

36. Potter, *War and Moral Discourse*, 61; see also 32.

37. Potter, *War and Moral Discourse*, 55–56.

38. Potter, *War and Moral Discourse*, 60.

39. Malloy, *Ethics of Law Enforcement*, 10.

40. Malloy, *Ethics of Law Enforcement*, 24.

cooperation might encourage other Christian ethicists to grapple with this problem of the control of, and response to, domestic violence."[41]

The first criterion with which Malloy deals, therefore, is "legitimate authority," i.e., war may be waged only by a recognized government. Adapting this to the police context, the police officer may use coercive force only when he or she truly represents the body politic.[42] Though sworn to uphold the law, police possess an enormous amount of discretion and cannot always consult with a superior or make a decision in advance; in many cases, therefore, they are authorized under oath to determine on the spot when to use force. Yet, such authority is derivative and is thereby withdrawn when other criteria for justifiable use of force are not satisfied. Criminologists Jerome Skolnick and James Fyfe corroborate this view: "[W]here police derive their authority from law and take an oath to support the Constitution they are obliged to acknowledge the law's moral force and to be constrained by it," and if an officer uses force in an inappropriate way, "he or she undermines the very source of police authority."[43]

Another criterion is that war may be fought only for a "just cause."[44] Because the object of the just-war tradition, in Malloy's account, includes both vindicating justice and restoring peace, traditional examples that he mentions are national defense and protecting allies. Importantly, Malloy does not include punishment here. So, adapting this criterion of just cause to the context of policing requires the existence of an operative legal code from which can be derived any situation where police use of force may be warranted. This, of course, presupposes the justice of the code as a whole. Therefore, when a just law is broken, intervention by police is justified.

Since the response, moreover, must be "proportionate" to the offense, police officers possess the discretionary ability to perhaps issue a warning for many infractions, or help persons in a conflict to talk and work things out, rather than make a forceful arrest. The pivotal role of the criteria of "proportionality" and "last resort" especially comes into view by considering the use of lethal force. According to Malloy, a police officer may fire a weapon only to protect life (one's own or someone else's), for a "life may be taken only when a life is at stake."[45] To kill someone unjustly is to judge him

---

41. Malloy, *Ethics of Law Enforcement*, ix.

42. Malloy, *Ethics of Law Enforcement*, 12.

43. Skolnick and Fyfe, *Above the Law*, xvi.

44. Malloy, *Ethics of Law Enforcement*, 12–13.

45. Malloy, *Ethics of Law Enforcement*, 17–18; 13, 22.

or her "guilty in an irrevocable manner," which is the reason that Malloy does not include punishment as an example of just cause. For him, the role of the police is not to punish but to apprehend or incapacitate the perpetrator. Thus, it should be a "reluctant decision to employ" force, especially lethal force, which is why it is a last resort. The police should exhaust all other possible methods, in other words, for handling a situation before resorting to force. Again, Malloy's view finds corroboration in what Kleinig describes as a process of the "tightening up of state legislative permissions or, in many cases, departmental policies and practices."[46] In the wake of a monumental Supreme Court decision in 1985, the justifiable use of deadly force has been limited to two categories: (1) the officer may shoot to defend herself or himself from grievous bodily injury, and (2) the officer may shoot to save another person from grievous bodily injury.[47] Departments no longer allow their officers to shoot fleeing felons, especially in situations in which the perpetrator no longer poses an immediate threat to anyone's life.[48]

It should be readily apparent that, for Malloy, the criteria coalesce as an interlocking framework, which is perhaps why he identifies himself as a "strict constructionist" just-war theorist.[49] That is, he requires that each and every criterion be met before justifying war, or in this case, the use of force by police. If any of the criteria cannot be satisfied, a "no" to the use of force must be the result. Still, it is Malloy's view that the classic criteria for the justified use of force are easier to observe and conform to in the domestic context of police work than they are in the international setting of military conflict.

Can a Pacifist Be a Police Officer?

What about Sherman's question to the pacifists? Can a pacifist be a police officer? The short, and common, answer is given by Potter: "If to be a Christian one must be nonviolent, then no Christian should assume the

46. Kleinig, *Ethics of Policing*, 112, 114–18.

47. Geller, "Police and Deadly Force," 218. Geller calls this a "defense-of-life" shooting policy. See *Tennessee v. Garner*, 471 US 1 (1985).

48. Whereas, in the eighteenth century the English jurist, William Blackstone, justified deadly force in stopping a felon who was fleeing, in recent years, "the rationale for the rule is gone; that while all felonies were capital crimes in the eighteenth century, relatively few are in the twentieth" (Hall, "Deadly Force, The Common Law and the Constitution," 27).

49. Malloy, *Ethics of Law Enforcement*, 28.

office of policeman, soldier, or magistrate."[50] Returning to his hypothetical Memphis police officer who has an opportunity to forestall the assassination of Martin Luther King Jr., Potter determines that "adherence to nonviolent ideals" by this officer "would not have marked a triumph of high morality; it would have been a suspicious and serious dereliction of duty."[51] Similarly, Malloy writes, "Anyone who rules out categorically firing a gun in the course of their work should not enter police work in the first place."[52] According to Malloy, a pacifist police officer, who is unwilling to shoot a weapon under any circumstances, would endanger fellow officers and civilians.

Pacifism, however, *has* been a viable and consistent tradition in the history of the Christian church. It was especially dominant in the first three centuries when Christian writers opposed participation in the military for a variety of reasons, including prohibitions against killing itself and/or prohibitions against idolatry and emperor worship.[53] Over subsequent centuries, pacifism was a mark of such Christians as the desert monks, Saint Francis, the historic peace churches of the Radical Reformation (e.g., Mennonites), and the Quakers. This being the case, what do *pacifists themselves* have to say in response to Sherman's query?

Actually, a variety of answers may be found among pacifists, most likely because pacifism comes in a variety of forms.[54] For example, a pacifist may oppose violence but not necessarily all force, or another pacifist may reject war but tolerate some violence short of war. The latter pacifist, that is, may claim that whereas all war involves violence, not all violence involves war. So, although most pacifists oppose all war, their miscellany of stances on violence, coercion, and force leads their views on policing to diverge into four discernible but overlapping positions. First, some pacifists, who reject all war and participation in war, likewise renounce all policing and participation in policing. Second, many pacifists exclude policing as a career for themselves while they accept policing as a valid and necessary

50. Potter, *War and Moral Discourse*, 56.

51. Potter, *War and Moral Discourse*, 56.

52. Malloy, *Ethics of Law Enforcement*, 17, 29.

53. See Hunter, "Christian Church and the Roman Army."

54. See Yoder, *Nevertheless*, where he identifies at least eighteen types or subtypes of pacifism. Cf. Cady, *From Warism to Pacifism*, 61–62; also, Child and Scherer, *Two Paths Toward Peace*, 68–71, where they identify a variety of pacifisms, including, for example, (1) "nonresistance"; (2) those who strictly prohibit all violence; (3) those who prohibit lethal violence; and (4) those who reject organized violence between nations.

institution in the wider society. Third, a growing number of pacifists accept "police actions" in the international arena, which indicates that they probably accept policing in the domestic arena. And fourth, some pacifists reject war although they accept policing—especially restrained, nonlethal policing—as a role for both others and themselves. I shall now turn to each of these pacifisms vis-à-vis Sherman's question.

Pacifists Who Answer "No"

To begin, some pacifists renounce violence in any form. Just as they reject all war and participation in war, so too do they repudiate all policing and participation in policing. This version of pacifism opposes killing in all circumstances. There is, in other words, an absolute (i.e., without exception) prohibition against killing. The sixteenth-century Anabaptists and Tolstoy represent this perspective, which has been identified as "nonresistance."[55] Out of obedience to the way of Jesus, these pacifists abdicate involvement in the coercive politics of civil society, thereby conceding the ongoing existence of evil in the wider world. Thus, while Tolstoy's answer that police violence is not much different from revolutionary violence could be attributed to the fact that he had in mind the Russian secret police, it ultimately arises from his interpretation of Jesus's Sermon on the Mount as calling for nonresistance. This grounds Tolstoy's opposition to all violence, including police violence. As he puts it with regard to military service: "It is not only Christians but all just people who must refuse to become soldiers—that is, to be ready at another's command (for this is what a soldier's duty actually consists of) to kill all those one is ordered to kill."[56] Even if employing violence as a soldier is done to protect one's own people or self, Tolstoy maintains that Jesus's call to nonresistant forgiveness and love of one's enemies nevertheless excludes soldiering. And because Tolstoy denounces all violence as intrinsically contrary to Jesus's teaching on nonresistance, by

---

55. See Niebuhr, "Why the Christian Church Is Not Pacifist," 28–46. Niebuhr acknowledges that this version of pacifism genuinely possesses internal integrity and corresponds faithfully to Jesus's teaching, but he (wrongly, I think) also claims that it is socially irresponsible. He contrasts this "genuine pacifism" against "heretical pacifism" which neglects sin and holds an over-optimistic view of human nature. On the influence of Niebuhr's grid of pacifisms (and how it is mistaken with regard to the question of responsibility), see Yoder, "How Many Ways Are There to Think Morally About War?," 104–6; and "Reinhold Niebuhr and Christian Pacifism," 101–17.

56. Tolstoy, "Advice to a Draftee," 212.

extension, pacifists themselves ought neither to participate as police, nor to legitimate policing in the wider society.

Pacifists Who Answer "No" and "Yes"

A second group of pacifists waive policing as a career for themselves while they condone policing as a valid and necessary institution in the wider society. For example, writing in response to some Mennonites at mid-century who approved of participation in international police-type forces instead of the military, Guy Franklin Hershberger deems that the coercion and violence of both the police and the military are not acceptable for pacifist Christians themselves. Even if the violence of policing involves more restraint and less bloodshed, he criticizes any "sanguine Mennonite with sufficient optimism to argue for political participation" in such state capacities as "sheriffs and policemen who use the gun sparingly."[57]

At the same time, however, Hershberger acknowledges that the police function, according to Romans 13, is a necessary one—for the maintenance of order and to execute God's wrath on wrongdoers—in society and in, if there is one, international society. But such a role remains "forbidden to non-resistant Christians who seek to follow Christ who taught men when smitten on the one cheek to turn the other also."[58] This is why, Hershberger suspects, the early Christians refused to perform the "police or punitive functions of the state." Moreover, while he concedes that the modern state possesses positive functions rather than only coercive police power, and while he acknowledges the necessity of the state and its police for the order of society, Hershberger nevertheless maintains that the state monopoly on coercion remains central. Indeed, although differences exist in degree between the police and the military, "the two are the same in kind."[59] Such being the case, he goes on to say that "the nonresistant Christian cannot consistently serve as a policeman any more than he can as a soldier." This answer echoes Tolstoy's, but it differs in that Hershberger tolerates policing in the wider society by those who are not pacifist Christians like himself.

A similar point of view is offered by Howard Zehr, who avows that the question about how Christian pacifists respond to crime is central to their

---

57. Hershberger, *Way of the Cross in Human Relations*, 181–83. Today Hershberger would have to include police*women* in his discussion.

58. Hershberger, *War, Peace, and Nonresistance*, 205.

59. Hershberger, *War, Peace, and Nonresistance*, 363–64.

"faith and experience."[60] Specifically, he believes that the pacifist's response of calling the police for protection or to make an arrest is "problematic."[61] There is recognized in Romans 13, he thinks, a need for police—"some people do indeed need to be restrained, some need the shock of apprehension"—but society, Zehr adds, relies excessively on the state's forceful response.[62] Of course, Zehr assumes in his analysis a "no" to the question about whether pacifist Christian themselves may be police. Given this, though, the next question that follows is whether pacifists may rely on nonpacifists to serve as police officers for their protection. For if the police are called, Zehr cautions, those pacifists who called them share some complicity in what they do, which is especially problematic if the police employ lethal force. Be that as it may, he declines to provide either a universal positive or negative answer to whether pacifist Christians should call the police. Zehr does advocate, after all is said and done, that pacifist Christians at least encourage the police to pursue more nonviolent methods and restraint "without necessarily expecting them never to use force."[63]

It is particularly in view of positions such as Hershberger's and Zehr's, which forbid policing by pacifists but accept it by nonpacifists for the good of society, that Wogaman's worry about possible equivocation initially surfaces. As James Child phrases it, "A consistent pacifist . . . must believe that calling the police, who will then come and use violent force, is a vicarious exercise of violent force on his own part."[64] Yet, when asked whether such pacifist Christians do not *de facto* depend upon other citizens to restrain criminal evil while refusing to do so themselves, a recent exponent of this variation of pacifism offers a common retort: "To this we may answer *Yes*, but without embarrassment. After all we do not *ask* anyone to act in ways in which we disapprove."[65]

---

60. Zehr, *Christian as Victim*, 3. For a similar view, see Jackson, *Dial 911*, 50–52, 107–11.

61. Zehr, *Christian as Victim*, 5.

62. Zehr, *Christian as Victim*, 20.

63. Zehr, *Christian as Victim*, 22.

64. Child and Scherer, *Two Paths Toward Peace*, 88.

65. Clark, "Case for All-Out Pacifism," 97.

Pacifists Who Answer "Yes" to International Policing

As alluded to in Hershberger's critical response against them, there is a third, growing set of pacifists who accept "police actions" in the international arena. For them, policing is a legitimate and desirable function in the wider, international sphere, and they accept possible pacifist participation in it. These pacifists hold that the differences between the traditional military and police models are significant enough for pacifists to accept police-type actions on the international level. For example, with historical precedent in the intervention of the United Nations in Korea, US troops in recent years have undertaken humanitarian interventions into other nations including Somalia and Bosnia. Such activity is often labeled as a "police action" instead of warfare, I suspect, because the former activity is understood as drawing on the analogy of the putatively more acceptable use of force in the civic realm. As Duane Cady astutely observes, "The point is that the smaller-scale acts of war have greater likelihood of being justified because the relevant factors are more manageable. This is why scale-reducing analogies are used, to persuade (oneself and others) that a given act of war is morally acceptable."[66]

Thus, many pacifists, out of genuine concern for justice and the welfare of others, now express an openness—however reluctantly—to forceful actions resembling police use of force: "The paradigm of police action, allowing for the use of violence in order to stop criminal activity, may enable some pacifists to accept military action, even killing, as a means of order."[67] Although they reject war, some pacifists apparently endorse a form of policing as a function in the international arena, assuming that there is a recognized international authority which will hold its police forces accountable to strict guidelines of restraint (in other words, actually, to the criteria of the just-war tradition). They believe that an international police power would differ in degree and kind from military power as we know it.

---

66. Cady, *From Warism to Pacifism*, 36.

67. Miller, "Casuistry, Pacifism, and the Just-War Tradition," 207. For another essay in the same volume that makes this observation, see Himes, "Catholic Social Thought and Humanitarian Intervention," 224–25. For examples of this type of pacifist, see Wallis, "Renewing the Heart of Faith," 10–14, and Nelson-Pallmeyer, "Wise as Serpents, Gentle as Doves?," 10–13. At mid-century, Addison suggested that the UN intervention in Korea was "rightly viewed . . . as the international equivalent of police work" (Addison, *War, Peace, and the Christian Mind*, 19).

Potter, however, takes issue with this form of pacifism. Indeed, he finds it "logically odd" that some "who call themselves pacifists" accept the notion of an international police force and would even "bear arms in a peacekeeping venture under international authority."[68] For Potter, as for Hershberger, the coercion intrinsic to both policing and military activity is not essentially different, which is why the violent functions of each context is considered analogous. In contrast to Potter, those pacifists who accept international policing emphasize the analogy between domestic policing and international policing, not the one Potter identifies between domestic policing and international *warfare*. These pacifists maintain that the difference between policing and war is not simply a matter of degree, but a difference that is profound and structural. In Potter's view, however, a "thoroughgoing pacifist, bound by an absolute rejection of killing under any and all circumstances," should participate neither in war nor in any policing capacity.[69]

Potter's assumption that the external violence of the state is analogous to its internal violence may be found in James Martineau's 1855 anti-pacifism sermon, described as "perhaps the best modern example of the 'police analogy' as a justification of war."[70] Just as the state, on behalf of its individual citizens, must use police to keep the peace and to protect threatened citizens against criminals, so too the state is responsible in the international sphere. In this view, the use of force in each sphere may differ in degree but not in kind. Given this analogy, therefore, if a Christian "has availed himself of the services of the police to arrest and the courts to try the offender against his person or goods; if, in short, he consents to have a place in civil society at all; he has engaged himself, by active coercion, in resistance to evil, and in his private capacity *gone to war* with the delinquencies he meets."[71] In Martineau's thinking, such pacifists either must rule out policing along with war, or, if they continue to accept policing, must honestly discontinue describing their ethical stance as pacifism and accept war as well.

But is Martineau's claim about the existence of this analogy valid? Perhaps a brief *excursus* would be appropriate at this point, for both pacifists and nonpacifists stand divided—even within their own camps—on this question. Of course, analogies are neither univocal nor equivocal; rather,

68. Potter, *War and Moral Discourse*, 66.
69. Potter, *War and Moral Discourse*, 66.
70. Marrin, *War and the Christian Conscience*, 119.
71. Martineau, "Rights of War," 121.

they involve attributes which are neither precisely the same nor yet simply different. Therefore, both the similarities and the dissimilarities between policing and war have been noted by various writers.[72] On the one hand, the analogy seems plausible for various reasons. To begin, it is commonly agreed that the state possesses a monopoly of physical power at its disposal to maintain peace both internally and externally. Moreover, nations are viewed as existing in relationship to other nations, just as persons do with other persons. Accordingly, they interact either justly or unjustly, thereby also holding moral agency and culpability. By the same token, in their interactions, the use of force, or the potential thereof, often compels nations to abide by international law, much like the use of force, or the potential thereof, compels individuals to abide by domestic law.

On the other hand, the analogy seems to break down in a number of ways. First, the "civic sense" that can be presupposed between nations such as Canada, England, and the United States does not exist among nations generally. There is no true community of nations. Second, the plausibility of the analogy hinges upon the existence of a recognized international authority with an international police force, neither of which, as of yet, exists. Simply put, there is no world federation similar to the federal system of the United States or any other national federal system. Third, the analogy appears to crumble when, given the absence of an impartial international authority and police force, and given the absence of universally recognized laws, one nation undertakes upon itself the role of the world's police officer. Within a nation, police must enforce the law within the parameters or limits of the laws themselves (laws that are known by the criminal to be applicable to him or her as well). Thus, the violence employed by police officers is subject to review by the authorities and often by civilian review boards. Fourth, the police are only one component in a criminal-justice system. Their role is to apprehend criminals for trial, not to act as judge, jailer, or executioner (i.e., not to punish)—all of which are not distinguished so neatly in warfare. Fifth and closely related to this, in the police function the violence is applied only to the alleged perpetrator of a crime, whereas in warfare the violence is directed more broadly at

---

72. See Addison, *War, Peace, and the Christian Mind,* 17–19; Cadoux, *Christian Pacifism Re-examined,* 40–45; Raven, *War and the Christian,* 116, 150–52; Calhoun, *God and the Common Life,* 234; Bainton, *Christian Attitudes Toward War and Peace,* 240–41. For more recent accounts of the difference between the civil use of force and warfare, see Cady, *From Warism to Pacifism,* 36; and Teichman, *Pacifism and the Just War,* 38–46. Also, see Yoder, *Politics of Jesus,* 204; and Hauerwas, *Dispatches from the Front,* 131–32.

armies and populations rather than, for example, only against a criminal dictator. Finally, there are significant differences in degree, and "questions of degree in matters of practical conduct often make all the difference between what is right and what is wrong."[73] For instance, the extent of damage, especially with regard to harming innocent civilians, is much greater in the international sphere; whereas domestic police use of force, at least in theory (the Philadelphia bombing of MOVE is counterevidence), tends to be more discriminating and controlled.

Because of these incongruities between policing and warfare, Robert C. Calhoun submits: "To approve police duty, even when it involves unavoidable violence, does not commit one to approval of . . . international or civil war."[74] For Calhoun, police are accountable to the law, proportionate in the application of force, and discriminating when distinguishing between criminal and innocent civilians. As a result, the police prefer to attempt any possible peaceful means before resorting to lethal force. Therefore, disagreeing with Martineau, Calhoun discerns the analogy to be more appropriate between domestic policing and international *policing*, rather than between policing and international *war*. And, acceptance of policing, be it domestic or international, he asserts, does not necessarily require acceptance of war, be it civil or international. Or, as Cadoux puts it, the analogy is "real and possibly even close, and must therefore be allowed for in any ethical assessment we may frame, but . . . it is not sufficiently close to constitute . . . a demonstration that, if one [i.e., domestic or international policing] is to be ethically justified, there cannot be any fault to find with the other [i.e., civil or international war]."[75]

I think it important to note that the ethical criteria employed here to evaluate the similarities and differences in both contexts of war and policing include such principles as just authority, just cause, last resort, proportionality, and discrimination. When, for example, Raven declares that his "duty as a Christian citizen to arrest a burglar or to protect a lonely woman from rape has no sort of bearing upon [his] duty to smash up the homes and torture the families" of an enemy nation, he implicitly assumes traditional just-war criteria rather than a principled pacifist point of view.[76] So, the question may

73. Cadoux, *Christian Pacifism Re-examined*, 43.

74. Calhoun, *God and the Common Life*, 234.

75. Cadoux, *Christian Pacifism Re-examined*, 43–44; cf. Addison, *War, Peace and the Christian Mind*, 19.

76. Raven, *War and the Christian*, 152. I do not know why Raven inserts the adjective "lonely" before "woman."

legitimately be asked of these pacifists who accept international policing, does admitting the real differences between policing and warfare mean pacifists are legitimate in approving of the violence in policing? For police action itself, just like war, is not always justifiable or right.[77] Even if the analogy between war and policing has both strengths and weaknesses, the use of force in either context requires justification. And the *ethical logic* or *framework* used to evaluate the justifiability of the use of force in either case, as Potter and Malloy claim, does seem to be analogous. Even Teichman, who emphasizes the dissimilarities between police violence and external state violence, concedes that the basic logic of restraint in the just-war tradition begins from the premise that the state's limited use of violence in a just war "is similar to its exercise of force in internal jurisdiction."[78] I suspect that this is why many pacifists converge with just-war advocates with regard to international police actions and humanitarian interventions.

Pacifists Who Answer "Yes"

Some of the pacifists who are now open to international police actions obviously presuppose a favorable disposition, on their part, toward domestic policing itself. This group, however, is not homogenous on this topic either. On the one hand, some of these pacifists reject war but accept police use of force, including the lethal use of force. On the other hand, however, *some* of these pacifists also reject war and accept policing, but only policing that is nonviolent and nonlethal.

An example of the former sort of pacifism was a mayor of South Bend, Indiana. Although a conscientious objector during the Vietnam War (citing religious and personal reasons of conscience), he made it clear to the local newspaper (in 1996, when he was under consideration for the office) that he believes the use of force "sometimes is necessary" in society. And, anticipating the possible questions about his pacifism and how it might affect his mayoral decisions, he points to his "strong support of the police department as an example of his understanding of that."[79] This seemingly contradictory stance is not new. Indeed, Quaker founder George Fox, for example, accepted the sword as a legitimate component of the police function of the state that when properly employed responds

77. Teichman, *Pacifism and the Just War*, 46.
78. Teichman, *Pacifism and the Just War*, 46.
79. Colwell, "Ex-POW Kernan Backs Objector."

to the Light of Christ that the criminal violates within herself or himself.[80] For Fox, violence is not equivalent to *any* use of the sword, but is rather the unjust use of the sword. In view of this, pacifists along this line hold that the lethal force justifiably used by police is not violence and certainly not violent like killing in war. As one exponent of this version of pacifism puts it, these pacifists cannot commit themselves to an "absolute rejection of killing in all circumstances."[81]

Like Fox, some pacifists, therefore, do not understand force as wrong or evil *per se*. Unlike Fox, however, other pacifists distinguish force from *lethal* force, with the latter often deemed as violence. Cady, for instance, argues that a pacifist may oppose violence, which is or could be lethal, but not necessarily exclude force, particularly nonlethal force. He objects to the view of pacifism that sees it as a monolithic, absolutist position holding "that it is wrong, always, everywhere, for anyone to use force against another human being."[82] Although this absolutist version is certainly one kind of pacifism, Cady notes that it is not the most commonly held version. As an alternative, he suggests that most pacifists today distinguish between violence, force, coercion, and power.

For this reason, a number of Christian pacifists describe their stance as *nonviolent resistance* rather than as Hershberger's or Tolstoy's *nonresistance*. Of course, parenthetically, it should be noted that Hershberger's understanding of pacifism as an absolute refusal to kill does not, by definition, rule out nonviolent resistance, although he himself may reject this. The reckoning of pacifism as nonviolent resistance, however, *has* gained acceptance as the twentieth century proceeded, especially with the examples of Gandhi, Martin Luther King Jr., and others.[83] With this type of pacifism in

---

80. Childress, "Answering that of God in Every Man," 25.

81. Erdahl, *Pro-Life/Pro-Choice*, 28, 82–83.

82. Cady, *From Warism to Pacifism*, 13, 61–62. Cf. Teichman, *Pacifism and the Just War*, 4–5, 40; and Addison, *War, Peace, and the Christian Mind*, 17–18, notes that not all pacifists are Tolstoyan, seeing force as intrinsically evil, especially those pacifists who accept force as exercised by police.

83. For cases of nonviolent resistance, see Miller, *Nonviolence: A Christian Interpretation*; Sharp, *Politics of Nonviolent Action*; and Sider, *Non-violence: The Invincible Weapon?* It should be briefly noted that the distinction between nonviolent resistance and nonresistance is viewed differently by nonpacifists like Reinhold Niebuhr and Paul Ramsey. They reject the view that nonviolent resistance is a Christian pacifist stance; that is, they see *nonresistance* as faithful to Christ's teachings. See Niebuhr, "Why the Christian Church Is Not Pacifist," 10; and Ramsey, *Basic Christian Ethics*, 69. Although Niebuhr criticized the nonviolent resistance methods as being not genuinely Christian,

mind, then, the efficacy of violence in policing, generally assumed by nearly everyone considered to this point, is called into question. That is, when the greater efficacy of nonviolence is granted, policing itself can be envisioned in a completely different way.

Accordingly, when pacifists are pressed, "*What if* you were in a police counterterrorism unit and you were trying to stop a sniper on a roof about to fire into a crowd of people?" Walter Wink responds that this scenario already assumes "a framework that virtually *requires* violence as its response."[84] And it is this framework itself that he calls into question. As an advocate of nonviolent resistance rather than passive nonresistance, Wink brings to our attention another way to resolve the police "what if" dilemma that coheres with the proposed distinction between force and violence.[85] According to Wink, *force* refers to "a truly legitimate, socially authorized, and morally defensible use of restraint to prevent harm being done to innocent people," whereas *violence* is excessive, injurious, or lethal force.[86] In order to promote policing that accords with his nonviolent perspective, Wink suggests that the just-war criteria be renamed "violence-reduction criteria" so that both just-war advocates and pacifists can cooperate in countering the police's current and "routine use of unnecessary violence."[87]

Therefore, contrary to the assumption behind the "what if" question, Wink demonstrates that policing does not necessarily *have* to be violent in order to be effective. After all, other options exist, including, for example, the strict gun control policy of Canada, the unarmed or minimally armed "bobbies" of the British police departments, and the improved training of police in nonviolent, less-than-lethal methods of control and restraint.

---

he did anticipate that the Gandhian methods would work in the American setting, for example, with regard to what would become the civil rights movement; see Niebuhr, *Moral Man and Immoral Society*, 252.

84. Wink, *Engaging the Powers*, 236. My thanks goes again to Lee Camp for bringing Wink's point to my attention. Similarly, Child and Scherer, *Two Paths Toward Peace*, 113–14, ask whether police *must* be armed as they are, citing counterexamples of the English "bobbies" and the nonviolent martial art of *aikido* as a method of protection and defense. See Ronald J. Sider and Richard K. Taylor's "Jesus and Violence: Some Critical Objections" in *Nuclear Holocaust and Christian Hope*, 117, 149–50; Sider, *Non-violence: The Invincible Weapon?* 3–4; Dombrowski, *Christian Pacifism*, 96–97; and Jackson, *Dial 911*, 50, who says of the British "bobbies": "They truly looked like *peace*-keepers and helpers."

85. Wink, *Engaging the Powers*, 227, 236, and 384.

86. Wink, *Engaging the Powers*, 236.

87. Wink, *Engaging the Powers*, 224, 227, 236–41.

Thus, for instance, in the case of a crazed gunman, the criminal can be immobilized and apprehended with a sedative dart or a jolt of electricity instead of a deadly bullet. And besides, most police work already is nonviolent, for police spend much of their time in a service capacity to the community, helping at an accident, or educating children about the dangers of drugs. For these reasons, some pacifists who share Wink's perspective conclude, "Nothing we have said implies or requires that Christians should not participate in police activity."[88]

Yet, do they think that Christians may use greater force as police officers when it sometimes may be required? For police work, as it is currently performed, continues to potentially require the resort to lethal force. Indeed, less-than-lethal tactics and methods sometimes turn out to be lethal (which is why such methods are referred to as less-than-lethal rather than nonlethal). In view of this, perhaps it boils down to the following stance for these pacifists:

> In many societies, we will not be able to serve as judges or police [officers], because these occupations have been ruled out by the obligations which they have been given either to take life or to sanction the taking of life. However, in those societies (such as the UK) which have rejected the death penalty and have a largely unarmed police force, these may be appropriate avenues of Christian involvement.[89]

And, similarly, Wink's parting thought on the question about whether a pacifist Christian can do police work is: "The answers are not self-evident, and are as much a matter of individual vocation and national location as of moral norms."[90]

In sum, it should by now be apparent that there is an assortment of pacifist perspectives, with overlap among them, on the issue of police and the use of force—and not all pacifists would agree with Tolstoy's implied evaluation of policing. Yet, these versions of pacifism may or may not be *Christian*. Some of the pacifist voices above identify themselves as Christian, but others do not. And, actually, there are representatives of both Christians and non-Christians in each type of pacifist perspective on policing covered to this point. Yet, while Sherman's questions about Rawlsians, Christians, and pacifism have been addressed, another voice that is

88. Sider and Taylor, "Jesus and Violence: Some Critical Objections," 117.

89. Swartley and Kreider, "Pacifist Christianity: The Kingdom Way," 57.

90. Wink, *Engaging the Powers*, 238–39; cf. Hauerwas, "Who Is 'We'?," 15.

specifically Christian and pacifist has not yet been heard in response to the question about policing.

Conclusion: A Yoderian Point of Departure

"The exposition I have chosen is to let the panorama of diverse theories unfold progressively, from the dialogue already in process, rather than proceeding 'foundationally' on the ground of what someone might claim as 'first principles.'"[91] Such was John Howard Yoder's approach when interpreting and treating ethical issues, and this is what I have endeavored to accomplish up to this point in the essay. For Yoder's concern about concrete moral questions usually involved a survey and analysis of the plurality of methods and positions represented in a discussion. Approaches that are teleological, deontological, virtue-oriented, contract-based, or narrative-dependent all fell within the scope of his careful consideration, and Yoder, in turn, would attempt some "mixing and matching according to the shape of a particular debate."[92] In doing so, Yoder perceived himself as not representing one method or "position" but, rather, a posture of love and creative witness. As he put it, "My conviction that war is wrong is not derived from a metaethical commitment to exceptionless prohibitions or to any other one mode of reasoning. I honor the people who have expressed themselves in those terms, while pointing out for present purposes that it is not the only way to argue."[93]

For Yoder, Christian pacifism or nonviolence is inseparable from the very life of the community of Christians formed and shaped by Jesus Christ's life, death, and resurrection. Such Christian nonviolence stems from the person and work of Jesus Christ, and it is the only example of pacifism up to this point in the essay for which Jesus Christ is indispensable. Its theological basis is in "the character of God and the work of Jesus Christ," whose death and resurrection "reveals how God deals with evil; here is the only valid starting point for Christian pacifism or nonresistance."[94] The new life inaugurated by Jesus Christ is not some ideal or absolute principle that requires Christian adherence to pacifism as a legalistic position. Rather, because of the Spirit present in the church since Pentecost, Christian pacifism, for Yoder, is not a

---

91. Yoder, "How Many Ways Are There to Think Morally About War?," 84.
92. Yoder, "Walk and Word," 87.
93. Yoder, "'What Would You Do . . . ?' Revisited," 2.
94. Yoder, *Politics of Jesus*, 239; and *Original Revolution*, 56.

81

"legalistic and absolutist sectarian pacifism" but, instead, part and parcel of the embodied Christian life of discipleship in the church.[95]

Yoder's Christian pacifism, therefore, at times overlapped with or encompassed elements of the other versions of pacifism, and the question of policing brings these points of contact into view. For example, like some of the pacifists surveyed above, Yoder acknowledged the biblical legitimacy of the police function by nonpacifists within the wider society.[96] Romans 13 (along with 1 Timothy 2 and 1 Peter 2), in his interpretation, recognizes the state's function as preserver of order and tranquility, which "obtain when the innocent are protected" in order that "all [people] might come to knowledge of the truth." In this way, the state's policing function within society receives legitimation; however, Yoder was quick to point out that Romans 13 does *not* apply at the international level of warfare. For, in policing, the innocent can be distinguished from the perpetrator, and a semblance of order can be maintained; whereas, in war neither of these are possible. Nevertheless, even with regard to policing itself, Yoder concluded that the state never possesses a blanket authorization to use force: "The use of force must be limited to the police function, i.e., guided by fair judicial processes, subject to recognized legislative regulation, and safe-guarded in practice against its running away with the situation. Only the absolute minimum of violence is therefore in any way excusable."[97] To discern whether a state's police force complies with this standard from Romans 13, Yoder suggested that we evaluate "one case at a time" and that we be on constant alert for the state's demonic side, when it succumbs to the temptation to overdo the police function, about which Revelation 13 warns.

In addition, similar to those pacifists who generally opposed policing by pacifists, Yoder made reference to the example of the early Christians, who believed that "the Christian as an agent of God for reconciliation has other things to do than to be in police service."[98] Yet by 170 CE some soldiers

---

95. Zimbelman correctly notes this in "Contribution of John Howard Yoder to Recent Discussions in Christian Social Ethics," 371, 378–79. See also Hauerwas, *Dispatches from the Front*, 117–18, 120. Cf. Cahill, *Love Your Enemies*, 2, where she accurately observes that many pacifists do not begin so much with an ethical reply to the violence question, but she incorrectly surmises that Yoder "arrives at a negative judgment on any Christian use of violence in any situation" (35).

96. Yoder, *Christian Witness to the State*, 36–37, 46–48; *Original Revolution*, 60. Cf. Bainton, *Christian Attitudes Toward War and Peace*, 13, 60.

97. Yoder, *Christian Witness to the State*, 36–37.

98. Yoder, *Christian Attitudes to War, Peace, and Revolution*, 31, 34; *Christian Witness*

who were Christians did not get excommunicated, for rather than fighting in war, the actual work of most soldiers during the *Pax Romana* consisted in road protection against bandits, transportation of mail, guarding prisoners, or fire-fighting service. As long as the Christian soldier had not killed anyone or burnt incense to Caesar, he was permitted to continue his living as a Christian and as a soldier. Indeed, Yoder considered the just-war tradition, developed initially by Ambrose and Augustine, as derived from this "function of the police in domestic peace-keeping."[99] Nevertheless, in both his scriptural interpretation and his reference to the practices of the early Christians, Yoder seemed to converge with those pacifists, like Hershberger and Zehr, who reject policing by Christian pacifists themselves, but accept it by nonpacifists for the sake of society.

At the same time, though, Yoder's reflections on pacifism and policing appeared to share more in common with those pacifists who express an openness to nonviolent policing, even by pacifists. Although earlier Yoder mentioned pacifism and nonresistance as synonymous terms, he came to see Christian pacifism as entailing nonviolent resistance. As Joel Zimbelman has observed: "In some later works (among those published after 1974), Yoder often employed the term 'nonviolent resistance' (rather than 'nonresistance') to specify the fundamental imperative of the Christian community."[100] Indeed, Yoder often stressed the fact that nonviolent resistance *can* be a way of effective Christian response, although he also pointed out that Christians do not measure the value of such resistance by its effectiveness. For him, given the numerous examples of successful nonviolently resistant movements and persons—including Gandhi and the civil rights movement led by Martin Luther King Jr.—"the door is open for nonviolent procedures of maintaining order" in a society.[101] And Yoder believed that more could be done along this vein.

Hence, on one occasion when he was asked about what to do in the face of crime and violence, Yoder replied with a question of his own: "Have

---

to the State, 56; "War as a Moral Problem in the Early Church," 8–9. Cf. Wink, *Engaging the Powers*, 211; Bainton, *Christian Attitudes Toward War and Peace*, 79–81; Swartley and Krieder, "Pacifist Christianity: The Kingdom Way," 57; Clark, "Case for All-Out Pacifism," 110; and Childress, "Moral Discourse about War," 131.

99. Yoder, *Priestly Kingdom*, 75; *Politics of Jesus*, 204.

100. Zimbelman, "Contribution of John Howard Yoder," 388.

101. Yoder, *Christian Attitudes to War, Peace, and Revolution*, 279. Also in this volume, he outlines four possible answers, without indicating his own view, to whether it is permissible to serve in an international police force (255).

you ever wondered whether some nonlethal method would be consistent with Jesus's teaching?"[102] And as an example of what he had in mind, Yoder followed up with another question: "Have you ever thought about *judo*?" Indeed, he sometimes suggested *judo* rather than *karate* as a method of defense, since the former involves grabs and holds rather than the latter's punches and kicks. On this distinction, Yoder echoed Scherer's advocacy of *aikido*, which is a "soft" martial art that emphasizes defense through guiding an aggressor in a way that his aggressive force works against him.[103] In this willingness to consider soft martial arts as examples of legitimate nonviolent force, Yoder appeared to be in agreement with those pacifists who advocate nonviolent resistance and who accept policing, either by themselves or by others, that employs less-than-lethal methods. But, again, Yoder cautioned such Christian pacifists to remember that pacifism should not deal with only the *means* question, for the claim that they can achieve without violence what violence usually promises to achieve, while sometimes true, is not necessarily the case. Still, this does not mean, in turn, that violence would be okay in such instances. Christian pacifism, for Yoder, "is one in which the calculating link between our obedience and ultimate efficacy has been broken, since the triumph of God comes through resurrection and not through effective sovereignty or assured survival."[104] So, although he evinced an openness to nonviolently resistant methods of defense, Yoder refused to see this as exhaustive of what it means to be a Christian pacifist.

Although a Christian pacifist, Yoder endeavored to critically and sympathetically engage in conversation with just-war interlocutors, giving them the benefit of the doubt and employing their moral language to whatever extent possible. His willingness to go the second mile to ecumenically engage just-war proponents was, in the final analysis, an expression of love of enemy, turning the other cheek, and affirming the dignity of the adversary. Indeed, Yoder had "greater respect" for those nonpacifists who view violence as evil (in contrast to nonpacifists who see violence as good, e.g., Rambo in war or Dirty Harry in policing), but who undertake responsibility for the protection of innocent neighbors against aggressive neighbors—"in short, what we have

102. Reported by Jackson, *Dial 911*, 51.

103. Child and Scherer, *Two Paths Toward Peace*, 111–13. On this point, however, I agree with Jeffrey K. Mann's view of aikido: "While aikido has strong peace-loving ethics attached to its founding a practice, it is not exactly nonviolent. It exists to one end of the spectrum of martial arts, with regard to force and brutality, but there is no shortage of pain and severity in its original practice" (Mann, *May I Kill?*, 142).

104. Yoder, *Politics of Jesus*, 239.

seen to be the police function of the state."[105] Thus, he considered himself as striving to honor the human dignity, the *imago Dei*, of those who adhere to, or at least verbally assent to, the just-war tradition, by inviting them to be honest with the restraints that the tradition purports to place upon the use of lethal force.[106] And he would, I think, do the same for those—like just-war theorists Potter and Malloy, or criminal-justice philosopher Kleinig—who are concerned about the ethic of the use of force in policing: "Wherever any new opening for the moral criticism of the use of violence arises, it is in some way a use of the just-war logic, and should be welcomed as at least an opening for possible moral judgment."[107]

That being the case, Yoder indicated an interest in Kleinig's "social peacekeeper" model as an alternative to the "crimefighter" model. The social-peacekeeper model couches policing within a wider framework of community and social practices of service, thereby hopefully curtailing the use of violence. As Kleinig puts it, "So understood, the peacekeeper model is broad enough to encompass most of the work that police do, whether it is crimefighting, crime control, or interventions in crisis situations. But what is more important is the irenic cast that it gives to police work."[108] Indeed, Kleinig confesses his respect for pacifists and their critiques of violence, which is why he maintains that there is a *prima facie* "presumption against the use of force."[109] To be sure, the peacekeeper paradigm does not rule out the use of force altogether, but through the social and community practices the model involves, the social-contractarian rules regarding the use of force are reinforced. Accordingly, Kleinig provides several criteria for justifying the use of force, criteria that clearly have functional analogs in the criteria of the just-war tradition. In the end, Kleinig hopes that the peacekeeper model will facilitate efforts to make police use of force "a last

105. Yoder, *Original Revolution*, 76.

106. Yoder, "Gordon Zahn Is Right," 1,5, 9; see also Yoder's *When War is Unjust*, 5; and Yoder, "On Not Being Ashamed of the Gospel, 285–300. Yoder also believed that when just-war proponents seriously adhere to the criteria of the tradition, fewer lives and values are destroyed. See, though, this volume's Introduction about his failure to respect the *imago Dei* of the women he harmed.

107. Yoder, *Original Revolution*, 132.

108. Kleinig, *Ethics of Policing*, 28–29.

109. Kleinig, *Ethics of Policing*, 96–98, 101. Yoder once asked me if I knew the provenance of Kleinig's perspective on the *prima facie* presumption against the use of force. It seems to echo Potter's understanding of the just-war logic. Cf. Child and Scherer, *Two Paths Toward Peace*, 27–30, where a "Minimal Justified Violence View" that involves a "presumption against violence" is similarly advocated.

(albeit sometimes necessary) resort rather than their dominant *modus operandi*."[110] And I think that Yoder would have welcomed Kleinig's work as an opening for holding police accountable in their use of force.

In sum, Yoder once asked, "If it is granted that nonresistant love is the way of the disciple, and if it is said at the same time that police force, within definite limits, is legitimate in the fallen world, can the Christian be the policeman?"[111] I have attempted to show how Yoder unpacked the two premises of this Sherman-like question. After all is said and done, however, Yoder refused to accept the straightforward "no" of Tolstoy, which is not to say that he gave an automatic "yes" either. Indeed, I suspect that Yoder would have expressed, in the end, a dissatisfaction with the way Sherman's questions at the beginning of this essay are phrased. For the question about whether a Christian or a pacifist can be a police officer is posed in legalistic terms. Yoder once suggested rephrasing the question: "Is the Christian *called* to be a police officer?" He speculated that if such a Christian believed that he or she truly possessed a calling to be both an agent of reconciliation as a Christian and an "agent of the wrath of God" as a police officer, then he or she must provide evidence—since the latter responsibility of using force "requires exceptional justification"—to the church of "such a special calling." At the time that he wrote these reflections, Yoder confessed that he had not met anyone "testifying to such an exceptional call."[112]

I think that Yoder's reflections were on the mark, especially given the present violent condition of American society and the current character of its police. For now, and for the foreseeable future, "what is still the most salient fact about the police, the very thing that calls for special justification and for special accountability, namely, [is] that the police have the authority to order us around and to use violence to back those orders up."[113] Yet, *in principle*, policing by Christians—perhaps even by pacifist Christians—cannot be excluded. If, on the one hand, the peacekeeping model proposed by Kleinig and, on the other hand, if stricter guidelines for the use of force are both implemented and followed—in other words, if we move from police officers to peace officers—it may become more possible for Christians and pacifists to serve such a calling.

110. Kleinig, *Ethics of Policing*, 29.

111. Yoder, *Christian Witness to the State*, 56–57.

112. Yoder, *Christian Witness to the State*, 56–57.

113. Reiman, "Scope and Limits of Police Ethics," 45; cf. Child and Scherer, *Two Paths Toward Peace*, 85–87.

Chapter Four

Just Cause and Preemptive Strikes in the War on Terrorism

Insights from a Just-Policing Perspective[1]

In 2003, the United States with some allies invaded Iraq, quickly toppling the brutal regime of Saddam Hussein. This act was justified, in the eyes of the administration of President George W. Bush, as part of the "war on terrorism," because the Iraqi government ostensibly posed an imminent threat with its weapons of mass destruction and had conspired with Al Qaeda, which had attacked the United States nearly two years earlier on September 11, 2001. These allegations were never substantiated, and the actual mastermind behind the terrorist attacks, Osama bin Laden, remained at large until he was killed by US forces in 2011.

Questions raised by a number of Christian ethicists in the aftermath of September 11th about whether a "war" approach to dealing with terrorism is most appropriate morally now appear spot-on. Of course, many theologians writing about how to respond to or prevent terrorist attacks have drawn on either pacifism or just-war theory, the two traditional Christian ethical perspectives on the use of force. In addition, a number of ethicists, including, interestingly, pacifists, have proposed the possible aptness of a "police" approach for dealing with terrorists as an alternative to warfare. The political theorist and just-war expert Michael Walzer refers to this as the "'dial 911' response to 9/11."[2]

In this essay, I explore this matter in four steps. In the first section, attention is devoted to calls by some theologians in the just-war camp for a

---

1. Originally published in *Journal of the Society of Christian Ethics* 26.2 (2006) 157–81.

2. Walzer, *Arguing about War*, xiv.

possible law enforcement approach for dealing with terrorists. Second, some representative examples of pacifist appeals to such a policing paradigm are surveyed. Third, a just-policing approach is examined, and I argue that the qualifier "just" is important and that this model actually remains at this time more consonant with just-war reasoning. Finally, given the growing interest in the possibility of a global police force, I draw on the discipline of police ethics and examine what just cause, especially with respect to preemptive strikes, might look like in a just-policing approach to dealing with terrorism. Thus, in this essay, I take inspiration from the subtitle of John Howard Yoder's *When War Is Unjust: Being Honest in Just-War Thinking*; however, I hope to offer an honest and accurate account of policing so as to help not only just-war ethicists to be honest in just-war thinking but also pacifists to be honest about pacifist thinking when it comes to each of their contemplations about the possible legitimacy of global policing.[3]

Pro-Police Just-War Ethicists?

In the wake of the terrorist attacks on September 11th, while most Christian ethicists who identify with the just-war tradition tapped its framework and rules for moral guidance concerning how to respond, some notable just-war experts also noted the possibility that a police or law enforcement approach might be more appropriate. In this section, I highlight a few such references to policing by just-war ethicists that I think are fairly representative. Attention is given especially to the possible reasons why these just-war ethicists think that a police approach might be more effective or ethical.

In an interview with the just-war ethicist Lisa Sowle Cahill and the pacifist ethicist Michael Baxter, where they offered their perspectives on the invasion of Afghanistan by the United States, Cahill expresses her interest in a police approach, suggested by a number of pacifists, as an alternative

---

3. Yoder, *When War Is Unjust*. As a Christian ethicist with previous experience in law enforcement, I find these recent suggestions for a possible police approach, particularly by pacifist theologians, to be quite intriguing. Indeed, these proposals are peculiar given that hardly any Christian ethicists have examined what such an approach might entail, especially with regard to the use of force. Edward LeRoy Long Jr. devotes several pages to considering a law enforcement or global policing model for addressing terrorism, similarly noting, "One can go through the indices of book after book in the field and find no entries for either law enforcement or police work. In comparison with the immense amount of thinking about the problem of war and the moral issues surrounding military service, this lacuna is telling" (Long, *Facing Terrorism*, 83).

to war in response to terrorism. "While our government has chosen to re-spond with war," she says, "I think . . . Baxter and others have made an interesting suggestion that it might be better to look at it as a police action."[4] Although Cahill in this interview still employs the principles of just war to muster a critique of the US war against Afghanistan, she opens the door to begin thinking about another approach for pursuing, apprehending, and stopping terrorists. Even though she has "more criticisms, reservations, and questions" than "feelings of support" about the war against al Qaeda and the Taliban in Afghanistan, she is "not prepared to entirely rule out the use of military means."[5] Indeed, she adds that she thinks even a police action would continue to involve the use of military means. Unfortunately, in this interview, this is all that Cahill had to say about the subject. It remains unclear as to why she is interested, as a just-war ethicist, in a police ap-proach; nor does she elaborate on the use of military means by a police type of force. Presumably, Cahill would expect such a police approach to comply more with the criteria that justify and govern the use of force, the very criteria that she employed to critique the war.

Likewise, shortly following the terrorist attacks, Jean Porter criticized the US's quick employment of the war model, and she implied instead the suitability of a law enforcement approach. "Like many others," Porter wrote, "I am troubled by the easy invocation of war, with its misleading implication that we are engaged in hostilities with whole nations, and not with independent groups of terrorists."[6] Because war in recent centuries presupposes the Westphalian model of sovereign, territorially defined nation-states, and because terrorist groups and cells are not nation-states, perhaps the threat and actions of terrorists more closely resembles criminal activity than warfare.[7]

Nevertheless, in the end Porter is willing to continue to invoke the just-war tradition to evaluate the US's war on terrorism: "But if our nation's leaders are going to style this conflict as a war, then we must remember that

---

4. Cahill and Baxter, "Is This Just War?," 360.

5. Cahill and Baxter, "Is This Just War?," 361.

6. Steinfels et al., "What Kind of 'War'?," 10.

7. Childress, "Just-War Tradition and the Invasion of Iraq," 4; Roth, "Law of War in the War on Terror," 2–7; Himes, "Intervention, Just War, and US National Security," 143, where he writes that much, though not all, of the campaign "on terrorism resembles activity similar to police work: intelligence gathering, interdiction of materials and fund-ing, detection leading to arrest, and prosecution of individuals."

even within war there are moral constraints on the use of force."[8] However, as I will demonstrate later in this essay, her just-war reminder that there are moral constraints on the use of force in war also ought to be remembered, even within policing.

Similar reflections about whether to employ a war or a policing approach as a legitimate and effective response to terrorism are provided by the just-war expert J. Bryan Hehir. A month after September 11th, he wrote, "But beyond the rhetoric there lie serious reasons to distinguish war from what is ahead of us. Even if one is convinced that there must be a military dimension to an effective response to terrorism, it is better not to locate the whole effort under war."[9] Unilateral war, in his view, would not be as effective. He also worries that the rhetoric of war may lead to an approach that is less measured and discriminating. What is needed instead is an international, cooperative effort that both addresses the roots of terrorism, which is a transnational phenomenon, and contains or captures terrorists with measured use of force. Though he does not rule out military force altogether, Hehir thinks that the approach he is advocating is basically a function of police and legal networks. As with Cahill and Porter, his concerns about a measured response that is discriminating and limited no doubt would be raised and addressed by simply taking seriously the moral criteria of the just-war tradition.

Pro-Police Pacifists?

Criticism of the war on terrorism was unsurprising, especially by those Christians who nonviolently seek to follow the biblical call to work for justice and peace. In the wake of September 11th, and before, during, and after the wars against Afghanistan and Iraq, the voices of nonviolent activists and pacifists protesting the military response to terrorism gained a wide, though not always sympathetic, hearing. Many among the peace movement and churches advocated nonviolent methods for dealing with terrorists and those providing them haven, ranging from sending humanitarian aid to inserting peace brigades. However, some prominent figures who espouse Christian nonviolence within popular, historic peace churches and scholarly circles contemplated the possibility of supporting a police approach for dealing with terrorists.

8. Steinfels et al., "What Kind of 'War'?," 10.

9. Hehir, "What Can Be Done? What Should Be Done?," 11.

For example, in the previous section, I noted the just-war ethicist Lisa Cahill's curiosity about the police approach suggested by Christian pacifists such as Michael Baxter. In the interview cited, when asked what he thought would be a more appropriate nonviolent or faith-based response to the situation in Afghanistan, Baxter responded, "I think the most interesting proposals have been to see this as more of a police action, in which the United States and other countries are going to round up a criminal who has committed a crime against humanity."[10] One of the reasons he gives for his interest is that he believes apprehending and bringing bin Laden to trial in the International Court of Justice would be the most effective thing to do. Unfortunately, Baxter does not say anything about the effect he envisions resulting here. In what ways would a police approach be more effective than going to war? Another reason he provides for thinking that a police approach is interesting is that it would not "really call for the kinds of operations the United States has launched against Afghanistan."[11] Here he presumably has in mind tactics such as aerial bombing or perhaps the use of tanks. Nevertheless, like some of the just-war ethicists in the previous section, he falls back on employing the sort of reasoning connected with the just-war tradition: "Of course, with such an effort, we'd have to be ready to sacrifice some US lives in the cause of pursuing this problem justly—according to the most strictly applied just war standards."[12] It seems here that Baxter views policing as an activity whose use of force involves a much stricter application of the criteria traditionally associated with the just-war tradition. If this is the case, perhaps a police approach will be more restrained in its use of force and thus less violent than war.

On the more popular front, Jim Wallis, the editor-in-chief of *Sojourners*, viewed the terrorist attacks on September 11th as a "crime against humanity" rather than as an act of war. He accordingly suggested exploring a "global police" force as an alternative to war for defending innocent lives and preventing future threats.[13] Similarly, theologian Rosemary Radford Ruether, in her regular column for *National Catholic Reporter*, avers "that war is exactly the wrong response to terrorism," and she likewise proceeds to recommend: "Not war but careful police work is then what is needed."[14] In

---

10. Cahill and Baxter, "Is This Just War?," 359.

11. Cahill and Baxter, "Is This Just War?," 359.

12. Cahill and Baxter, "Is This Just War?," 359.

13. Wallis, "Hard Questions for Peacemakers," 29–33.

14. Ruether, "Wrong Response to Terrorism," 21. For similar reflections, see Patterson,

her view, the combined efforts of international police and intelligence agencies can more effectively discover terrorist cells or networks and prevent them from carrying out further attacks. As for the historic peace churches, Gerald Schlabach has noted that a number of their leaders in the wake of September 11th were prompted "to affirm international rule of law as the best framework for responding to terrorism . . . [which] implies international law enforcement mechanisms—that is, policing."[15]

The well-known Christian pacifist and theological ethicist Stanley Hauerwas, in an interview soon after the terrorist attacks, indicated that he "would certainly like to start envisioning the possibility of that kind of police force," because in his view a police operation would be a less violent alternative, which he says would be "good."[16] Moreover, he and the Irish just-war moral theologian Enda McDonagh have extended an invitation to Christian leaders and theologians to participate in a "serious conversation" about the outlawing of war internationally, which, even though they neglect to mention or consider it, presumably would require some sort of enforcement mechanism, i.e., policing.[17] Similarly, Timothy A. McElwee, a professor of peace studies and the former director of the Church of the Brethren Washington Office, has called for the development of a global peace system that would supplant war through "international law enforcement initiatives," such as the International Criminal Court and "the use of UN civilian police."[18]

Although many pacifist individuals and groups are considering supporting policing as a more effective or ethical approach to dealing with terrorists, debate continues within their ranks over the question of the possible place for, and moral legitimacy of, the use of force in such a model. Wallis correctly recognizes that international policing to protect the innocent, to prevent terrorist attacks, and to apprehend terrorists "involves using some kind of force," which poses a serious problem, he says, "for those

---

"Experts Say Bombing Is Risky Strategy," 3–4; Hoover, "Pacifism on the Record," 9–11, 26; Trollinger, "Nonviolent Voices," 18–22; Hanson, "Police Power for Peace," 7, 34; and Fahey, *War and the Christian Conscience*, 63, 65.

15. Schlabach, "Just Policing, Not War," 19. See also Schlabach, "Just Policing: How War Could Cease to Be a Church-Dividing Issue," 19–75; and Schlabach, *Just Policing: Proposal for a Divided Church in a Violent World*.

16. Wallis, "Interview with Stanley Hauerwas."

17. Hauerwas and McDonagh, "Abolishing War?"; Hauerwas, "Reflections on the 'Appeal to Abolish War,'" 135–47; and Hauerwas et al., "Case for Abolition of War," 17–35.

18. McElwee, "Instead of War," 159.

of us committed to nonviolent solutions."[19] Indeed, some pacifists wonder if an acceptance of policing remains congruent with their tradition on nonviolence. For example, Tom Ryan, a Quaker from State College, Pennsylvania, told Tina Moore of the Associated Press wire service on September 26, 2001, that internal debate existed among Quakers concerning how to respond to the terrorist attacks. "We're a peace church," he notes, "but there are some people who are worried whether that's enough, or whether some sort of police action is consistent with our beliefs."[20]

With regard to this question of consistency, another Quaker, Matt Reilly, who feels that a limited, police action type of war might be justified, adds nevertheless, "I feel less Quakerly." As for Hauerwas, because *lethal* force may be necessary if, for instance, bin Laden refuses to surrender without a fight, his support of a police approach stops at the point where it requires him to "carry a gun."[21] Thus, according to Joseph Fahey, "many pacifists believe in police forces and the coercive power of domestic and international law. But they think it is immoral and counterproductive to use violence as a method to secure justice."[22] Yet it is not clear that all pacifist Christians agree with the second part of Fahey's observation or with Hauerwas's drawing a line at lethal force. Indeed, it appears that some pacifists are open to the possibility of coercive force that normally would be deemed as violence.

Of course, some precedent exists of pacifists who accept police actions in the international arena. As Cahill has observed, "Pacifists generally are opposed not only to war, but to any form of direct physical violence, although they may make exceptions to this bias by permitting police action."[23] For example, the church historian Roland Bainton once noted that "certain pacifists" in the 1950s endorsed the UN intervention in Korea "on the ground that it was not war but only police action."[24] In addition, during the last decade, in the context of the discussion over the moral legitimacy of humanitarian interventions, Duane Cady has observed that because many pacifists "tend

19. Wallis, "Hard Questions for Peacemakers."

20. Quoted in Hoover, "Pacifism on the Record," 10; see also Wallis, "Hard Questions for Peacemakers," 31.

21. Wallis, "Interview with Stanley Hauerwas."

22. Fahey, *War and the Christian Conscience*, 65.

23. Cahill, *Love Your Enemies*, 2.

24. Bainton, "War and the Christian Ethic," 209. At midcentury, James Thayer Addison suggested that the UN intervention in Korea was "rightly viewed . . . as the international equivalent of police work" (Addison, *War, Peace, and the Christian Mind*, 19).

not to hesitate over controlled and restrained uses of force by police officers in the apprehension of criminals," they may endorse small-scale military activities resembling large-scale police work.[25]

Evidently, as John Howard Yoder astutely observed, there exists "a wide gamut of varying, sometimes even contradictory, views" among pacifists.[26] Hence a spectrum of pacifist perspectives arises with regard to policing. At one end, complete pacifists reject not only all war but also all policing and participation in policing. In addition, other principled pacifists still oppose war and continue to waive policing as a career for themselves, but at the same time they accept policing by others as a necessary institution in society. Moreover, still other Christian peacemakers reject war but accept policing and even possible participation in policing, though only if it is nonlethal and basically nonviolent. Pacifists in this category often distinguish between coercive and violent force, accepting the former while rejecting the latter. McElwee, for example, who believes "nonmilitary yet coercive forms of law enforcement hold great promise for promoting international conflict transformation and respect for human rights," accordingly finds it "useful and necessary to distinguish between the pursuit of peace and justice through police action and military action."[27] Finally, some pacifists support local and global policing that may entail the use of lethal force, including their own possible participation in such policing. As one exponent of this version of pacifism puts it, these pacifists cannot commit themselves to an "absolute rejection of killing in all circumstances."[28] Accordingly, just-war theorist Richard B. Miller notes with regard to those pacifists on this end of the spectrum: "The paradigm of police action, allowing for the use of violence in order to stop criminal activity, may enable some pacifists to accept military action, even killing, as a means of order."[29]

It is important to note that many pacifists who are more open to the possibility of policing hold that the differences between war and policing are significant enough for them to accept police-type actions on the international level. For this reason, they tend to disagree with those persons who claim that war and policing are *analogous*; instead, these pacifists generally regard war and policing as two different *kinds* of activities. In

25. Cady, "Pacifist Perspectives on Humanitarian Intervention," 69.

26. Yoder, *Nevertheless*, 9–10.

27. McElwee, "Instead of War," 159.

28. Erdahl, *Pro-Life/Pro-Choice*, 28, 82–83.

29. Miller, "Casuistry, Pacifism, and the Just-War Tradition," 207.

their view, warfare and police activity differ in several ways.[30] For example, the use of force in policing is aimed at perpetrators rather than more broadly at populations. Also, police use of force intends the apprehension rather than punishment of the suspect. Punishment is the task of the courts and the prisons, not the police. In addition, the use of force by police is subject to review and constraint by higher authorities, the law, and often by civilian review boards. There is thus more accountability with regard to the use of force in policing.

Adding to these differences, Schlabach provides a list of psychosocial dynamics that he believes distinguish policing from war.[31] Unlike policing, war involves a rally-around-the-flag phenomenon that slips into nationalism and crusading. War also leads to "going berserk" and an adrenaline rush. Moreover, in war the sacrifices of the dead may become the reason for continuing to fight even when no other good reasons to be at war continue to exist, because of the belief that we should not let the fallen die in vain. Because of these kinds of apparent incongruities between policing and warfare, Robert L. Calhoun years ago posited, "To approve police duty, even when it involves unavoidable violence, does not commit one to approval of . . . international or civil war."[32]

So, in sum, there appear to be a number of different reasons offered for possible support of a police approach by various Christian pacifists. First of all, they rightly feel that something actively needs to be done to address and confront the threat of terrorism. Moreover, there seems to be agreement that violence should be restrained and kept to a minimum. Policing would appear to do this more than war. Also, there would be institutions associated with policing that would hold it accountable, and others, including pacifists, could also use the strict principles governing police use of force in order to hold police accountable in their use of force. In this respect, pacifists would be following the lead of Yoder when he spoke of using "middle axioms" with the aim of reducing violence.[33]

---

30. Raven, *War and the Christian*, 116, 150–52; Cadoux, *Christian Pacifism Reexamined*, 43; Bainton, *Christian Attitudes toward War and Peace*, 240–41; Teichman, *Pacifism and the Just War*, 38–46; Yoder, *Politics of Jesus*, 204; Hauerwas, *Dispatches from the Front*, 131–32; and Long, *Facing Terrorism*, 82.

31. Schlabach, "Just Policing: How War Could Cease to Be a Church-Dividing Issue," 28–31; and Schlabach, "Just Policing, Not War," 19–20.

32. Calhoun, *God and the Common Life*, 234.

33. Yoder, *Christian Witness to the State*, 33, 47.

Furthermore, many pacifists consider warfare and policing as two different kinds of activities. Schlabach's recent work on just policing, in addition, is primarily motivated by an ecumenical hope that discussions about this topic by pacifist and just-war Christians will help them to converge enough to come to "see more clearly how war could cease to be a church-dividing issue."[34] After all, it is rather remarkable that both pacifist and just-war ethicists, as shown above, for example, by the interest expressed by both Baxter and Cahill, are enthusiastically beginning to explore the question of policing at this time.

Nevertheless, the nonpacifist Christian ethicist J. Philip Wogaman disagrees with the view that the police use of force and the use of force in war are all that different. Indeed, he adds that pacifists' *acceptance* of—and especially if this includes their possible *participation* in—police actions may be a form of "equivocation."[35] Perhaps it is for this very reason that Judith Rock, who is a Christian, a college professor, and a part-time police officer, admits that she, in becoming a police officer, is "no longer a complete pacifist."[36] She appears to be torn by this. On the one hand, she seems to wish to continue to claim for herself the descriptive adjective of "pacifist"; yet on the other hand, she believes that by being a police officer who might have to use force, including deadly force, she must acknowledge that she is not an *absolute* pacifist. She seems to cling to some sort of pacifism, or she at least leans strongly in that direction, but she can no longer describe herself as a "complete pacifist." The Mennonite J. Denny Weaver agrees with this observation, pointing out that pacifists who accept and possibly participate in policing that involves the use of force, even if it is limited, whether nonlethal or lethal and whether locally or globally, instead are "practically" or "almost" pacifists who actually have "just-war outlooks but with more stringent application of just-war criteria than is usually the case."[37] His assessment here is in line with Yoder's view that the rules governing police use of force resemble the criteria of the just-war tradition.[38] Or, as Hauerwas has similarly acknowledged, "a police force is the

34. Schlabach, "Just Policing: How War Could Cease to Be a Church-Dividing Issue," 19.

35. Wogaman, *Christian Ethics: A Historical Introduction*, 280.

36. Rock, "Voices of My Selves," 395.

37. J. Denny Weaver, "Why the 'Almost' Is Still Important," in Kauffman, *Just Policing*, 90.

38. See Yoder, *Christian Witness to the State*, 36–37; Yoder, *Politics of Jesus*, 203–4; and Yoder, *Priestly Kingdom*, 75.

best institutionalization of what just war should be about."[39] It is interesting that neither Yoder nor Hauerwas has indicated instead that a police force is the best institutionalization of what pacifism should be about. A more appropriate way to put it, in my view, would be to say that *just* policing would be the best exemplification of what just war should be about.

Just and Unjust Policing: Being Honest in Thinking about the Police

To simply call for a *police* approach is insufficient. As the Rodney King beating by some Los Angeles police officers in 1991 and other similar incidents should remind us, not all policing is *just* policing. There are, after all, such things as police *brutality* and *excessive* force, and these cannot be what Christian ethicists, pacifist or not, have in mind when suggesting the extension of a police approach from the domestic to the international sphere.

To be sure, a blatant example of unjust policing was the bombing of the radical African American group MOVE by the Philadelphia police in 1985. MOVE was founded in the early 1970s, and its members adopted the surname "Africa," advocated animal rights, opposed technology, and lived together communally in a West Philadelphia rowhouse, usually in friction with neighbors and police. When a shoot-out occurred in 1978 with the Philadelphia police, the result was one officer's death and the imprisonment of several MOVE members. Relocating to another house, the remaining members installed loudspeakers outside that they used to demand the reopening of their fellow members' legal cases. When neighbors complained about the noise, trash, and evidence of weapons, the Philadelphia police decided to take action.

On May 13, 1985, five hundred heavily armed police officers surrounded the MOVE house, demanding the surrender of four members on charges including harassment, rioting, and possessing explosives. A ninety-minute gun battle ensued that ended in a stalemate. Thereupon, the police resorted to dropping a bomb from a helicopter on the MOVE house. It ignited a tremendous fire that quickly consumed the building. The blaze, which the police allowed to burn, ultimately engulfed and destroyed sixty-one other houses in the neighborhood and killed eleven MOVE members, including six adults and five children.[40]

39. Quoted in Wallis, "Interview with Stanley Hauerwas."
40. See Wagner-Pacifici, *Discourse and Destruction*, 29, 66.

Moreover, the call for a police approach by Christian ethicists begs the question of what *model* of policing is most congruent with just policing. Only in recent decades have criminologists begun to examine police ethics in general and police use of force in particular. John Kleinig, a philosophical criminal-justice ethicist, identifies several models of policing that are currently circulating among criminologists, along with their correlative perspectives on the use of force.[41] At opposite ends of the spectrum are the "crime fighter" and the "social peacekeeper" models. The primary model of policing that developed within the United States during much of the twentieth and the early twenty-first centuries has been the former model, which is often referred to as the "military model," as reflected in the recent mantra by politicians on fighting a "war on crime." Indeed, when referring to "real" police work, many police officers have in mind crime fighting—as do the film industry and much of the American public. So, while there is certainly, as Chris Hedges has convincingly demonstrated, a myth of war that can lead to the jettisoning of moral precepts, I would add that a similar danger arises, perhaps to a lesser degree, with the mythology of the popular *Dirty Harry* movies and the like that probably has had as much of an impact on our culture's view of policing and the actual practice of some police officers in ways that parallel some of the psychosocial dynamics Schlabach associates with war.[42]

Within this paradigm, the use of coercive force is the *raison d'être* of policing, as reflected in everything from institutional organization (sergeants, lieutenants, etc.) to equipment (uniforms, helmets, semiautomatic rifles, tear gas, flash grenades, etc.). This model might encourage an "us versus them" attitude, which is why a growing number of criminologists warn that the crime-fighter model of policing may be the soil from which sprouts the seeds of police brutality and excessive force.[43] Everyone is viewed as a potential "enemy," which makes it easier, according to the criminologist Paul Chevigny, for police "to abuse those who are the enemy, easier even to kill or torture them."[44] It is therefore hard to imagine

---

41. Kleinig, *Ethics of Policing*, 24.

42. See Hedges, *War Is a Force That Gives Us Meaning*. For a narrative of police work that sometimes utilizes language reminiscent of what Hedges describes with regard to war, see Sasser, *Shoot to Kill*.

43. Kappeler et al., *Mythology of Crime*, 131.

44. Chevigny, *Edge of the Knife*, 255–56.

support for this model of policing either domestically or internationally by Christian ethicists, pacifist or not.

Indeed, perhaps there is a danger in the frequent use of these martial metaphors, for, as James Childress warns, metaphors "shape how we think, what we experience, and what we do by what they highlight and hide."[45] If we are not careful, he says, metaphors can possibly use us as much as we make use of them. As he sees it, those who unreflectively invoke the metaphors of war, in fields ranging from policing to medicine, unfortunately forget that there are also supposed to be moral constraints with regard to waging war. In so doing, they tend to slide into a crusade, realist, or excessively militaristic mentality. To avoid this danger, Childress does not necessarily call for banning the use of military metaphors altogether. Rather, he suggests that these "negative or ambiguous implications of the war metaphor . . . can be avoided if . . . the metaphor is interpreted in accord with the limits set by the just-war tradition."[46] I note this because while in my work I have been critical of the crime-fighter, or military, model of policing, I have attempted to use the framework and criteria of the just-war tradition in an effort to provide police officers, especially those who are Christians, with guidelines that it is hoped will help them avoid using unjustified and excessive force. I think, moreover, that these guidelines possibly have more teeth when situated within another model of policing, namely, the social-peacekeeper approach.

Although the crime-fighter model has become prevalent in the United States, it is not the only option. Among other possibilities, Kleinig recommends the social-peacekeeper model, which is more in keeping with the historical roots of policing in England and the United States. I associate this approach with just policing.[47] This model highlights numerous services that police perform in the community. In her actual daily work, a police officer does many things, including helping injured accident victims, assisting people with mental illnesses, finding runaways, searching

45. Childress, *Practical Reasoning in Bioethics*, 5, 7, 9.

46. Childress, *Practical Reasoning in Bioethics*, 9.

47. The phrase "just policing" has been made more widely known recently through the work of Gerald Schlabach. Even though my own work on policing preceded his, I focused primarily on the just use of force by police. In March 2000, however, while teaching at Simpson College, I was invited by the professor emeritus and social ethicist Roger Betsworth to give a presentation that I titled "Just Policing" to an adult education group at First United Methodist Church in Indianola, Iowa, and I believe that is the first time I used this phrase.

for lost children, informing people of the deaths of loved ones, directing traffic, and talking persons out of committing suicide. Police spend most of their time performing these kinds of activities rather than forcefully fighting crime. Schlabach basically defines just policing as being "embedded, indebted, and accountable within [a] community," which then means that "it has an inherent tendency to minimize recourse to violence."[48] Note that he does not rule out altogether the ongoing place for the use of violent force within just policing. However, within this overarching social peacekeeping framework, the use of force in policing is instrumental rather than central, and it is governed stringently by criteria for when and how to employ it morally and legally. Indeed, Kleinig suggests that had the Los Angeles police officers who participated in the beating of Rodney King understood themselves "primarily as social peacekeepers, for whom recourse to force constituted a last and regrettable option, events would almost certainly have turned out very differently."[49]

Therefore, while I grant some of the differences between policing and warfare, it is my view that these are mainly differences in *degree* rather than in kind. Moreover, I might add that many of the psychosocial dynamics that Schlabach lists actually are evident in police culture. Indeed, in a footnote he acknowledges as much: "While the rituals surrounding police work include flags, oaths, and appeals to honor, they manage to proceed in far less feverish ways."[50] This admission would seem to imply that the differences between policing and warfare have more to do with degree than kind. Hence, though the beating of Rodney King and the bombing of MOVE were both police actions, they are considered unjust morally for a number of reasons that echo criteria associated with the just-war tradition, including last resort, proportionality, right intention, and discrimination. Recognition of this resemblance between the criteria for the justified use of force in both just policing and just war is nothing new, even though few Christian ethicists have explored this substantially.

Indeed, the mode of reasoning and the criteria justifying and governing the use of force in both contexts, just policing and just war, are

48. Schlabach, "Just Policing: How War Could Cease to Be a Church-Dividing Issue," 23.

49. Kleinig, *Ethics of Policing*, 96. For an extension of this social peacekeeping model of policing to the international sphere, see Winright, "Community Policing as a Paradigm for International Order," 130–52.

50. Schlabach, "Just Policing: How War Could Cease to Be a Church-Dividing Issue," 63.

similar or analogous. Put differently, just policing and just war are, as Joseph Capizzi asserts, two different species within the same genus, which is the justified use of force.[51] This interpretation resembles that of Paul Ramsey, who argued that the "moral economy" of the just-war tradition is "*morally* if not *legally* binding upon the use of force between nations," and it also "regulates the use of force within political communities, where it is both *morally* and *legally* binding."[52] This point by Ramsey addresses a number of the purported dis-analogies identified by pacifists who wish to argue that policing and war are different in kind. For instance, Schlabach writes, "War can never be subject to the rule of law in the way that policing is."[53] Regardless of this *jurisprudential* state of affairs (and his assertion here could be disputed), the *ethical* mode of reasoning employed to evaluate whether the use of force is just rather than unjust, proportionate rather than excessive, discriminating rather than indiscriminate is the same in each sphere, in both just policing and just war.

This is why Ralph Potter, in his classic work on just war, maintains that just-war reasoning applies "to all situations in which the use of force must be contemplated," and he proceeds to suggest its aptness as "a mode of thinking for assessing the use of domestic police power."[54] Likewise, Edward Malloy has persuasively demonstrated the way in which "the 'just war' or 'justified violence' tradition" provides a "helpful ethical framework for analysis . . . adapted to the problem of police use of force."[55] He goes on to say that he is "convinced that the classic criteria for the justified use of violence are much *easier* to satisfy in the domestic context of police work than they are in the international setting of war."[56] Note that he does not deny altogether the applicability of just-war criteria to international conflicts; rather, he acknowledges that the same mode of ethical reasoning and criteria for the use of force ought to be employed in either context, though it might be easier to apply and adhere to the criteria within the domestic sphere of policing. Indeed, this ethical framework for justifying and evaluating police use of force would also extend to, and perhaps be easier to satisfy, in the international context of global policing.

51. Capizzi, "War Remains Church Dividing," 76–77.
52. Ramsey, *Just War: Force and Political Responsibility*, 144.
53. Schlabach, "Just Policing, Not War," 20.
54. Potter, *War and Moral Discourse*, 49–50.
55. Malloy, *Ethics of Law Enforcement*, 10.
56. Malloy, *Ethics of Law Enforcement*, 24; emphasis added.

So let us imagine for a moment a day when we ban war internationally, as Hauerwas and McDonagh have proposed, and as the Catholic bishops of Vatican II called for when they wrote, "It is our clear duty, then, to strain every muscle as we work for the time when all war can be completely outlawed by international consent."[57] Then if a rogue nation or terrorist group breaks this law and commits an act of aggression, there would need to be a global police force that can hopefully prevent such an act from happening in the first place or can respond to the crime and apprehend the perpetrator(s). Given that the use of force may be necessary by such an international police institution, moral (and legal, because in this hypothetical situation an international institution exists) criteria for when and how such force can be employed justly would also be needed. In this scenario, though war has been abandoned as a method of conflict resolution, the just-war mode of reasoning has not necessarily been set aside, even if we instead are referring to just policing. Hauerwas's partner in appealing for the abolition, or outlawing, of war, McDonagh, previously has written as much, though it does not receive explicit attention in their call for the abolition of war: "Accepting, in common with the majority of Christians past and present, the need for the violence of restraint in society, one is operating with criteria similar to those of the just war."[58]

Accordingly, whether we call for a just-war or a global just-policing approach for dealing with terrorism today, we are nevertheless employing the same basic mode of ethical reasoning and framework of criteria for justifying and evaluating the use of force. In the remainder of this essay, therefore, I explore what difference, if any, a global just-policing approach would make with regard to the question of just cause and preemptive strikes.

Just Policing and Preemptive or Preventive Uses of Force

One of the main areas of contention concerning the US-led war against Iraq, which the Bush administration claimed was another front in the global war on terrorism, had to do with whether it was a preemptive or preventive war, as well as whether this would be morally or legally licit vis-à-vis the principle of just cause.[59] In September 2002, the Bush administration issued

57. Paul VI, "Gaudium et Spes," §82.

58. McDonagh, *Church and Politics*, 71.

59. Fiala, "Citizenship, Epistemology, and the Just War Theory," 104.

The National Security Strategy of the United States, which referred to a new policy, dubbed the "Bush Doctrine," of preemptive war, which provided the foundation for the US invasion of Iraq in March 2003.

Given the new situation with the ongoing terrorist threat since September 11th and the proliferation of weapons of mass destruction, which are easily concealed for covert delivery, *The National Security Strategy* claims that the United States must adapt its understanding of the concept of imminent threat and defend itself through preemptive attacks against "emerging threats before they are fully formed."[60] Though some support for this policy has been expressed by some theological thinkers, it appears that most church leaders and theologians joined a chorus of voices criticizing the administration's position. Indeed, before the war, the United States Conference of Catholic Bishops stated, "We are deeply concerned about recent proposals to expand dramatically traditional limits on just cause to include preventive uses of military force to overthrow threatening regimes or to deal with weapons of mass destruction."[61]

As is evident in the bishops' statement, much of the criticism has to do with the way that the administration interchangeably uses or conflates "preemptive" with "preventive."[62] The standard distinction between these concepts was detailed in Michael Walzer's classic work, *Just and Unjust Wars.*[63] Preemptive strikes, though highly scrutinized by international law and ethics, may be permissible in the face of a clear and present danger, or a grave and imminent threat; whereas preventive wars, which seek to maintain a balance of power by attacking a state that may pose a threat further in the future, have been condemned in ethics and international law. According to Drew Christiansen, SJ, the Bush administration therefore appears to broaden preemptive strikes to encompass preventive war "when attack is neither imminent nor grave in the sense of threatening either the nation's survival or a crippling blow to its defensive capacity."[64]

---

60. White House, *National Security Strategy of the United States,* 4.

61. United States Conference of Catholic Bishops, "Statement on Iraq," 407. For similar concerns about expanding just cause beyond self-defense, see Casey, "Just War and Iraq? Ethical Theory Says No," 94, 96. For treatments supportive of the Bush doctrine, see Weigel, "Just War Case for the War," 7–10; "Moral Clarity in a Time of War," 20–27; and Novak, "Argument that War against Iraq Is Just," 593, 595–98.

62. Surlis, "War in Iraq," 605–6.

63. Walzer, *Just and Unjust Wars,* 74–85; and Walzer, *Arguing about War,* 146–47. See also Wester, "Preemption and Just War," 20–39.

64. Christiansen, "Whither the 'Just War'?" 9. Also see "Pre-emptive War?," 3; and

However, even some of the criticisms of the "Bush Doctrine" continue to confuse matters by also using these concepts of preventive and preemptive interchangeably. For example, in its recent *Compendium of the Social Doctrine of the Church*, the Vatican refers to the UN Charter and states that *"engaging in a preventive war without clear proof that an attack is imminent cannot fail to raise moral and juridical questions."*[65] Instead of applying the standard of imminent and clear threat to the traditionally accepted, though highly scrutinized, idea of preemptive strikes, the Vatican here applies the same standard to the traditionally condemned practice of preventive war. Can the policing approach that ethicists, including pacifist ones, have contemplated shed any new light here?

J. Daryl Charles provides the following scenario involving "dialing 911." He writes, "Suppose a stalker-murderer were on the prowl in your neighborhood," and he then asks, "Would you call the police to respond?"[66] Indeed, he goes even further and asks whether the police would need to wait until an attack is under way before they respond with force. Likewise, just-war theorist John Langan, SJ, before the invasion of Iraq, used the following similar analogy, though it involved a less immediate threat. He described a neighborhood with a house inhabited by an enigmatic owner, who engages in heated arguments with his neighbors and has mysterious strangers visiting, including chemical trucks delivering ominous, unmarked packages. Because disturbing stories, moreover, circulate that the homeowner is a recently released convict with a long history of criminal activity, Langan asks,

Himes, "Intervention, Just War, and US National Security," 147–48. For an ethical critique of preventive war and preemptive strikes earlier in the twentieth century, see Ryan and Boland, *Catholic Principles of Politics*, 257.

65. Pontifical Council for Justice and Peace, *Compendium of the Social Doctrine of the Church*, 218; italics in original. Pope Benedict XVI, when he was still Cardinal Joseph Ratzinger, prefect of the Congregation for the Doctrine of the Faith, stated that preventive war "does not appear in the *Catechism of the Catholic Church*" (quoted in Christiansen, "Whither the 'Just War'?," 9). In international law, the accepted norm is that nations may resort to armed force only in defense against aggression already under way; as such, preemptive strikes are prohibited. According to the United Nations Charter, the use of force is prohibited except when specifically authorized by the Security Council under chapter VII, article 42, or for actions of self-defense under article 51 in response to an attack on the territory of a member state. See Atack, *Ethics of Peace and War*, 64–65; and Sofaer, "On the Necessity of Pre-emption," 209–26.

66. Charles, *Between Pacifism and Jihad*, 114–15.

"What are the neighbors to do?"[67] He then provides the following course of action involving dialing 911:

> The standard answer in an American suburb is to contact the police, who, if they think the matter should be taken seriously, will investigate the man and the house, obtaining a search warrant if they have reason to believe that a crime has been committed. The police will conduct a search using no more force than is necessary and will arrest the man if they determine that a serious crime has been committed. . . . If the man refuses the search warrant or resists arrest, there may be a difficult interval, perhaps even a siege or shoot-out, until overwhelming force is brought in and order is restored. Harm to the neighbors is prevented, and the threat from a dangerous criminal is removed.[68]

To most of us, I suspect, Langan's scenario describes the situation with Iraq better than does Charles's hypothetical case. As such, the preemptive use of force by the United States, though perhaps theoretically a possible option at some point during what Langan vaguely refers to as a "difficult interval, perhaps even a siege or shoot-out," was not yet justifiable. Although I am in much more agreement with Langan than Charles with regard to just-war theory overall, I highlight this ambiguity for Langan, because it remains unclear in his account, as Charles might ask, whether the police would need to wait until the suspect shoots first during the "difficult interval." For some possible clarification on this question, I now turn to work in police ethics on the use of force.

Kleinig notes that though the *functional* origins of policing may be traced to ancient communal self-policing, modern policing began *institutionally* with Sir Robert Peel's establishment of the "New Police" of Metropolitan London in 1829.[69] Due to increasing urban crime and riots, against which the earlier night watchmen and constables were ineffective because of their lack of enforcement capability, and against which the military was brutally effective with its excessive use of force, Peel organized the first modern police department. The primary object of this first police department, as explicitly reflected in Peel's General Instructions from 1829, was the *prevention* of crime, and emphasis was placed on the use of persuasion, with physical force as a last resort and using only the

---

67. Langan, "Should We Attack Iraq?," 8.
68. Langan, "Should We Attack Iraq?," 8.
69. Kleinig, *Ethics of Policing*, 11. See also Ascoli, *Queen's Peace*, 89–90.

minimum necessary for preventing or stopping a breach of the law.[70] In Peel's approach, the police would be citizens working in partnership with their community. Their patrol duties involved walking regular beats in neighborhoods, but also included: traffic control; the prevention of cruelty to children and animals; finding missing persons; the care of the poor and destitute; extinguishing fires; the inspection of weights, bridges, and buildings; and even waking people up for work. As such, the officers of the London Metropolitan Police, according to the police historian Samuel Walker, "were proactive rather than reactive."[71] Such an approach to policing is an exemplification of what I described above as community policing or, as Kleinig calls it, the social-peacekeeper model.

In the beginning days of World War II, the eminent scholar of police history and principles, Charles Reith, in his book *Police Principles and the Problem of War*, called for a retrieval of Peel's model of policing and an extension of its principles to the international level as a move toward the abolition of war. In the introduction, he wrote:

> What is needed urgently, at the moment, is not only understanding and appreciation of the values of our police conception and its history, but the practical vision of the possibilities of their lessons in the wider sphere of the rebuilding of a stricken world. The subject of this volume is the use that may be made of the "preventive" principle of police in solving the recurring wars among the nations.[72]

Notwithstanding the rhetoric of a "war on crime" in the United States in recent decades, the understanding of "preventive" in traditional policing does not involve using force first against some possible future threat. Its analogue is not preventive war. Rather, the preventive principle of policing might support the creation of an international police force that attempts to work with people and various organizations to address problems before they give rise to conflict within the international community.

At the same time, however, in the wake of the League of Nations' failure to stop the outbreak of World War II, Reith recognized the need for the capacity to use force to enforce international law if rogue or recalcitrant nations pose a threat to other nations, ethnic groups, or international order. He warned: "Observance of international laws cannot be secured without

70. Ascoli, *Queen's Peace*, 80, 85, 87. The General Instructions of the London Metropolitan Police may be found in Kleinig and Zhang, *Professional Law Enforcement*, 25–27.

71. Walker, *Popular Justice*, 60; emphasis in the original.

72. Reith, *Police Principles and the Problem of War*, viii.

provision of force for compelling it."[73] Such a use of force by a global police institution, however, would be governed by the moral principles of policing, so that it would be the *force of law* rather than the *law of force*.

Kleinig helpfully details the development of deadly force policy for police since its inception, showing how the moral and legal guidelines have gotten tighter and stricter over time.[74] Initially, the common law tradition sanctioned the use of deadly force for either "defense of life" or in cases of a "fleeing felon." Behind both of these rests the principle of proportionality, whereby "police may be justified in using force to apprehend suspects, provided that the force is proportionate to the seriousness of the alleged offense or harm threatened."[75] Of course, in earlier times, many felonies—including not only murder but also arson, rape, burglary, larceny, sodomy, and others—were considered capital crimes punishable by death. Thus, a police officer using deadly force against a fleeing felon was considered justified as "the premature execution of the inevitable judgment."[76] Over time, however, the felony/misdemeanor distinction came to be understood differently, and, furthermore, with the gradual trend toward abolishing the death penalty, fewer felonies were considered capital offenses. Given these developments, "in many cases in which the 'fleeing felon' privilege was exercised, the use of deadly force no longer anticipated a subsequent death sentence."[77]

The benchmark Supreme Court decision in 1985, *Tennessee v. Garner*, subsequently argued that the use of deadly force against a fleeing felon constituted a seizure under the Fourth Amendment of the US Constitution and therefore had to satisfy a reasonableness requirement.[78] To determine what counts as "reasonable," the Court proposed inquiring "whether the totality of the circumstances justified a particular sort of search or seizure."[79] Because police officers must make split-second judgments under pressure

73. Reith, *Police Principles and the Problem of War*, 147.

74. Kleinig, *Ethics of Policing*, 96–122.

75. Kleinig, *Ethics of Policing*, 111.

76. Boatwright, "Legalized Murder of a Fleeing Felon," 583; quoted in Kleinig, *Ethics of Policing*, 112.

77. Boatwright, "Legalized Murder of a Fleeing Felon," 583.

78. *Tennessee v. Garner*, 471 US 1 (1985).

79. *Tennessee v. Garner*, 471 US 8–9. Sofaer, an expert in international law, writes, "The standard generally applicable to pre-emptive self-defence is, rather, the same general rule applicable to all uses of force: necessity to act under the relevant circumstances, together with the requirement that any action be proportionate to the threat addressed" (Sofaer, "On the Necessity of Pre-emption," 220).

in dangerous circumstances, the analysis of police conduct must be done in view of the circumstances existing at the time of the arrest and not in retrospect.[80] Ultimately, such a consideration hinges upon a balancing test, or "the balancing of competing interests," weighing the individual suspect's "fundamental interest in his own life" against the state's "interest in effective law enforcement" on behalf of the safety of society.[81]

In the Supreme Court's view, the interest in life should prevail except where "it is necessary to prevent . . . escape and the officer has probable cause to believe that the suspect poses a significant threat of death or serious physical injury to the officer or others."[82] Accordingly, the use of lethal force to stop an unarmed, nonthreatening, fleeing suspect, as had happened when a Tennessee police officer shot a fifteen-year-old burglar named Edward Garner, who was fleeing the scene, seemed unreasonable to the Court. With the *Garner* decision, says Kleinig, a "turning point" occurred, where "we have arrived at a situation in which the police use of deadly force has been significantly limited—one in which the fleeing felon privilege has been all but subsumed under the defense-of-life privilege."[83] Dorothy Guyot notes in her book, *Policing as Though People Matter*, the "emerging standard" as a result of *Garner* "is that an officer is justified in shooting only in immediate defense of life."[84]

In 1989 another seminal Supreme Court case, *Graham v. Connor*, reaffirmed the use of the Fourth Amendment reasonableness standard for analyzing the use of force by police.[85] It added that the "objective reasonableness" of a police officer's use of force should be "judged from the perspective of a reasonable officer on the scene rather than with the 20/20 vision of hindsight."[86]

These developments are reflected in state statutes and departmental policies around the United States today. For example, the *Manual of the Los Angeles Police Department* bases its use of force policy on a "reverence

---

80. *Tennessee v. Garner*, 471 US 26 (1985).

81. *Tennessee v. Garner*, 471 US 9 (1985).

82. *Tennessee v. Garner*, 471 US 1, 105 (1985). Michael P. Orsi has very briefly suggested extending this use of "probable cause" to just-war theory, especially for a post-September 11th world; see Orsi, "Expand 'Just War' Theory," 107.

83. Kleinig, *Ethics of Policing*, 114, 116.

84. Guyot, *Policing as Though People Matter*, 168.

85. See Petrowski, "Use-of-Force Policies and Training," 25–32.

86. *Graham v. Connor*, 490 US 396 (1989).

for the value of human life" that allows police officers to employ "whatever force that is reasonable and necessary to protect others or themselves from bodily harm," but only "when all reasonable alternatives have been exhausted or appear impracticable," in order "to protect himself or others against the immediate threat of death or serious bodily injury or to apprehend a fleeing felon who has committed a violent crime and whose escape presents a substantial risk of death or serious bodily injury to others."[87]

It is important to note, however, that even though clear legal guidelines have developed for justifying and limiting their use of lethal force, police officers are not required under the Fourth Amendment to wait until a suspect shoots first in order to confirm that an imminent and grave threat exists. The key is threat assessment, and the Federal Bureau of Investigation (FBI) identifies four categories for agents to assess when they have probable cause to believe that a subject poses a threat of serious injury, including: (1) the subject possesses or is attempting to get access to a weapon under circumstances indicating an intention to use it against the agent or others; (2) the subject is armed and running to get tactical advantage; (3) an unarmed subject nevertheless has the capability of inflicting death or serious injury and is demonstrating an intention of doing so; and (4) the subject is fleeing an area of violent confrontation where he inflicted or attempted to cause the death or serious injury of the agent of others.[88] According to Thomas D. Petrowski, who is a legal instructor at the FBI Academy, "In use-of-force training, the concept of striking after the threat is realized but before the assault commences often is referred to as preemptive force."[89] Actually, in his view, any lawful use of force is preemptive, regardless of whether an assault was initiated, because it "is employed to prevent—that is, preempt—future harm."[90]

Conclusion: Insights from a Just-Policing Perspective

If policing and its principles for the use of force were to be extended as a model for dealing with the threat of terrorism, it appears that preemptive strikes would still be justifiable by such a global police force as a form of

87. Los Angeles Police Department, *Manual of the Los Angeles Police Department*, 414–16.

88. Petrowski, "Use-of-Force Policies and Training (Part Two)," 25–26.

89. Petrowski, "Use-of-Force Policies and Training (Part Two)," 27.

90. Petrowski, "Use-of-Force Policies and Training (Part Two)," 28.

anticipatory defense against a grave and imminent threat to life. This, however, has had "a recognized historic and narrowly defined place" in the just-war tradition.[91] Indeed, the mode of reasoning and the criteria that keep surfacing with regard to the just use of force by police officers seem to me basically the same as what comes to us from the just-war tradition. As such, I might recommend following the suggestion of Kenneth R. Himes, OFM, that we refer to this as "a general theory of armed intervention."[92]

Moreover, the distinction between preemptive and preventive bequeathed by this tradition should, in my view, be maintained, especially by those just-war ethicists working toward the abolition of war and the creation of a global police force. Also, though I think that many pacifist Christians— especially in their work and experience with nonviolent resistance and peacemaking endeavors that attempt to curtail conflict at its source—should be able to contribute to and support Peel's "preventive" policing practices as extended by analogy to the international sphere, I suspect that they will continue to find problematic the "enforcement" aspect with its capacity to use force, preemptively or not. Obviously, more criteria besides just cause should be considered to determine whether a war is just, just as other criteria such as proportionality and last resort surfaced during the survey of police use of force. However, due to the bubbling interest in contemplating a police approach, and due to the widespread criticisms of preemptive strikes and preventive wars, I thought it appropriate to focus here on just cause vis-à-vis just policing for some possible insights.

Before concluding, however, Walzer provides us with an important reminder that the "dial 911":

> response would have been a perfectly plausible response if anyone were answering the phone. In a global state with a monopoly on the legitimate use of force, calling the police would be the right response to violence. Crime, the pursuit of the criminal by the police, and the trial and punishment of the criminal—these three would exhaust the field of action; we would read about war only in the history books. But that is not a description of the world we live in, and even if a global state ought to be our goal . . . it is a great mistake to pretend that we are already there.[93]

91. Wester, "Preemption and Just War," 26–27.

92. Himes, "Intervention Just War, and US National Security," 149.

93. Walzer, *Arguing about War*, xiv. For an article that considers whether the UN Security Council should engage in preventive military actions, see Lango, "Preventive Wars, Just War Principles, and the United Nations," 247–68.

In the meantime, according to Gregory Foster, "We are left to ponder whether the mere presence of a tyrannical dictator (even one with hostile intentions), suspected weapons of mass destruction, and unfulfilled UN mandates constitute a truly just cause for the preemptive use of force."[94] Threat assessment is the key area needing as much attention in just war or global just policing as has been given to it in domestic policing. Simple capability or possession of weapons themselves are not sufficient reasons to use deadly force in policing, and this should be the case with regard to thinking about preemptive strikes against terrorist or rogue state threats as well.

Whether we have just policing or just war, we should still be able to employ the mode of moral reasoning that leads Langan to say that a convincing case was not made for "the view that Saddam Hussein is actually on the verge of using weapons of mass destruction,"[95] and that therefore in this particular case the use of force was unjustified. If so, then shifting from just war to just policing would not really introduce a new mode of moral reasoning or different moral criteria constraining the use of force, or offer pacifists a panacea for dealing with recalcitrant terrorist groups or rogue nations—even though I do think that institutionalizing policing internationally, so that someone would answer the 911 call, would at least provide the sort of accountable framework within which violence would be more measured.

94. Foster, "Just-War Doctrine: Lessons from Iraq," 11.

95. Langan, "Should We Attack Iraq?," 11. The editors of *America* agree; see "Preemptive War?" This was also the assessment of the United States Conference of Catholic Bishops prior to the war: "Based on the facts that are known to us, we continue to find it difficult to justify the resort to war against Iraq, lacking clear and adequate evidence of an imminent attack of grave nature" ("Statement on Iraq," 407). See also Himes, "Intervention, Just War, and US National Security," 145.

Chapter Five

Just Policing and the
Responsibility to Protect[1]

B rian Steidle, a former United States Marine captain who served in
Kosovo and who subsequently became a human rights activist, journal-
ist, and photographer shares the following experience from when he served
as a monitor for the African Union in the Darfur region of western Sudan:

> Ahmed and I headed toward a large nim tree on the outskirts
> of Wash al tool, where 250 homeless women and children had
> stopped earlier in the day to share in the small piece of shade. They
> had escaped the initial conflict in Alliet, a town of 15,000 we had
> just visited. The village was the most recent to fall prey to Gov-
> ernment of Sudan troops in what was now described by Western
> diplomats—publicly, if belatedly—as genocide . . .
>
> The baby's breathing was labored, and she was wheezing no-
> ticeably. Upon closer inspection, I realized that this tiny human
> being had been shot in the back—the child had gaping entry and
> exit wounds that accentuated her struggle to breathe. Her guard-
> ian looked up at me with a blank gaze.
>
> "What's her name?" I stammered, my sense of disbelief au-
> dible in my tone.
>
> "Mihad Hamid," she said after a quick translation of my
> question.[2]
>
> . . . In Baraka, 10 villagers had been tortured and brutally
> murdered by the Janjaweed . . . Several bloody corpses filled a
> shallow grave. They were lined up in a row and covered with grass

1. Originally published in *Ecumenical Review* 63.1 (2011) 84–95.

2. Steidle and Steidle Wallace, *Devil Came on Horseback*, xi. See also de Waal, *War in Darfur and the Search for Peace.*

mats. Images from the Holocaust and Rwanda filled my mind. I looked closer. Every single man in this countless row of African civilians had had his eyes plucked out and his ears cut off.[3]

During that six-month stint as one of three United States military observers assigned to Darfur, Steidle witnessed many horrific atrocities, which are documented in his book, *The Devil Came on Horseback*. The title refers to the Janjaweed, a faction accused of much of the genocide in Darfur. According to the United Nations, 200,000 people have been killed, 2.5 million have been driven from their homes to refugee camps, and 4 million have been directly affected by the conflict in the Darfur region of Sudan and neighboring Chad.[4] In view of such crimes against humanity, a new international norm, "the responsibility to protect" (R2P), has emerged.

The phrase first appeared in a 2001 report by that title[5] issued by the International Commission on Intervention and State Sovereignty, an initiative of the Canadian government to reflect on how to move beyond the moral and jurisprudential obstacles surrounding what was referred to as "humanitarian intervention" during the 1990s in connection with "the kinds of catastrophic assaults on individuals and communities that the world has witnessed"[6] in countries such as Rwanda, Bosnia, and Kosovo. The United Nations subsequently studied this proposal, and at the 2005 World Summit, member states endorsed R2P. A report in January 2009 from UN Secretary-General Ban Ki-moon on "Implementing the Responsibility to Protect" led to further debate, and a resolution by the General Assembly in July 2009 committed the body to more discussion of R2P.[7]

For its part, the World Council of Churches (WCC), as a component of its Decade to Overcome Violence, has studied, debated and come to affirm R2P. The recommendations of a report from the Commission of the Churches on International Affairs under the title "The Responsibility to Protect: Ethical and Theological Reflections" were endorsed by the WCC central committee in 2003. This was followed by the adoption in February

---

3. Steidle and Steidle Wallace, *Devil Came on Horseback*, 88.

4. United Nations, "United Nations and Darfur."

5. International Commission on Intervention and State Sovereignty, "Responsibility to Protect."

6. Ninth Assembly of the World Council of Churches, "Vulnerable Populations at Risk," paras. 2, 7.

7. United Nations General Assembly, "2005 World Summit Outcome Document"; Hamann and Muggah, "Implementing the Responsibility to Protect"; Global Centre for the Responsibility to Protect, "Responsibility to Protect A/RES/63/308."

2006 of the statement "Vulnerable Populations at Risk: Statement on the Responsibility to Protect," during the WCC's ninth assembly at Porto Alegre, Brazil.[8] Subsequently, in 2009, the WCC invoked R2P to spark international concern about Israel's actions in Gaza.[9] The Roman Catholic Church also has begun to refer to R2P, with Pope Benedict XVI mentioning it in his address to the General Assembly of the UN on April 18, 2008, and, also, in his major social encyclical *Caritas in Veritate*, which was issued on June 29, 2009, calling for R2P's implementation.[10] Although there certainly continues to be debate about the concept in the international public square as well as within the churches, R2P has gained some purchase.[11]

Gareth Evans, who conducted pioneering work on R2P, believes it provides a "new way of talking about the whole issue of humanitarian intervention."[12] R2P nuances and qualifies national sovereignty, which is no longer understood as an absolute right to non-interference. Instead, state sovereignty entails responsibilities on the part of a nation to its own citizens; however, if a state fails to fulfill its primary responsibility to protect its own citizens, this responsibility transfers to the international community. The focus, as former WCC general secretary Konrad Raiser puts it, is on "the human security of all people everywhere," especially those most at risk.[13] R2P seeks to prevent and stop four crimes—genocide, war crimes, crimes against humanity, and ethnic cleansing—and involves three primary obligations: *the responsibility to prevent* (addressing the root and direct causes of conflict putting populations at risk); *the responsibility to react* (responding to egregious threats to human security through appropriate measures, including coercive measures such as sanctions and, in extreme cases, forceful military intervention); and *the responsibility to rebuild* (assisting with recovery, reconstruction, and reconciliation, as well as addressing the causes of the threat that the intervention averted or stopped).

8. Ninth Assembly of the World Council of Churches, "Vulnerable Populations at Risk."

9. World Council of Churches Executive Committee, "Statement on the Gaza War."

10. Benedict XVI, "Address to the United Nations"; *Caritas in Veritate*. So far, little work has been done in Catholic circles on R2P. For a recent article that attempts to introduce Catholics to the topic, see Hollenbach, "Humanitarian Intervention," 9–11.

11. For a helpful recent article on how R2P offers a normative vocabulary for motivating action and as a policy agenda still needing implementation, see Bellamy, "Responsibility to Protect," 143–69.

12. Evans, "Responsibility to Protect," 5.

13. Raiser, "Ethics of Protection," 11.

A 2001 statement, "The Protection of Endangered Populations in Situations of Armed Violence: Toward an Ecumenical Ethical Approach," presented to the WCC Central Committee, emphasized a Christian ethic of "just peacemaking" to prevent conflict, build peace, resolve disputes and reconcile adversaries.[14] This paradigm was made popular in recent years by American Baptist ethicist Glen Stassen, whose edited book[15] contains essays exploring ten proactive practices that have been empirically shown as realistic and effective for preventing wars, whether between or within nations. These include nonviolent direct action, cooperative conflict resolution, advancing democracy and human rights, fostering just and sustainable economic development, strengthening the United Nations and other international efforts and institutions, and more. As this new paradigm has gained traction among churches in the WCC, they now "agree on one thing: the importance of preventive efforts designed to avoid or tackle a crisis before it escalates."[16]

The 2001 statement from the WCC Central Committee, however, noted an ongoing debate that "revealed clearly the different theological perspectives among member churches with respect to violence and nonviolence."[17] Four years later, Evans observed that "the question of military action remains, for better or worse, the most prominent and controversial one in the debate."[18]

In particular, Christians who emphasize nonviolence—especially those in the historic peace churches—remain reluctant to express their support for the use of force to protect the vulnerable.[19] This attitude should not be surprising, given that similar disagreement lingered among the contributors, consisting of both pacifists and proponents of just war,

---

14. Central Committee of the World Council of Churches, "Protection of Endangered Populations in Situations of Armed Violence," esp. paras. 17, 49, and 50. The Central Committee received and commended the document to the churches for "further study, reflection and use—as they may deem appropriate—in their continuing dialogues."

15. Stassen, *Just Peacemaking*.

16. Weiderud, "Foreword," vii.

17. Central Committee of the World Council of Churches, "Protection of Endangered Populations in Situations of Armed Violence," para. 1.

18. Evans, "Responsibility to Protect," 5. See also Kerber, "Responsibility to Protect," 115.

19. Neufeldt-Fast, "Christianity and War," 120; Workshop for Peace Theology of "Church and Peace" and of the "International Fellowship of Reconciliation" (German Branch), "S4C—Suffer for Christ"; Fehr, "Responsibility to Confront Evil."

to Stassen's volume on just peacemaking. The chapter that sparked the most controversy was written by Michael Joseph Smith, a professor of government and foreign affairs at the University of Virginia. In language very similar to R2P, he called for the strengthening of the UN by developing "the capacity to identify, prevent, and, if necessary, to intervene in conflicts within and between states that threaten basic human rights."[20] Although a consensus was reached about the importance of just peacemaking practices, unanimity was not achieved concerning the possible legitimacy of forceful interventions. So, too, it appears, is this the case at present among WCC members concerning R2P.[21]

In an effort to get beyond this impasse, some—including members of the historic peace churches—have suggested that viewing R2P as a form of policing rather than a military action might offer a fruitful avenue to pursue. Mennonite Ernie Regehr writes, "Just as individuals and communities in stable and affluent societies are able in emergencies to call on armed police to come to their aid when they experience unusual or extraordinary threats of violence or attack, churches recognize that people in much more perilous circumstances should have access to protectors."[22] Indeed, the 2006 WCC statement from Porto Alegre quotes this line almost verbatim and goes on to posit that force "deployed and used for humanitarian purposes" should be seen as "more related to just policing" than to "military war-fighting."[23] To be sure, similar calls for a "police" rather than a "war" approach to dealing with terrorism arose from a number of prominent Christian writers in the wake of the September 11th, 2001, attacks on the United States. Jim Wallis, the editor-in-chief of *Sojourners*, admonished US

20. Michael Joseph Smith, "Strengthen the United Nations and International Efforts," in Stassen, *Just Peacemaking*, 166.

21. In its 2001 decision on the "protection of endangered peoples" document, the WCC Central Committee stated "that on the substance of the concern to protect populations caught in situations of armed violence described in the following background document there was broad agreement, but that some differences remain with respect to the use of armed force for the protection of endangered populations in situations of armed violence." Similarly, the 2006 statement from the Ninth Assembly of the World Council of Churches, "Vulnerable Populations at Risk," also notes in para. 2: "The use of force for humanitarian purposes is a controversial issue. . . . While some believe that the resort to force must not be avoided when it can alleviate or stop large-scale human rights violations, others can only support intervention by creative, non-violent means."

22. Regehr, "Comments from Ernie Regehr," 105.

23. Ninth Assembly of the World Council of Churches, "Vulnerable Populations at Risk," paras. 13, 17.

Christians to view the terrorist bombings as a "crime against humanity" that should be addressed by "global police" responsible for preventing future threats and defending innocent lives.[24]

Likewise, Stanley Hauerwas, an influential pacifist Christian theologian, said that he "would certainly like to start envisioning the possibility of that kind of police force" as a "good" alternative to war.[25] Some notable just-war experts also suggested that a police approach might be more appropriate for dealing with the threat of terrorism.[26] Political theorist Michael Walzer refers to such appeals to a "police" approach as an alternative to military action as the "'dial 911' response to 9/11."[27]

Such appeals are curious given that little serious attention has been paid within the churches and the discipline of theological ethics to the ethics of policing, especially with regard to the use of lethal force. As Christian ethicist Edward LeRoy Long Jr. has noted, "One can go through the indices of book after book in the field and find no entries for either law enforcement or police work. In comparison with the immense amount of thinking about the problem of war and the moral issues surrounding military service, this lacuna is telling."[28] Therefore, before drawing parallels between R2P and policing in order to generate further consensus among Christians and churches in the WCC, careful consideration must first be given to the ethics of policing. In what follows, I will argue that similarities do indeed exist between R2P and "just policing"; however, I will also show that this model of policing retains the possibility for the legitimate use of force—in accordance with strict rules governing such use of force that are analogous to those found in just-war reasoning. It may therefore be unlikely to persuade all those within the WCC fellowship who have negative views about R2P to change their opinion. Nevertheless, while pacifists may not be able to participate in actions resembling policing, especially when lethal force may be involved, there may be ways in which they can support efforts by others to make just war more like policing.

24. Wallis, "Hard Questions for Peacemakers," 29–33.

25. Wallis, "Interview with Stanley Hauerwas."

26. As seen in the previous chapter of this present volume, examples include Catholic moral theologians Lisa Sowle Cahill, Jean Porter, and J. Bryan Hehir.

27. Walzer, *Arguing About War*, xiv. In the United States, "911" is the telephone number for calling the police.

28. Long, *Facing Terrorism*, 83.

Models of Policing

Simply invoking an analogy with the police is insufficient, for surely not all policing is ethical. No Christian ethicist or church, for example, would morally defend a *police state* and its totalitarian oppression. There are also many police institutions around the globe that are viewed as corrupt and untrustworthy by citizens, such as in El Salvador and Afghanistan.[29] Nor is all police use of force necessarily moral, as evinced by the excessive force and police brutality associated, for instance, with the famous Rodney King beating by Los Angeles police officers in 1991. When reference is made to the police, therefore, we need to be clear about the kind of policing we have in mind. That the 2006 WCC statement on R2P from Porto Alegre specifies "just policing" indicates some awareness of this point. It is important to clarify this issue because some objections to R2P from persons in the historic peace churches hinge on the view that policing is still about violence and thus no more moral than war-fighting.[30]

One approach to policing often correlated with violence is known as the "crime fighter" or "military" model. John Kleinig, a philosopher who specializes in police ethics, describes how this type of policing, which regards the use of force as its *raison d'être*, came to the fore during the twentieth century, especially in the United States.[31] Similarly, criminologist Egon Bittner observes, "The conception of the police as a quasi-military institution with a war-like mission plays an important part in the structuring of police work in modern American police departments."[32] Not only do American police tend to regard themselves as crime fighters in the war on crime, but, as criminologists Jerome Skolnick and James Fyfe note, the "military metaphor also colors the public's expectations of the police."[33] Such an approach emphasizes "the *primacy* of force in coping with crime and criminals."[34] While the crime fighter model of policing revolves around the use of force, it also colors police officers' attitudes

29. According to David H. Bayley and Robert M. Perito, 43 percent of people surveyed in El Salvador believe corruption is pervasive among public servants, including the police; 42 percent of Afghans respond similarly (Bayley and Perito, *Police in War*, 101).

30. See, for example, articles by Alexis-Baker, "Gospel or a Glock?," 23–49, and "Community, Policing, and Violence," 102–16.

31. Kleinig, *Ethics of Policing*, 24–25.

32. Bittner, *Functions of the Police*, 52.

33. Skolnick and Fyfe, *Above the Law*, 113. See Kleinig, *Ethics of Policing*, 283.

34. Scheingold, *Politics of Law and Order*, 101–2.

towards others. In this approach, an "us versus them" attitude tends to come into play.[35] Everyone is viewed as a potential "enemy." This makes it easier, warns Paul Chevigny, for police "to abuse those who are the enemy, easier even to kill or torture them."[36] Indeed, Skolnick and Fyfe claim a "causal connection" exists between "the idea that cops are like soldiers in wars on crime" and the use of excessive force, and believe that the war model of policing constitutes "a major cause of police violence and the violation of citizens' rights."[37] Obviously, this model cannot be what Christian ethicists and churches have in mind when suggesting policing as a way to make R2P more acceptable to WCC members.

Other models exist that are purported to be less violent. Kleinig, for example, proposes the "social peacekeeper" approach to policing.[38] Elements of this model have been implemented in recent decades, including in the United States, in what have been commonly referred to as community policing or problem-oriented policing.[39] More recently, in their *The Police in War: Fighting Insurgency, Terrorism, and Violent Crime*, which examines the need for policing in the immediate aftermath of conflict, David H. Bayley and Robert M. Perito refer to this basic approach, which they advocate, as "core policing."[40] Such policing seeks, as the motto says, to "serve and protect" the public. Pivoting on a partnership between the police and the community, it involves training and practices that seek to foster a relationship of mutual trust, bonds of empathy, and a common purpose between police and people. This approach is also more proactive than reactive, involving a more preventive approach to crime that strives to identify, understand, and address the root causes of crime. As theological ethicist Gerald Schlabach puts it, community policing involves being "embedded, indebted, and accountable within [a] community," which he believes entails that "it has an inherent tendency to minimize recourse to

---

35. Kappeler et al., *Mythology of Crime*, 131.

36. Chevigny, *Edge of the Knife*, 255–56.

37. Skolnick and Fyfe, *Above the Law*, xviii, 12–13, 115–16.

38. Kleinig, *Ethics of Policing*, 27–29. Other models of policing include the "emergency operator" and the "social enforcer," but Kleinig argues that both of these continue to regard the monopoly of coercive force as the distinguishing essential feature of policing (25–27).

39. Kleinig, *Ethics of Policing*, 28, 78, 229–33. For more on community policing, see Friedmann, *Community Policing*; For a critical assessment of community policing, see Stephens and Doerner, "Peace in the 'Hood'"; and Stephens, "Future of Policing," 77–93.

40. Bayley and Perito, *Police in War*, 73–74, 83–86, 98–102, 113–18.

violence."[41] Kleinig noted that although the use of force is not ruled out absolutely, it is governed stringently by moral and legal criteria for when and how to employ it.[42] This social-peacekeeper model of policing—or as I have named it, just policing—appears to coincide more with R2P, especially with its first prong emphasizing the "responsibility to prevent" through just peacemaking practices, as well as with the second prong about the "responsibility to react" through, as a last resort in extreme circumstances where necessary, forceful intervention.

John Howard Yoder, Just-War Theory, and R2P

If R2P indeed may be viewed as an extension of just policing, most WCC members should be able to support it. Of course, not everyone will agree with it, particularly those in the historic peace churches who regard the use of lethal force, even by police, as incompatible with Christian ethics. As a Protestant much influenced in his pacifism by the Mennonite tradition, Stanley Hauerwas comments that his support of a police approach to dealing with international conflict stops at the point where it requires him to "carry a gun."[43] Moreover, Mennonite J. Denny Weaver argues that pacifists who accept and possibly participate in policing that involves the use of force, even if it is more limited than war-fighting, are "practically" or "almost" pacifists who actually have "just-war outlooks but with more stringent application of just-war criteria than is usually the case."[44] Yet, might it be possible to offer their moral support for R2P even if they never actually participate in this particular prong of it? I think so.

My teacher, the Mennonite theological ethicist John Howard Yoder, who was the pacifist who most influenced my other teacher, Hauerwas, used to show his respect for the dignity of his fellow Christians who subscribe to the just-war tradition by engaging them in conversations on their terms and encouraging them to think more seriously about what it would really mean to honor and adhere to this mode of moral reasoning about when war is, or *is not*, justified. As Mark Thiessen Nation notes, not only were pacifists "strengthened through Yoder's pacifist writings," but other Christians "were

41. Schlabach, "Just Policing: Response to the Responses," 23.

42. Kleinig, *Ethics of Policing*, 99–102; *deadly* force policy is further discussed at 107–22.

43. Wallis, "Interview with Stanley Hauerwas."

44. Weaver, "Why the 'Almost' Is Still Important," 90.

strengthened in their resolve to use violence only in a disciplined fashion."[45] Indeed, Yoder believed that Christian pacifists and just-war proponents should waste less time attacking each other and instead "spend more energy . . . [on] their responsibility to challenge the realists, crusaders, and rambos on their 'right' who in fact are shooting up the world."[46]

One area where pacifists and just-war theorists have responded to Yoder's call to forge an alliance has been the fruitful work on just peacemaking, which certainly connects with the "responsibility to prevent" and, in my view, "the responsibility to rebuild" prongs of R2P. But I think that just policing represents another area where most pacifists and just-war theorists may come together and support, at least morally, R2P, including its second prong, "the responsibility to react." While Yoder was not sure if pacifists could participate in actions resembling policing, especially when lethal force may be involved, he thought pacifists should support efforts by others to make just war more like just policing. "The closer one comes to the domestic model," he wrote, "where restrained violence is like that of the police officer, the more applicable, by analogy, is the just-war language, and the more credible is its claim to be providing real guidance."[47] Or, as Hauerwas expresses it, "a police force is the best institutionalization of what just war should be about."[48] A number of just-war ethicists in recent decades have shared this perspective, even though policing generally has not received substantial attention in the field of Christian ethics.

Accordingly, some just-war ethicists highlighted how the just war mode of reasoning can be discerned analogously in moral accounts of any political use of force, both domestically and internationally. Irish moral theologian Enda McDonagh has written, "Accepting, in common with the majority of Christians past and present, the need for the violence of restraint in society, one is operating with criteria similar to those of the just war."[49] This interpretation echoes that of the twentieth-century United States Methodist theologian, Paul Ramsey, who argued that the "moral economy" of the just-war tradition is *morally* if not *legally* binding upon the use of force between nations," and it also "regulates the use

---

45. Nation, *John Howard Yoder*, 194.

46. Yoder, "How Many Ways Are There to Think Morally about War?," 107.

47. Yoder, *When War Is Unjust*, 69.

48. Quoted in Wallis, "Interview with Stanley Hauerwas."

49. McDonagh, *Church and Politics*, 71; published in Ireland as *The Demands of Simple Justice*. See also Potter, *War and Moral Discourse*, 49–50.

of force within political communities, where it is both *morally* and *legally* binding."[50] Likewise, Catholic ethicist Edward Malloy believes "the 'just war' or 'justified violence' tradition" provides a "helpful ethical framework for analysis . . . adapted to the problem of police use of force." He is "convinced that the classic criteria for the justified use of violence are much easier to satisfy in the domestic context of police work than they are in the international setting of war."[51] While he knew that many invoke just-war language as a smokescreen for wars that are unjust, Yoder constantly asked just-war advocates how they might make the claims of the just-war tradition truly operational in a way that has "teeth" (he also called this a "strict constructionist" approach) so as to lead to less violence, less injustice, and less loss of life in the world.[52] Just policing would appear to be what all of these theologians have in mind, even though they did not yet name it as such. That is, while the reasoning and the criteria are basically the same in either just war or just policing, their application in just policing has more teeth given the community and legal framework, under which police use of force is subject to more constraint, review and accountability.

R2P endeavors to do the same. As Raiser observes, "Even the military component follows a logic that is closer to the role of police; their task is not to 'win' and to liquidate an enemy, but rather to stop armed violence and to bring to justice those responsible for acts of violence."[53] Although much warfare, especially in the past bloody century, has not exemplified such moral concern—even when they are purported to be "just" wars—for the enemy, the logic of the just-war tradition going back to Augustine rests behind both the just policing and R2P frameworks for the moral use of force.[54]

Augustine held that the aim of a just war—its right intent—should be to restore peace. In his letter to Boniface, a Roman general in Africa who, after his wife's death, desired to retire and become a monk, Augustine wrote, "War should be waged only as a necessity and waged only that through it

50. Ramsey, *Just War*, 144.

51. Malloy, *Ethics of Law Enforcement*, 10, 24.

52. Yoder, *When War Is Unjust*, 3.

53. Raiser, "Ethics of Protection," 15.

54. Roger Williamson has noted, "The [2001] report is set within the intellectual framework of the just war tradition, which includes criteria relating both to the decision to use military force and on the conduct of war." Williamson, "Further Developing the Criteria for Intervention," 60. See also Stålsett, "Notes on the Just War Tradition," 28–30, who observes that the criteria for R2P in the various reports are in line with the "tradition on the justifiable use of coercive force" (29).

God may deliver men from that necessity and preserve them in peace. For peace is not to be sought in order to kindle war, but war is to be waged in order to obtain peace."[55] Like his teacher Ambrose, Augustine anchored just war in loving defense of an innocent neighbor who is under attack.[56] Augustine did not have in mind revenge and vengeance; rather—and this tied back to his understanding of right intent—the hope was to have evil persons repent and reform, and thereby restore the peace.[57] He did not think that just war contradicted Jesus's injunction to love one's enemies. Just war is a form of love in going to the aid of an unjustly attacked innocent party; however, it is also an expression of love, or "kind harshness," for one's enemy neighbor.[58] It aims at turning the enemy from their wicked ways, making amends, and helping the enemy to rejoin the community of peace and justice. Augustine wrote, "Therefore, even in waging war, cherish the spirit of a peacemaker, that, by conquering those whom you attack, you may lead them back to the advantages of peace."[59]

But, one may ask, how is this a benefit or how is it loving for those enemies who are killed on the battlefield? Augustine replied, "Let necessity, therefore, and not your will, slay the enemy who fights against you."[60] A mournful mood should accompany this action, moreover. In his view, the "real evils in war are love of violence, revengeful cruelty, fierce and implacable enmity, wild resistance, and the lust of power,"[61] all of which would be at odds with restoring a just peace.

Paul Ramsey argued that "the *logic*, the heart and soul, of such protective love" is the basis for the Christian just-war tradition.[62] For Ramsey, whenever a choice must be made between the unjust perpetrator and the innocent victim, circumstances dictate that the latter is to be preferred. As Augustine put it, necessity requires such action. Necessity here, however, should be understood in the strict sense of employing lawful and indispensable means, and not in the way that was critiqued by Yoder, namely,

---

55. Augustine, "Letter 189," in Holmes, *War and Christian Ethics*, 62–63. For a helpful treatment of Augustine here, see Bell, *Just War as Christian Discipleship*, 28–31.

56. Augustine, "Letter 47," in Schaff, *Confessions and Letters of St. Augustine*, 293.

57. Augustine, *Augustine: Political Writings*, 135.

58. Augustine, *Augustine: Political Writings*, 38.

59. Augustine, "Letter 189," 63.

60. Augustine, "Letter 189," 63.

61. Augustine, "Reply to Faustus the Manichean," 64.

62. Ramsey, *Speak Up for Just War or Pacifism*, 72.

"that one may legitimately break the rules whenever one 'really has to,' which tends to boil down to being useful (saving lives, shortening the war) rather than to the real lack of any other means."[63] The latter was the reasoning that supposedly justified the United States' decision to drop atomic bombs on Hiroshima and Nagasaki.

What, it may be asked, has happened to the Christian call to love the enemy neighbor? In Ramsey's view, such love is not altogether extinguished or absent. What he referred to as the "twin-born" justification for war involves a preferential love for the wronged innocent neighbor, but it must also extend to the wrongdoing guilty neighbor, entailing the principle of noncombatant immunity.[64] In other words, the criteria governing when and how the use of force may be morally used—whether in just war, just policing, or, we might rightly add today, R2P—exist out of love for both the innocent and the guilty neighbors.

Conclusion

In his disturbing book, *Killing Civilians: Method, Madness, and Morality in War*, Hugo Slim shares the story of the Liberian village of Bakedo, a mostly Muslim community of Mandingo people of traders and farmers in West Africa. In June 1990, a massacre happened near the mosque nestled in the town's center. Rebels of Charles Taylor's National Patriotic Front of Liberia opened fire at point-blank range, killing thirty-six people—men, women, and children—who they had pushed onto the floor of the "palava hut" near the mosque.

Panic then ensued as people all over the village ran for the forest or scrambled to hide in their houses. As people fled, the sentries posted at the exits of the village shot them one by one, killing men, women, and children outright or wounding others who then ran on into the bush where many of them later bled to death. Soldiers inside the village stormed every hut, killing anyone they found and firing up into the thatched roofs where people were hiding, their blood then dripping to the floor below.[65]

The surviving villagers think they counted 350 people killed in that half hour. What should Christians who are called to be like the Good Samaritan do when a crime such as this is happening? I believe that much

63. Yoder, *When War Is Unjust*, 28.

64. Ramsey, *Just War*, 143–44.

65. Slim, *Killing Civilians*, 9–10.

can be done, including the practices of just peacemaking, to prevent such scenarios from happening in the first place; unfortunately, force is sometimes necessary to put a stop to horrific crimes that are already underway against the innocent. This is analogous to a police officer responding to an emergency call and arriving at the scene to find that the armed suspect is already in the process of shooting at civilians in a park.

Of course, not all pacifist Christians will accept this approach, although some will. As Yoder astutely observed, there exists "a wide gamut of varying, sometimes even contradictory, views" among pacifists.[66] A spectrum of pacifist perspectives arises with regard to policing. The church historian Roland Bainton once noted that "certain pacifists" in the 1950s endorsed the UN intervention in Korea "on the ground that it was not war but only police action."[67] In addition, during the 1990s, in the context of the discussion over the moral legitimacy of humanitarian interventions, Duane Cady observed that because many pacifists "tend not to hesitate over controlled and restrained uses of force by police officers in the apprehension of criminals," they may endorse small-scale military activities resembling large-scale police work.[68] At the same time, I recognize that some Christian pacifists continue to raise significant objections to any lethal use of force, regardless of whether it is employed by police or by the military. Yoder himself would be skeptical that Christians are called to participate in such activities.[69] Nevertheless, he still maintained, "Wherever any new opening for the moral criticism of the use of violence arises, it is in some way a use of the just-war logic, and should be welcomed as at least an opening for possible moral judgment."[70]

In the early years of the Second World War, a scholar of police history, Charles Reith, in his book *Police Principles and the Problem of War*, called for an extension of policing principles to the international level as a move towards abolishing war by an international league or union of nations.[71] In this work, Reith retrieves two major prongs that were initially emphasized

66. Yoder, *Nevertheless*, 9–10.

67. Bainton, "War and the Christian Ethic," 209. At mid-century, James Thayer Addison suggested that the UN intervention in Korea was "rightly viewed . . . as the international equivalent of police work" (Addison, *War, Peace, and the Christian Mind*, 19).

68. Cady, "Pacifist Perspectives on Humanitarian Intervention," 69.

69. Yoder, *Christian Witness to the State*, 56–57.

70. Yoder, *Original Revolution*, 132.

71. Reith, *Police Principles and the Problem of War*.

by Sir Robert Peel's New Police, which he organized in London in 1829: the *preventive principle* of policing and the *capacity to enforce* the law. By the "preventive" principle of policing, Reith had in mind the prevention of crime, which was emphasized by Peel. The London Metropolitan Police, according to police historian Samuel Walker, "were *pro*active rather than *re*active,"[72] much like the social peacekeeping model Kleinig advocates and the just-policing approach outlined here—and consistent with the "responsibility to prevent" prong of R2P.

At the same time, however, in the wake of the League of Nations' failure to stop the outbreak of the Second World War, Reith recognized the need for the capacity to use force to enforce international law if rogue or recalcitrant nations pose a threat to other nations, ethnic groups, or international order. He warned, "Observance of international laws cannot be secured without provision of force for compelling it."[73] Such force, however, would be governed by the moral principles of just policing, so that it would be the *force of law* rather than the *law of force*. Again, this approach would be congruent with the kind of policing envisioned by Peel, who highlighted the use of persuasion, with physical force as a last resort and using only the minimum necessary for preventing or stopping a breach of the law, the social-peacekeeper or just-policing approach to policing, or the "responsibility to react" prong of R2P.

72. Walker, *Popular Justice*, 60; emphasis in the original.
73. Reith, *Police Principles and the Problem of War*, 47.

Chapter Six

The Police in War[1]

At the close of the first decade of the twenty-first century, the United States demonstrated that even though it can easily achieve military victory in war, winning the peace has been more difficult though it is just as important. When the US Army's Third Infantry Division reached downtown Baghdad on April 9, 2003, cheerful crowds inundated the streets, looted stores, ransacked government buildings, and plundered residences of officials of Saddam Hussein's regime. With no Iraqi police to maintain law and order—and with US military forces standing by and watching—the celebratory chaos was replaced by armed gangs and organized criminal groups that continued to dismantle shopping centers and public institutions of anything of value, including the National Museum of Antiquities, where irreplaceable ancient collections were stolen, and the wards of Baghdad's hospitals, where mobs removed patients from their beds and carried off vital medical equipment that was in use to treat the wounded. The seventeen thousand soldiers from the Third Infantry, a mechanized division with tank crews neither equipped nor trained to conduct foot patrols to police an urban environment, had orders not to intervene because looting was not viewed as a military threat. Crime and lack of security thus became the primary concerns of most Iraqi citizens.

Things might have gone differently. Retired US Army General Jay Garner and the staff of the Pentagon's Office of Reconstruction and Humanitarian Affairs, who were responsible for planning and managing the post-conflict phase of operations, prior to the intervention recommended a coalition of

1. Originally published as a review of *The Police in War: Fighting Insurgency, Terrorism, and Violent Crime*, by David H. Bayley and Robert M. Perito (Boulder: Lynne Rienner Publishers, 2010), in the *Journal of Military Ethics* 10, no. 1 (2011) 71–73.

US-led international constabulary and police forces to help reestablish the rule of law; however, the Bush White House and Department of Defense officials rejected this suggestion, instead repeating the assumption that Americans would be welcomed with flowers and candy. Lessons that should have been learned from both the failures and the successes concerning policing in previous US military interventions went unheeded.

A Police Proposal

This important book, *The Police in War: Fighting Insurgency, Terrorism, and Violent Crime*, by two seasoned and respected criminal-justice experts, David H. Bayley and Robert M. Perito, should provide practical guidance about the role of police for politicians, military commanders, and operational decision-makers charged with securing the peace in the immediate aftermath of future military interventions. Although not a book on military ethics as such, its proposal for a form of policing that both protects and earns the support of local populations is congruent, I think, with recent attention being given by just-war theorists to *jus post bellum* (post-war justice) criteria and commitments.[2] Moreover, while Bayley and Perito do not articulate an explicit moral theory, they offer a policing model—they call it *core* policing, and I would associate it with what has been named by others, myself included, *just policing*—that they regard as consistent with the values of human rights and democracy, along with clear rules governing and limiting the use of force. "In order for governments to gain public support," they write, "the responsibility for security should be entrusted as much as possible to police deployed among the population who minimize the use of force and who act in accordance with human rights standards."[3]

While the first chapter examines the unsuccessful attempts with police reconstruction by the United States in Iraq and Afghanistan, with particular attention devoted to what went wrong and why, the second chapter surveys peace and stability operations in Panama, Somalia, Haiti, Bosnia-Herzegovina, and Kosovo, gleaning insights about what sort of policing either failed or succeeded in contributing to the establishment of a just peace. In postintervention situations, local police are often "unprepared, unwilling, or unfit to provide police services," resulting in further

---

2. See, for example, Allman and Winright, *After the Smoke Clears*.
3. Bayley and Perito, *Police in War*, 51.

looting, disorder, and crime.[4] Moreover, when the intervening military forces fail to provide a safe and secure environment, local popular support wanes and jeopardizes the mission's success. Therefore, intervention forces should include a police component capable of restoring public order and securing the rule of law. Such a policing presence, especially as it transitions to international oversight, should be civilian rather than military in nature, and thus accountable to the rule of law. At the same time, local police should be recruited, vetted, and trained in police academies and afterwards mentored by exemplary officers.

Importantly, Bayley and Perito do not offer a one-size-fits-all blueprint but rather a basic framework that is detailed though flexible enough for adaptation according to circumstances and context. In the third chapter, they discuss the role of police in current US counterinsurgency and counterterrorism efforts, with attention given to what might be learned from other nations' experiences with policing, such as the Operation Delphinus and the Safer Neighborhoods programs developed by the London Metropolitan Police in 2006. The fourth chapter specifies the different types of police operations (uniformed patrol; nonuniformed criminal investigators; stability police units to deal with riots; armed police units to undertake offensive operations against insurgents, terrorists, gangs, and violent criminals; covert intelligence agents; and border police) that are feasible on a continuum of security levels during peacebuilding missions (war; insurgency; subversion; disorder; normal crime).

Another Model of Policing

The fifth chapter unpacks further what Bayley and Perito envision by core policing, which they rightly note is similar to community policing, and they helpfully outline a curriculum, which includes attention to ethical values and conduct, for training police. This is followed by a comparative examination of the content of training curricula around the world at this time, especially in view of how they are congruent or not with Bayley and Perito's recommendations, in the sixth chapter. Of course, on the ground in post-conflict settings wider institutional reform is necessary for the creation of "a legitimate and community-oriented police force,"[5] so the seventh chapter offers suggestions

4. Bayley and Perito, *Police in War*, 48.
5. Bayley and Perito, *Police in War*, 127.

concerning justice sector reform (not only police but also the courts and prisons) and ministerial reform (e.g., Interior Ministry).

The eighth chapter summarizes their analysis and draws out its implications for current US efforts at stabilization and reconstruction, including a call for the creation of an entirely new Stability Operations Agency in the United States.[6] One of the key points that Bayley and Perito reiterate is that "military action, whether carried out by foreigners or locals, is a poor tool for winning hearts and minds because it is more destructive and less discriminating than police action and directed by remote commanders rather than by local citizens."[7] Although they do not discuss it, there are, however, a variety of extant models of policing, with some that correlate with brutality and excessive force. Bayley and Perito are not advocating policing of the sort that we witnessed years ago with the beating of Rodney King by Los Angeles police officers. Nor do Bayley and Perito have in mind the kind of oppressive policing associated with totalitarian police states. Core policing, in their view, earns the support of local populations because the police make themselves available to citizens, respond effectively to their requests, and demonstrate fairness in their actions.

As a just-war ethicist possessing previous professional experience in law enforcement, I welcome Bayley and Perito's much-needed book. With helpful diagrams and figures illustrating key points, it will indeed continue to inform my own ongoing work in both just policing and *jus post bellum*, and I hope that it reaches a wide audience.

6. Bayley and Perito, *Police in War*, 160.
7. Bayley and Perito, *Police in War*, 152.

Chapter Seven

Militarized Policing

The History of the Warrior Cop[1]

M ichael Brown is dead, a young black man gone before he could start college and begin life as an adult. The life of Darren Wilson, the white police officer who shot and killed the unarmed Brown, has been forever changed, too. Since the August 9th shooting, protesters in Ferguson, Missouri, have faced a heavy-handed, heavily armed police response. This has prompted much national conversation about both racism and the growing militarization of American police forces.

The latter subject had been getting some attention lately, even before the events in Ferguson. Radley Balko's book *Rise of the Warrior Cop* is a notable example.[2] But as Balko acknowledges, the militarization of the police is not a new development. Over the years, others have noted it as well.

The best book on the subject, in my view, is John Kleinig's *The Ethics of Policing*.[3] Kleinig examines the moral foundations of policing, the use of force, and several extant models of policing. The two primary models, at opposite ends of the spectrum, are the "crime fighter" and the "social peacekeeper." During the twentieth century, the former, which is also known as the "military model" of policing, became the primary paradigm in the United States.

---

1. Originally published in *Christian Century* 131.19 (September 17, 2014) 10–12.

2. Balko, *Rise of the Warrior Cop.*

3. Kleinig, *Ethics of Policing.*

From Martial Metaphor to Military Model

In the popular book *Shoot to Kill*, former police officer Charles W. Sasser evinces the extent to which this military metaphor has had an impact on the self-definition of American police. He writes that police are "soldiers in a strange war that will never end," risking their lives as a "final defense against the forces of darkness and evil" in the "continuing war against crime" while they patrol "the combat zone that is modern America."[4] Sasser notes that thousands of American cops are assaulted each year "with everything from fists and broken street signs to knives and, of course, guns."[5] Police feel like they are always potentially in danger, and in order to deal effectively with such threats they want certain crime-fighting tools—including weapons, equipment such as helmets and body armor, and the ability to use force when necessary.

And it's not just police themselves who regard their work as fighting a war on crime. As Jerome Skolnick and James Fyfe write in *Above the Law*, the "military metaphor also colors the public's expectations of the police."[6] In addition to the political rhetoric of "getting tough on crime," Americans are likely influenced by popular depictions of policing, which focus mostly on crime fighting. According to Stuart A. Scheingold, in his *The Politics of Law and Order*, TV and movie viewers often see "heroic males regularly and successfully using lethal violence as a way of avenging wrongs," conveying the message that violence is an American "way of life" for dealing with interpersonal conflict and social problems.[7]

Police, too, are affected by such media portrayals of policing. In *The Badge and the Bullet*, Peter Scharf and Arnold Binder name these media depictions "the mythology of police work," especially with regard to viewing the gun as "the primary symbol of law enforcement," the "tool of the trade," and the "culturally defined essence of police work."[8]

This military approach gained traction in 1974 with the formation of Special Weapons and Tactics teams in many American police departments. SWAT teams are outfitted with special gear, including helmets, semiautomatic assault rifles, tear gas, and flash grenades. They represent a model

4. Sasser, *Shoot to Kill*, 7.

5. Sasser, *Shoot to Kill*, 15.

6. Skolnick and Fyfe, *Above the Law*, 113.

7. Scheingold, *Politics of Law and Order*, 63.

8. Scharf and Binder, *Badge and the Bullet*, 29, 32, 36, 38.

that regards the use of force as the key characteristic of policing; put differently, it views coercive power as the *raison d'être* of policing.

Might Makes Right?

Criminologists have warned that the military model of policing may be the soil from which sprout the seeds of police brutality and excessive force. There is the belief "that being a law enforcement officer is akin to the work of a soldier on the frontlines," write Victor Kappeler, Mark Blumberg, and Gary Potter in *The Mythology of Crime and Criminal Justice*.[9] "This pervasive sense that their mission is a dangerous one cannot help but affect the way that police officers deal with the public."[10]

The military model alienates the police from the public, often leading to the dehumanization of the very people the police are pledged to serve and protect. Everyone is viewed suspiciously and cynically as a potential enemy. In turn, this makes it easier, according to Paul Chevigny in *Edge of the Knife*, for police "to abuse those who are the enemy, easier even to kill or torture them."[11]

Likewise, Skolnick and Fyfe assert that a "causal connection" exists between "the idea that cops are like soldiers in war on crime"[12] and the use of excessive force. Indeed, the war model of policing constitutes "a major cause of police violence and the violation of citizens' rights" and it "encourages police violence of the type that victimized Rodney King."[13]

It should be noted, however, that in actual daily work, a police officer deals with a large array of problems and incidents: intervening in domestic disputes, helping injured accident victims, dealing with people with mental illness, finding runaways, searching for lost children, informing people of the deaths of loved ones, directing traffic, stopping suicide attempts. The police spend the majority of their time—estimates range from 70 to 90 percent—in these kinds of activities, rather than using force to fight crime.

Yet, when I used to work in law enforcement, I recall that most of my fellow recruits in the police academy seemed to look forward to and enjoy the firearms training the most.

9. Kappeler et al., *Mythology of Crime and Criminal Justice*, 131.

10. Kappeler et al., *Mythology of Crime and Criminal Justice*, 131.

11. Chevigny, *Edge of the Knife*, 255–56.

12. Skolnick and Fyfe, *Above the Law*, xviii.

13. Skolnick and Fyfe, *Above the Law*, 115–16.

Police as Peacekeepers

"Unless and until police see themselves primarily as peacekeepers rather than as crimefighters," Kleinig writes, "firearms will tend to be used unnecessarily."[14] In his view, the social-peacekeeper model of policing better encompasses most of the responsibilities and tasks of police in society, and although there remains a place for the possibility of the use of force against an uncooperative or threatening suspect, "its instrumental or subservient character is emphasized" in this model.[15] Indeed, Kleinig suggests that had the Los Angeles police officers who participated in the beating of Rodney King understood themselves "primarily as social peacekeepers, for whom recourse to force constituted a last and regrettable option, events would almost certainly have turned out very differently."[16]

This social-peacekeeper model has its historical roots in England, with its emphasis on community service and peacekeeping. Although the functional origins of policing may be traced to ancient communal self-policing (i.e., night watches), modern policing began institutionally with Sir Robert Peel's establishment of the "New Police" of Metropolitan London in 1829 (the term "Bobby" is here derived from "Robert").[17]

According to David Ascoli in *The Queen's Peace*, Peel "was stubborn to the point of obsession that his 'New Police' should be seen to be free of all taint of militarism," which is why they were required to wear a "quiet" uniform consisting of "a blue shallow-tail coat with white button" and not the British military's red coat.[18] The primary object of this first police department, as explicitly reflected in its General Instructions from 1829, was the prevention of crime, and emphasis was placed on the use of persuasion, with physical force as a last resort—and using only the minimum force necessary for preventing or stopping a breach of the law.

Initially there was skepticism among the British public, with some calling the New Police derogatory epithets such as "Blue Locusts," "Blue Drones," and "Blue Devils." Yet Ascoli notes that when a riot broke out at Hyde Park Corner in 1830, the mob was "met by only passive police resistance, a tactic which seems to have bewildered the rioters who, bent on violence, were

14. Kleinig, *Ethics of Policing*, 117.
15. Kleinig, *Ethics of Policing*, 29.
16. Kleinig, *Ethics of Policing*, 96.
17. Ascoli, *Queen's Peace*, 89–90.
18. Ascoli, *Queen's Peace*, 89–90.

hoping for violence in return."[19] Because of their restraint in the use of force, the Metropolitan Police gained widespread public acceptance.

Also, the police were citizens working in partnership with their community. Their patrol duties—which consisted of walking regular beats in neighborhoods—included traffic control, the prevention of cruelty to children and animals, finding missing persons, the care of the poor and destitute, extinguishing fires, the inspection of weights, bridges, and buildings, and even waking people up for work.

This was the model of policing that was transplanted to Boston and New York City in the nineteenth century. Even so, when police began to wear uniforms and a badge in the 1850s, many worried that the police would turn out to be essentially a standing army, though police departments did not recruit from the military at that time. According to Robert Fogelson, in his *Big-City Police*, Americans "had a strong conviction that the police should have an essentially civilian orientation."[20] The ethos changed after the Civil War, when the surplus of firearms began to find its way into the hands of the police. Then, in the early twentieth century, well-armed gangsters such as Al Capone motivated the police to begin to arm themselves even more.

In the 1990s this militaristic approach was moderated by community policing, basically another name for the social-peacekeeper model. Yet ongoing talk of a "war on crime" and a "war on drugs" kept the military model alive, and it was resuscitated especially by the "war on terror" and the surplus of military weapons and equipment that police departments have received following the wars in Iraq and Afghanistan.

I believe we need a larger paradigm shift back to the community-policing or social-peacekeeper model. If anyone doubts its effectiveness or believes it is unrealistic, consider how successful it has been in Nicaragua, which is the poorest country in Central America but has the lowest crime rates—and, unlike other Central American nations with more militaristic police and higher crime, hardly any children seeking refuge in the United States.

Along with this general paradigm shift, we need further clarification of use-of-force guidelines. Since the 1980s, with important Supreme Court decisions such as *Tennessee v. Garner* (1985), police cannot use lethal force to stop the escape of a fleeing criminal suspect unless the "officer has probable cause to believe that the suspect poses a significant

19. Ascoli, *Queen's Peace*, 89–90.
20. Fogelson, *Big-City Police*, 45.

threat of death or serious physical injury to the officer or others."[21] That rule is the basis on which Wilson's use of deadly force against Brown will be evaluated. Moreover, the "totality of the circumstances" will be considered, based on the "perspective of a reasonable officer on the scene, rather than with the 20/20 vision of hindsight."

Ambiguity arises in the *Tennessee v. Garner* decision, however, because Justice Byron White, writing for the majority, added that "if the suspect threatens the officer with a weapon or there is probable cause to believe that he has committed a crime involving the infliction or threatened infliction of serious physical harm, deadly force may be used if necessary to prevent escape, and if, where feasible, some warning has been given."[22] This ambiguity needs to be addressed.

In the end, what's needed is policing that reflects the force of law. Right now, it too often reflects the law of force.

21. *Tennessee v. Garner*, 471 US 1 (1985).
22. *Tennessee v. Garner*, 471 US 1 (1985).

Chapter Eight

Demilitarize the Police![1]

Across the country, police departments act more like an occupying army than keepers of the peace.

As a former reserve police officer who has taught ethics at two police academies, I followed the news very closely after eighteen-year-old Michael Brown was shot to death by police officer Darren Wilson in nearby Ferguson, Missouri. When I saw the military equipment of the St. Louis County Police—especially the sharp shooter on top of an armored vehicle aiming his rifle at the protesters—I said to my wife, "This may turn out to be very, very bad."

US Senator Claire McCaskill, of Missouri, argued in the midst of the protests that St. Louis County should "demilitarize the police response" in Ferguson, telling reporters, "The police response has been part of the problem."[2] I agree.

The militarization of the police has been trending over the past few decades. When the thin blue line resembles an occupying force, it exacerbates racial tensions in neighborhoods and communities, making things worse for everyone, including the police.

Some communities are starting to push back. For instance, the city council of Davis, California, recently directed its police department to get rid of a mine-resistant, ambush-protected vehicle (worth $700,000) that it had received free from the US military's surplus program.[3]

How did the militarization of the police happen? Radley Balko, in his troubling book *Rise of the Warrior Cop*, observes that "no one made a

1. Originally published in *Sojourners* 43.11 (December 2014) 10–11.

2. Klimas, "Sen. Claire McCaskill: Police Are the Problem."

3. Nagourney, "Police Armored Vehicle Is Unwelcome."

decision to militarize the police in America. The change has come slowly, the result of a generation of politicians and public officials fanning and exploiting public fear by declaring war on abstractions like crime, drug use, and terrorism. The resulting policies have made those war metaphors increasingly real."[4]

Beginning in the early 1970s, police agencies received grants and equipment from the federal Law Enforcement Assistance Administration, an agency in the Department of Justice. Agency director Don Santarelli worried that police departments "didn't value education or training. They valued hardware."[5] At that time Birmingham, Alabama, had asked for an armored personnel carrier, and Los Angeles even requested a submarine. Cities across the country wanted training and gear for SWAT (special weapons and tactics) teams.[6]

In 1987, an office in the Pentagon was established to oversee transfers of war equipment to civilian law enforcement agencies. After the terrorist attack of September 11th, the Department of Homeland Security began to provide police departments funding to purchase armored vehicles, body armor, aircraft, and other military equipment. Companies that make and sell military-grade hardware have made quite a profit on the program.

The problem with the military metaphor for policing is that citizens are viewed as the enemy. Coercion, rather than persuasion, is central. Conflict, rather than cooperation, is expected. These, in turn, increase the likelihood of police brutality and excessive force.

The modern institution of policing began in 1829 with the establishment of the Metropolitan Police of London by Sir Robert Peel, who made sure his police were different from the military. The police were not armed in the same way, and officers were citizens who knew and interacted with their fellow citizens. The use of force was governed strictly and considered a last resort.

Such a model is commonly known today as community policing, which involves police presence in the community, working with fellow citizens, and treating others respectfully. Community policing can be very effective at re-establishing trust within society as well as at protecting people.

To be sure, policing in US cities can be very dangerous, especially with so many guns circulating in our society. Although officers must be able to

4. Balko, *Rise of the Warrior Cop*, 42.
5. Balko, *Rise of the Warrior Cop*, 96.
6. Balko, *Rise of the Warrior Cop*, 96.

protect themselves, David H. Bayley and Robert M. Perito argue in their book, *The Police in War,* in doing so they should not give the impression that war is their business.[7]

7. Bayley and Perito. *The Police in War.*

Chapter Nine

Faith, Justice, and Ferguson

Insights for Religious Educators from a Law Enforcement
Officer Turned Theological Ethicist[1]

Although for nearly two decades I have been a Catholic theological
ethicist, I also possess experience in law enforcement. Indeed, I am
a former corrections officer and reserve police officer who has taught ethics
at two police academies, including at the St. Louis County and Municipal
Police Academy and the Des Moines City Police Academy, and ethics for
prison staff at the Eastern Reception, Diagnostic and Correctional Center in
Bonne Terre, Missouri, where executions by the state are conducted. Nearly
three-and-a-half decades ago, as a first-generation college student interested
in pursuing a career in either law or ministry, I worked full-time as a corrections officer, mostly on the midnight shift, at a maximum-security jail, for
the same metropolitan sheriff's department where my mother was a patrol
officer, while I attended classes full-time during the day. In those years, I
found myself wrestling with questions about ethics, theology, and violence.
Hence, after graduating, rather than go to law school, I went to Duke Divinity
School and then to the University of Notre Dame, thereby fusing my interests
through the study of moral theology. Somewhat more related to the field of
religious education, though, along the way I was also a youth minister, got
some experience in college campus ministry, and since then have regularly
and enthusiastically spoken to adult religious education groups in local parishes and churches about a wide range of ethical topics and issues, including
this one having to do with faith, justice, and Ferguson.

---

1. Originally presented as an invited lecture for the Peace and Justice Taskforce of the
Religious Education Association in November 2017 in St. Louis, Missouri, and published
in *Religious Education* 113.3 (May–June 2018) 244–52.

At Notre Dame, one of my early course papers explored the ethics of the use of force by police officers—a lacuna in Catholic moral theology and more widely in Christian ethics, which I thought was curious given that many Catholics are in law enforcement and, like me, likely have questions about possible tensions between their faith and their job, particularly with regard to the use of force—and it was also my first peer-reviewed journal article on the subject.[2] This was followed by my PhD dissertation, "The Challenge of Policing: An Analysis in Christian Social Ethics," and many subsequent articles and book chapters about what I came to call "just policing" as opposed to "unjust policing."[3]

So, it is with this background that when I first heard on the local news—I have taught at St. Louis University for over a dozen years now—about how eighteen-year-old Michael Brown was shot to death by police officer Darren Wilson on August 9th, 2014 in nearby Ferguson, I initially had two concerns. First, based on the eyewitness accounts at the time, I wondered whether Wilson's lethal actions were justified in accordance with use-of-force guidelines and jurisprudence. Second, because most citizens in Ferguson are African Americans, and most of the police there are not, I wondered what role race played, not only in this individual incident but also institutionally in the Ferguson Police Department. After all, the problem of racism in US law enforcement involves more than a few bad apples; sometimes the tree itself is diseased.

Militaristic Missteps

Moreover, during the protests that happened over the subsequent days, a third concern arose. When I saw the St. Louis County Police and its military equipment—the helmets, the camouflaged uniforms—and especially the sharpshooter on top of an armored vehicle aiming his rifle at the people who were protesting, I said to my wife, "This is bad, and it may turn out to be very, very bad." Years ago, I qualified as a shotgun sharpshooter, and I received training in riot control, with the baton and shield, but I am glad I was never placed in a situation like what unfolded in Ferguson. As Brittany Ferrell, a protester who was interviewed by Leah Gunning Francis, in her important book *Ferguson and Faith: Sparking Leadership and Awakening Community*, described it: "I began to see photos of K-9 units and . . . video

2. Winright, "Perpetrator as Person," 37–56.
3. Winright, "Challenge of Policing."

recordings of police officers calling protestors 'animals' and telling them that they'll 'blow their f-ing brains out.' And that's when I was like this is violence from the people that are supposed to protect the community."[4] Her realization of the dissonance between police who are supposed to "serve and protect" their fellow citizens and the hostile military-like police on the scene in Ferguson is extremely significant.

The militarization of the police correlates with an overemphasis on the use of force, and when the thin blue line resembles an occupying force it exacerbates an "us versus them" mentality and racial tensions. It only makes things worse for everyone, including the police. Thus, I quickly wrote an opinion piece for the ecumenical magazine, *Christian Century*, which turned out to be the cover story with a photo of a police officer, who looked a lot more like a soldier in combat, and the caption "Militarized Policing: The History of the Warrior Cop."[5] Soon I wrote another one for *Sojourners* magazine,[6] and *US Catholic*[7] published an interview with me about the ethics of policing. As one of the handful of theological ethicists with experience in law enforcement who has written on this topic, I became very busy, especially since the St. Louis area was "ground zero" for its police shootings.

As Rev. Heather Arcovitch put it when interviewed by Gunning Francis, "This is much more than this one officer and one young man. This is a whole systemic thing that we can't move away from anymore. This is happening and we need to not look away."[8] Indeed, since the shooting in Ferguson, other shootings by police in St. Louis and across the United States have been in the news. On August 19, 2014, two St. Louis police officers shot and killed knife-wielding Kajieme Powell, a twenty-five-year-old black man who allegedly did not pay for two energy drinks at a nearby store and who was acting "erratically."[9] Then, on October 9th, in the neighborhood where my parish is located, right around the corner from my office, eighteen-year-old African American VonDerritt D. Meyers Jr. was shot by an off-duty St. Louis police officer, an incident that sparked more protests, including a week-long occupation on the campus of St. Louis University.[10] And similar

---

4. Francis, *Ferguson & Faith*, 59.

5. Winright, "Militarized Policing," 10–12. See chapter 7 of this book.

6. Winright, "Demilitarize the Police!," 10–11. See chapter 8 of this book.

7. Winright. "Keeping the Peace," 18–22.

8. Francis, *Ferguson & Faith*, 41.

9. Holleman and Brown. "St. Louis Police Fatally Shoot Man."

10. Barbash and Phillip, "Fatal Shooting of 18-year-old."

instances of police use of force elsewhere have also gotten national—and international—attention, from Columbia, South Carolina, to St. Paul, Minnesota, and many (too many) more.

Ministry of Presence for Protesters (and for Police)

One of the courses that I have taught for nearly two decades is "Black Theology and Social Change," so I was also closely following the protests in Ferguson, St. Louis, and elsewhere. One of my students who took that course, Alisha Sonnier, was a leader in the Black Lives Matter movement, and her thoughts about it are also shared in Francis's book. Also, many of my friends who are members of the clergy have been active in the demonstrations against the police. Pastor Nelson Pierce's words accurately reflect their efforts: "Several clergy used their relationships, status, and strength for the benefit of the young people to say to the police and to the justice system, 'These are our people, and we are going to work to get them [out of jail].' This was important for the young people to see. . . . It was also important for the police and others to see."[11] Such a ministry of presence with young people of color and their allies who care about justice, I believe, has important implications for the church and for religious education. As Ferrell observed, "I feel like there's this perpetuated idea that 'church' is something you go to, and it's been proven wrong within the last six months, because the church has come to us whether we welcomed it or not. It was there. We became church."[12] In Francis's interviews in her book, others—both young demonstrators and clergy—shared similar reflections from their experience out on the streets. Of course, because "[j]ustice is a constitutive dimension of the preaching of the Gospel,"[13] the church cannot be neutral or unbiased, but must take a preferential option for the poor and stand with the oppressed. I believe in, and agree with that, which is why my recent publications on policing have been critical of militarized, racist, "us-versus-them" policing.

And, yet, I have also worried about the church mirroring that "us-versus-them" attitude right back at the police,[14] as evident in quotes such

11. Francis, *Ferguson & Faith*, 97.
12. Francis, *Ferguson & Faith*, 63.
13. World Synod of Catholic Bishops, "Justice in the World."
14. Winright, "Police and the Community."

as this one from John Stratton: "And it was very tense in the moment right before we knelt down and prayed. The police were dumbfounded when we did that. They didn't know what to do."[15] I fear that by referring to the police as "they" risks forgetting that police officers are also "us," for like my mother, myself, and many others, police officers, too, sit on our pews, attend Sunday school or other religious education opportunities, and worship in our churches. What can the church—and religious educators—do on behalf of faith and justice for all who are involved in the Fergusons of the United States? It may be like walking a tightrope, as evident in these words from Rev. Carlton Lee: "I was acting as a bridge . . . trying to hold the hands of the protestors while yet holding the hands of the police and saying, 'What's our common ground?' However, I noticed it was only going to be a handful of police that you can discuss this with. You had a handful of protestors that you can discuss it with. But, for the most part, neither side wanted to listen."[16] I think that one way to find common ground, perhaps, is to turn our attention to the history of policing.

Policing's Past

It has always struck me as curious that few theological ethicists had seriously considered policing, especially since that word "police" is used in a number of ways, negative as well as positive. After all, nobody wants to live in a "police state." That phrase definitely has a negative connotation. However, on the other hand, the Korean War was supported even by many pacifists because it was viewed as a "police action." There the phrase seems more positive. Similarly, after the terrorist attacks on 9/11, a number of pacifists and nonviolent activists, including Stanley Hauerwas[17] and *Sojourners's* Jim Wallis,[18] proposed a "police" model for responding to and dealing with terrorism. And, yet, Wallis was arrested in Ferguson while demonstrating against the police. Indeed, only a handful of theologians, ethicists, and other Christians have really examined the ethics of policing—which is all the more incredible given that police are authorized to use force, including lethal force.

---

15. Francis, *Ferguson & Faith*, 12.

16. Francis, *Ferguson & Faith*, 34.

17. Wallis, "Interview with Stanley Hauerwas."

18. Wallis, "Hard Questions for Peacemakers," 29–33.

In his classic work on just-war theory from forty-five years ago, Harvard ethicist Ralph Potter observed, "Seldom have American Christian scholars . . . addressed themselves seriously to the task of helping public officers reflect upon the mode of reasoning appropriate to their office that would guide them in determining when they should act, how they should act, and why."[19] Potter believed that police officers need ethical guidance to help them to understand and evaluate the use of force in a way that coheres with moral principles. No theological ethicist devoted attention to the concerns raised by Potter until 1982 when Edward A. Malloy published his slim volume, *The Ethics of Law Enforcement and Criminal Punishment*, which included as its first chapter a brief treatment of "Ethics and the Use of Force."[20] Indeed, Malloy observed that while much theological attention has been given to whether, when, or how Christians morally should participate in war, "there is a noticeable deficiency in applying such analysis to the domestic context of crime and punishment," including policing.[21] He regarded his brief attempt at examining the ethics of policing and the use of force as a preliminary one that "might encourage other Christian ethicists to grapple with this problem of the control of, and response to, domestic violence."[22] Very few theological ethicists, however, have followed up on Malloy's invitation.

As the above references to "police state" and "police action" imply, there is no univocal understanding of the police. In fact, to distinguish between unjust and just policing it is important to note that the institution of policing as we know it today in the United States has not always existed. It is a human construct, and historically there have even been different models of policing. Only in the past forty years or so have scholars of criminology begun to examine police ethics in general and the use of force specifically. One of the contributions to this discussion is John Kleinig's book *The Ethics of Policing*. A philosopher specializing in criminal-justice ethics at John Jay in New York City, he examines the moral foundations of policing and the specific problem of the use of force.[23] Kleinig identifies various models of policing that are currently extant and criminologists that are associated with them. The two main models at opposite ends of the

19. Potter, *War and Moral Discourse*, 60.
20. Malloy, *Ethics of Law Enforcement*.
21. Malloy, *Ethics of Law Enforcement*, 2.
22. Malloy, *Ethics of Law Enforcement*, ix.
23. Kleinig, *Ethics of Policing*.

spectrum from each other are the "crime fighter" model and the "social peacekeeper" model. Falling somewhere in between these two poles, two other models—the "emergency operator" and the "social enforcer"—also are competing in criminological circles. In what follows, I give attention only to the "crime fighter" and the "social peacekeeper" models, due to limited space, although I deal with them elsewhere.[24]

The primary model of policing that developed and prevailed among police institutions within the United States during much of the twentieth century has been the crime-fighter model. As Kleinig notes, it is also often referred to as the military model. According to Joycelyn Pollock-Byrne, police take "very seriously" their role as crime fighters, so much so that this forms and shapes their self-understanding.[25] Indeed, when referring to "real" police work, law enforcement officers generally have in mind crime fighting, with the use of force occupying a central role in their job. For this reason, it is regarded as synonymous with a military model for policing. "The conception of the police as a quasi-military institution with a war-like mission," observes Egon Bittner, "plays an important part in the structuring of police work in modern American departments."[26]

Nor are the police in the United States the only ones to regard policing as crime fighting and a war on crime, but the "military metaphor also colors the public's expectations of the police."[27] Popular depictions of policing on television and in movies focus more on crime fighting and highlight the use of force. Audiences of such television dramas and movies often see "heroic males regularly and successfully using lethal violence as a way of avenging wrongs," conveying the message that violence is a "way of life" in America for dealing with interpersonal conflict and social problems.[28] Police, too, are affected by such media portrayals of policing. "Fed on movies and television shows such as *Dirty Harry*, *Lethal Weapon*, and *Hill Street Blues*," new police officers, believes Fyfe, who was writing in the 1990s, "are likely to believe that they are entering a world where death lurks around every corner, where every contact with a citizen may prove fatal."[29] Peter Scharf

24. Tobias Winright, "Community Policing as a Paradigm for International Order," in Schlabach, *Just Policing, Not War*, 130–52.

25. Pollock-Byrne, *Ethics in Crime and Justice*, 73.

26. Bittner, *Functions of the Police in Modern Society*, 52.

27. Skolnick and Fyfe, *Above the Law*, 113.

28. Scheingold, *Politics of Law and Order*, 63.

29. Fyfe, "Training to Reduce Police-Civilian Violence," 175.

and Arnold Binder name these media depictions "the mythology of police work," especially with regard to viewing the gun as "the primary symbol of law enforcement," the "tool of the trade," and the "culturally defined essence of police work."[30] I remember this mentality firsthand when I was in law enforcement in the 1980s—and the aforementioned movies and TV shows were popular—and I also witnessed it again in the early 2000s when I did another stint in law enforcement.

Most recently, Radley Balko, in his *Rise of the Warrior Cop: The Militarization of America's Police Forces*, has documented this trend. As he observes, "No one made a decision to militarize the police in America. The change has come slowly, the result of a generation of politicians and public officials fanning and exploiting public fears by declaring war on abstractions like crime, drug use, and terrorism. The resulting policies have made those war metaphors increasingly real."[31] Balko surveys how such martial language came to shape policing, not only how police officers came to view themselves and their work but also the US public's expectations of law enforcement. From President Richard Nixon, who was the first to refer to the "war" on drugs, to Ronald Reagan, George H. W. Bush, Bill Clinton, and George W. Bush, the militarization of the police coincided with these so-called wars underway within the domestic United States.

In addition, beginning in the early 1970s, police agencies received grants and equipment from the federal Law Enforcement Assistance Administration, which Don Santarelli directed. He worried about what the police departments requested: "They didn't value education or training. They valued hardware."[32] At that time, Birmingham asked for an armored personnel carrier, and Los Angeles even requested a submarine. And they wanted training and gear for special weapons and tactics (SWAT) teams, the first of which was established by Daryl Gates in Los Angeles, with their special gear, including semiautomatic assault rifles, tear gas, and flash grenades, and with many cities and towns across the country quickly forming their own. And what about the helmets and camouflage uniforms that we saw in Ferguson? As Balko puts it, "There seemed to be little purpose for it other than to mimic the military."[33]

---

30. Scharf and Binder, *Badge and the Bullet*, 31–32, 38.

31. Balko, *Rise of the Warrior Cop*, 42.

32. Balko, *Rise of the Warrior Cop*, 96.

33. Balko, *Rise of the Warrior Cop*, 293.

In 1987 an office in the Pentagon was established to oversee transfers of war equipment to civilian law enforcement agencies.[34] After the terrorist attack of September 11th, the Department of Homeland Security provided anti-terrorism grants for police departments to purchase armored vehicles, body armor, aircraft, and other military equipment. Companies that make and sell military-grade hardware are now quite profitable, too. The military-industrial complex has spawned a similar industry in policing. According to Martin Edmonds, the "militarization" of the police and "their being armed with specialized equipment and weapons is an increasingly frequent phenomenon almost everywhere."[35] Indeed, Balko speculates that the "police today may be more militarized than the military."[36]

This view of policing assumes "the *primacy* of force in coping with crime and criminals."[37] This model reckons the use of force as the key characteristic of policing or, put differently, it regards coercive power as the *raison d'être* of policing. And, as one group of criminologists observes, the "belief that being a law enforcement officer is akin to the work of a soldier on the frontlines . . . [and] this pervasive sense that their mission is a dangerous one cannot help but affect the way that police officers deal with the public."[38]

Indeed, the military or crime-fighter model alienates the police from the public, often leading to the dehumanization of the very people that police are pledged to serve and protect. Everyone is viewed suspiciously and cynically as a potential "enemy," and a criminal suspect is especially regarded as such, often called "scum" or "animal" or other dehumanizing words. One police officer put it this way: "Because when you get into that mentality, there are no innocent people. There's us and there's the enemy."[39] In turn, this makes it easier, according to Paul Chevigny, for police "to abuse those who are the enemy, easier even to kill or torture them."[40] When police view the public as a whole cynically and suspiciously, according to Christopher Daskalos, "the chances of police misuse of force are greatly increased" and the temptation to use excessive force is "exacerbated."[41] Likewise, Skolnick

---

34. Balko, *Rise of the Warrior Cop*, 293.

35. Edmonds, *Armed Services and Society*, 7.

36. Balko, *Rise of the Warrior Cop*, 335.

37. Scheingold, *Politics of Law and Order*, 101–2.

38. Kappeler et al., *Mythology of Crime and Criminal Justice*, 131.

39. Balko, *Rise of the Warrior Cop*, 241.

40. Chevigny, *Edge of the Knife*.

41. Daskalos, "Current Issues in Policing," 67.

and Fyfe assert that a "causal connection" exists between "the idea that cops are like soldiers in wars on crime" and the use of excessive force.[42] That so many criminologists over the past three decades have warned about this approach to policing is significant—and yet, this is precisely the type of policing we have seen in Ferguson, St. Louis, and elsewhere.

However, this crime-fighter or military model of policing is not the only one available. John Kleinig proposes the "social peacekeeper" model of policing, which he sees as rooted in the origins of policing.[43] Whereas the *functional* origins of policing may be traced to ancient communal self-policing, modern policing began institutionally with Sir Robert Peel's establishment of the "New Police" of Metropolitan London in 1829 (this is why a London police officer is called a "Bobby"). Prior to that time, there were night watches, and there were constables and shire reeves (from which we derive the word "sheriff"). With industrialization and urbanization during the eighteenth and nineteenth centuries, these approaches were viewed as ineffective, and the military was used to quell riots, often with a great deal of violence. Peel organized the first modern police department, therefore, to more effectively—and less violently—prevent crime and protect the public.

Initially, there were doubts and fears among the population that the police would be violent like the military. But Peel "was stubborn to the point of obsession that his 'New Police' should be seen to be free of all taint of militarism," which is why they were required to wear "a quiet" uniform consisting of "a blue shallow-tail coat with white buttons" rather than the British military's red coat."[44] Even then, at first, the New Police were called derogatory epithets such as "Blue Locusts," "Blue Drones," and "Blue Devils." To counter these concerns, Peel emphasized that the primary object of this first police department, as explicitly reflected in its General Instructions from 1829, was the *prevention* of crime, and emphasis was placed on the use of persuasion, with physical force as a last resort and using only the minimum necessary for preventing or stopping a breach of the law.[45] Most importantly, in Peel's approach, the police would be citizens working in partnership with their community. A considerable part of their patrol duties, involving publicly walking regular beats in neighborhoods, also included traffic control, the prevention of cruelty to children and animals,

42. Skolnick and Fyfe, *Above the Law*, xviii.

43. Kleinig, *Ethics of Policing*, 27–28.

44. Ascoli, *Queen's Peace*, 89–90.

45. Ascoli, *Queen's Peace*, 89–90.

finding missing persons, the care of the poor and destitute, extinguishing fires, the inspection of weights, bridges and buildings, and even waking people up for work. As such, the London Metropolitan Police "were *pro-active* rather than *reactive*."[46] Only within that overarching community peacekeeping framework were the New Police required occasionally to stop a crime in progress and to use force to apprehend criminals. Also, as Ascoli notes, when a riot broke out at Hyde Park Corner in 1830, the mob was "met by only passive police resistance, a tactic which seems to have bewildered the rioters who, bent on violence, were hoping for violence in return."[47] Because of their restraint in the use of force, the Metropolitan Police came to be accepted by the British public.

The social-peacekeeper approach advanced by Peel was also transplanted to the United States, beginning in New York in 1845, followed by Boston and Philadelphia—although in the South policing's roots were connected more with slave patrols. When police began to wear uniforms and badges in the 1850s, many citizens worried that the police would turn out to be essentially a standing army. Yet police departments did not recruit from the military at that time, and Americans "had a strong conviction that the police should have an essentially civilian orientation."[48] The ethos changed after the Civil War, when the surplus of firearms began to find its way into the hands of the police. Then, in the early twentieth century, during the 1920s, well-armed gangsters such as Al Capone motivated the police to begin to arm themselves even more. This era was the dawn of the crime-fighter or military approach to policing.

An Appeal for a (New) Peel

Kleinig's call for the social-peacekeeper model of policing, therefore, attempts to reclaim key elements and practices of policing that were emphasized in the genesis and much of the first century of modern policing. By situating policing within this social-peacekeeping context, Kleinig is confident that crime will be more effectively dealt with, and the use of force by police will be less likely and less excessive. Indeed, he argues that the social-peacekeeper approach "acknowledges the nonnegotiable force

---

46. Walker, *Popular Justice*, 60; emphasis in the original.

47. Ascoli, *Queen's Peace*, 98.

48. Fogelson, *Big-City Police*, 45.

at police disposal without transforming it into the police *raison d'être*."[49] In his view, the social-peacekeeper model of policing better encompasses most of the responsibilities and tasks of police in society, such as being first responders at traffic accidents or searching for a missing child, and in this model the fact that police are armed is merely "a contingent matter."[50] In this way, although there remains a place for the possibility of the use of force against an uncooperative or threatening suspect, "its instrumental or subservient character is emphasized."[51] Thus, the use of force by police is "a last (albeit sometimes necessary) resort rather than their dominant *modus operandi*."[52] Indeed, Kleinig suggests that had the Los Angeles police officers who participated in the beating of Rodney King (he was writing in the 1990s) understood themselves "primarily as social peacekeepers, for whom recourse to force constituted a last and regrettable option, events would almost certainly have turned out very differently."[53]

This social-peacekeeper model may be more familiar to us as *community policing*, and Kleinig occasionally notes their intersection. One of the chief characteristics of community policing is that it involves a partnership between the police and the community. Put simply, it seeks to foster a relationship of mutual trust, bonds of empathy, and a common purpose, rather than an adversarial "us versus them" mentality. Police and the citizens share a stake in the common good and welfare of their community. The police are part of the community, fellow citizens, and therefore work in cooperation with the community. As such, many community-policing programs establish decentralized substations throughout the community, while encouraging police to purchase homes and reside in these neighborhoods. They get police out of their cars, walking beats, riding bicycles, in order to get to know, listen to, and interact face-to-face with citizens. In addition, community-policing programs promote the hiring of recruits who reflect or possess an understanding of the diverse communities that they will serve.

At the same time, as part of this partnership, community residents also have a role to play in peacekeeping and crime prevention. Through neighborhood-watch programs, safe houses, and other community-service organizations, citizens share responsibility with police for the welfare and

49. Kleinig, *Ethics of Policing*, 27.
50. Kleinig, *Ethics of Policing*, 293.
51. Kleinig, *Ethics of Policing*, 29.
52. Kleinig, *Ethics of Policing*, 29.
53. Kleinig, *Ethics of Policing*, 96.

common good of their community. Police officers also are encouraged to become involved in such community activities as coaching sports teams or participating in town and neighborhood meetings. Together the police, citizens, and community groups can explore and possibly implement creative solutions to local problems that may give rise to crime. In these ways, community policing is more proactive than reactive, thereby involving a more preventive or problem-oriented approach to crime. That is, community policing seeks to identify, understand, and address the root causes of crime that may be found in the community. Community policing attends to the wider social framework or patterns of activities that play a role in leading to crime. Thus, citizens, civic groups, and the police strive together to help any community members who are at risk of resorting to criminal activity. Also, when someone commits a crime, he or she will be treated as a fellow community member rather than some external enemy. In this model, if force is necessary to apprehend the suspect, it should be in accordance with strict criteria governing use of force, for both when and how it is used.

In my view, the social-peacekeeper model of policing, also known as community policing, is more consonant with principles of Catholic social teaching, especially human dignity, solidarity, subsidiarity, and the common good. It also seems more consistent with recent Catholic emphasis on restorative justice[54] and on just peace and nonviolence.[55] As Rev. Krista Talve rightly put it in her interview with Francis: "If you're in a community, get to know your police officers and make sure they know your children and your neighbor's children. Get to know them. Make sure, if there are kids of color in your community, that there are programs that help them to know the police and the police to get to know them by name, so that nobody makes judgments that aren't true. . . ."[56] Pope Francis similarly understands the vocation of policing as about community service. Recently, he told Italian police officers, "A vocation of service can never simply be against criminals; it must be on behalf of communities" in order to maintain "the confidence and esteem that the people place in you."[57] This sounds a lot like the social-peacekeeper model of policing to me.

So, as religious educators, theologians, and clergy, let's initiate a conversation with our police departments and officers about how we can

54. Conway et al., *Redemption and Restoration*.

55. Dennis and McCarthy, "Jesus and 'Just War?'"

56. Gunning Francis, *Ferguson & Faith*, 146.

57. Winright, "A Vocation to Serve and Protect."

work together for a more just approach to policing in our communities and neighborhoods. Let's keep in mind that police, too, are members of our parishes. Let's educate our young people so that those who aspire to becoming police officers will do so for the right reasons. Let's promote a social-peacekeeper model of community policing.

Postscript

As I was preparing to go over the copyedits so that this manuscript could then be sent to the typesetter, additional killings of Black persons by police officers disrupted our "new normal" of being quarantined in our homes due to the global pandemic.[58] On May 25, 2020, George Floyd, a forty-six-year-old Black American man, was killed in Minneapolis, Minnesota, during an arrest for allegedly using a counterfeit $20 bill. Video footage of white police officer Derek Chauvin holding his knee on Floyd's neck for nearly nine minutes, as Floyd echoed Eric Garner's "I can't breathe," won't soon be forgotten. If there is such a thing as an anti-icon, something that is the opposite of a sacred icon, this image of Chauvin nonchalantly kneeling, with his hands in his pants pockets (something I was trained not to do, especially when in a potentially dangerous environment), certainly qualifies. As a Christian and a theologian, I believe both Chauvin and Floyd, like all human persons, are *imago Dei*—image of God. The image of Chauvin slowly pressing the breath and life from Floyd, however, is demonic. This is a word I rarely and reluctantly use, since I worry about its being elided into demonizing others. Nevertheless, what the writer of

58. In addition to the killing of George Floyd in Minneapolis, Minnesota, there was the fatal shooting of Breonna Taylor in Louisville, Kentucky, and the murder by a former police officer and his son of Ahmaud Arbery near Brunswick, Georgia. A few days after Floyd's death, the annual convention of the College Theology Society was held virtually, due to the pandemic, on May 28–30, 2020. The society's board of directors, on which I served as vice president, issued a statement on US racism: http://www.collegetheology. org/2020-Statement-on-US-Racism. Likewise, on December 8, 2014, following the police killings of Rekia Boyd, Eric Garner, Michael Brown, John Crawford, seven-year-old Aiyana Stanley-Jones, and twelve-year-old Tamir Rice, 456 Catholic theologians signed a Statement of Catholic Theologians on Racial Justice: https://catholicmoraltheology.com/ statement-of-catholic-theologians-on-racial-justice/.

Ephesians had to say seems apt: "For our struggle is not against enemies of blood and flesh, but against the rulers, against the authorities, against the cosmic powers of this present darkness, against the spiritual forces of evil in the heavenly places" (6:12, NRSV).

In his *An Ethic for Christians and Other Aliens in a Strange Land*, lawyer and lay Episcopal theologian William Stringfellow (1928–85) wrote about these "powers," viewing them as fallen though created by God. Rather than being promotive of life, their devotion is to death. Examples include governments, ideologies, economic systems, and corporations that dehumanize, deceive, and brutalize human beings—especially vulnerable and marginalized persons such as the poor and persons of color.[59] Ultimately, though, even these "powers," which were created by God, are to be recreated—that is, redeemed—by Christ. I know, this seems impossible, especially when we consider something such as the governmental institution of the police. Like the father of the convulsing boy said to Jesus, I confess, "Lord, I believe; help my unbelief!" (Mark 9:24, NKJV).

Not even a deadly pandemic could occlude the righteous pandemonium and protests, mostly led by Black people but with participants of other pigmentations, young and old, proclaiming "Black Lives Matter!" Unlike the earlier cases about which I wrote in the chapters selected for this volume, where attention was devoted to reforming the police and reorienting them as community police, the calls for "defunding" and "abolishing" the police resounded through the media, from newspapers and magazine articles to blog pieces and cable news shows. Not all demands for either defunding or abolishing the police concurred concerning what is meant or entailed by these words, though. For the sake of this brief postscript, I will refer only to one such appeal by a fellow Catholic theological ethicist, leaving for my next book a more thorough and thoughtful treatment of these specific questions about the future of policing.[60]

---

59. William Stringfellow, *An Ethic for Christians and Other Aliens in a Strange Land* (Eugene: Wipf & Stock, 2004; originally published in 1973), 75, 81, 112–13, 124, 150. When I was a doctoral student at the University of Notre Dame, I wrote a paper on Stringfellow for one of my courses. I think his work remains timely and relevant.

60. In addition to the article by Michael Jaycox that I address in what follows, a similar essay that I will engage in the future, especially because, unlike Jaycox's, it deals with just-war theory, is Nathaniel Grimes and Vincent Lloyd, "Challenging the Police: Abolition and Christian Ethics," *The Bias Magazine: The Voice of the Christian Left*, undated, https://christiansocialism.com/abolish-police-christian-ethics-just-war/.

In "A Catholic Case for Police Defunding and Abolition," Michael Jaycox, who teaches Christian ethics at Seattle University and who stayed at my house during the protests in Saint Louis several years ago to conduct interviews (as a participant-observer) of the protesters, argues actually more for the latter: "We must imagine a world without policing."[61] Jaycox holds that calls for reform are a cul-de-sac, that the abolition of policing "is more consistent with a commitment to the common good, and that Catholic ethicists can appreciate the rationale for this position by listening to Black women who have been in the forefront of the abolitionist cause." Among the Black women Jaycox cites are Angela Y. Davis and Ruth Wilson Gilmore, both of whom claim that the history of policing is inextricably intertwined with anti-Black racism, white supremacy, and the mass-carceral state.[62] For them and others Jaycox mentions, attempts to reform the police are not only insufficient but completely misguided. They simply perpetuate and exacerbate rather than address and redress the root causes of the social problems that have been mistakenly and maliciously delegated to the police. Therefore, abolition is the aim, and even defunding the police is but a step in that direction. To be sure, not all pleas for defunding have abolition in mind; many instead seek reallocation of funds to other persons, such as social workers and youth workers, and to other programs, such as community centers and social services.[63]

On abolitionism, although I agree that much, perhaps even most, of the history of policing in the United States has been tethered to anti-Black racism, white supremacy, and hegemony of the wealthy, I am not yet convinced that this is entirely accurate historically. Moreover, many abolitionists urge moving toward a "world without policing," even though such calls tend to focus on the United States, but I suspect that a comparative analysis of the police in other nations would reveal that this institution and its practices are neither as univocal nor as universal as abolitionists may assume.[64] On

---

61. Jaycox, "Catholic Case for Police Defunding and Abolition," para. 1. The fruit of his research in Saint Louis may be found in Jaycox, "Black Lives Matter and Catholic Whiteness: A Tale of Two Performances."

62. See, e.g., Davis, "From Michael Brown to Assata Shakur, the Racist State of America Persists"; Goodman, "Angela Davis on Abolition, Calls to Defund Police, Toppled Racist Statues & Voting in 2020 Election"; Kumanyika, "Ruth Wilson Gilmore Makes the Case for Abolition"; and Kushner, "Is Prison Necessary? Ruth Wilson Gilmore Might Change Your Mind."

63. See, e.g., Ray, "What Does 'Defund the Police' Mean and Does It Have Merit?"

64. See, e.g., the website of the organization For a World Without Police, https://

defunding—and here, I am in agreement with the words "reallocation" and "redistribution"—I am more supportive. However, I worry that reducing and minimizing the police's role and responsibilities only to the use of force might instead reinforce the popular view of both the police and the public, at least in the United States, that this is their *raison d'etre*. In other words, I remain convinced by John Kleinig's social-peacekeeper model of the police in which other more positive responsibilities of officers contextualize, moderate, and restrain their use of force. According to Kleinig, "So understood, the peacekeeper model is broad enough to encompass most of the work that police do, whether it is crimefighting, crime control, or interventions in crisis situations. But what is more important is the irenic cast that it gives to police work."[65] So, to delegate more responsibilities to mental health care professionals, for example, is a good thing. Police do not possess the education and training of such a professional, although they should have at least a baseline or rudimentary (and regular) training in this area. Also, the police and other professionals should work more closely together, both on and off the streets. Nevertheless, there may be instances when there simply is no time to call for a "time out" and to defuse a situation, such as when there is an active shooter. On August 4, 2019, when Connor Stephen Betts fatally shot nine people and wounded seventeen others in the popular Oregon District of Dayton, Ohio, the police responded within thirty-two seconds of his first shot, fatally shooting him and, I believe, saving the lives of others.[66] Hopefully, such an example will become extremely rare, especially if police are formed and shaped by the more irenic social-peacekeeper approach, but both abolitionists and those who call for defunding the police must account for this possible scenario (I say *possible*, yet with the prevalence of guns and the gun culture in the United States at present, it is unfortunately *probable*, but this is another, though related, project to be tackled).

From a Catholic theological and ethical perspective, the social principle known as the common good is relevant. According to the Second Vatican Council's document *Gaudium et Spes*, the common good is "the sum of those conditions of social life which allow social groups and their individual members relatively thorough and ready access to their own fulfillment . . .

---

aworldwithoutpolice.org/. For a helpful comparative analysis of the police around the world, see Haberfeld and Cerrah, *Comparative Policing*. The history and practices of the police in twelve countries are examined in this volume. See also Ralph, "To Protect and Serve: Global Lessons in Police Reform."

65. Kleinig, *Ethics of Policing*, 28–29.

66. Ansari, "Dayton Police Provide Minute-by-Minute Timeline of Shooting."

[entailing that every] social group must take account of the needs and legitimate aspirations of other groups, and even of the general welfare of the entire human family."[67] Indeed, Jaycox extends this definition to mean that "a credible Catholic commitment to pursuing the common good would have to include, at minimum, ensuring whatever social conditions are necessary for Black freedom from white violence." Given their history and experience, the police, in Jaycox's view, "cannot be part of how we ensure these social conditions.[68]" He rightly notes that Catholic social teaching regards the state as being responsible for protecting the common good, but Jaycox interprets this as not necessarily entailing "the police system." While I support Jaycox's turn to the common good, I hesitate to exclude the police. And even were we able to do so, there would remain the need not only for "resolving conflict" but, on hopefully rare occasions, for stopping it. That is, regardless of what we name them—police officers, peace officers (my preference), law-enforcement officers, social peacekeepers (I also prefer), etc.—this function of being able to intervene, possibly with the use of force (though hopefully less lethally, as do the police in, for example, Scotland[69]), remains necessary on this side of the final eschaton.

Part of the problem are the police unions, and Jaycox correctly calls for disbanding them even though Catholic social teaching supports the right of people to organize through unions against economic exploitation. With Jaycox, I do not see how police unions today have anything to do with helping working class people to oppose social injustices. Instead they serve and protect the power and interests of the police status quo.[70]

Before concluding his essay, Jaycox devotes attention to two possible objections to his argument: first, one might argue that "police reform is more realistic than police defunding and abolition"; and second, one might argue that "policing should not be defunded or abolished because there would no longer be a deterrent to crime."[71] While Jaycox appreciatively highlights my work as an advocate for police reform, nowhere do I argue that what I am calling for is "more realistic" or that there is a need for policing as a "deterrent" to crime. On realism, I have been called an

67. Paul VI, "Gaudium et Spes," §26.

68. Jaycox, "Catholic Case for Police Defunding and Abolition," para. 6.

69. Baker, "U.S. Police Leaders, Visiting Scotland, Get Lessons on Avoiding Deadly Force."

70. Michaels, "Infuriating History of Why Police Unions Have So Much Power."

71. Jaycox, "Catholic Case for Police Defunding and Abolition," para. 9.

"idealist" (and worse) by some police simply for the reforms I am advocating. Jaycox claims that reformers' "models" of policing are not "ideals," that these are "surface-level remedies," and that these are incapable of "counteracting a systemic, deeply-ingrained culture of anti-blackness in police departments." These are serious challenges, indeed. For now, I am less inclined to see the problem and its solution in such an either/or binary. In my next project, I hope to provide a deeper and more thorough analysis of the *culture*—including the recruiting and training—of the police, along with a constructive proposal for cultivating a social peacekeeping culture.[72] On Jaycox's criticism of those who are concerned that the abolition of the police would remove a deterrent to rampant crime, again, I simply have not made such an argument even if others have done so. Indeed, the social-peacekeeper model, or community-policing approach, would work together with community members, organizations, and other intermediary associations to address the root causes of crime, including those crimes that Jaycox rightly notes tend not to be policed, which "benefit the racially and economically dominant classes."

As I press the keys to conclude this postscript, I am in a tap house and wine bar adjacent to my apartment building in downtown Saint Louis. Directly across the street I see a painting of George Floyd on boards that were placed over a window of a bicycle shop during protests here earlier this summer. The words "One man can change the world" are also painted with it. Unfortunately, more than one man—and one woman, as well as minors—have died due to unjustified and unjust use of force by police. I pray that Floyd's and their unjust deaths do, indeed, change at least how policing is viewed, institutionalized, and practiced in the United States and elsewhere where such reform is needed in the world.

---

72. For a similar effort, see Rosa Brooks, "Stop Training the Police Like They're Joining the Military," *The Atlantic* (June 10, 2020), https://www.theatlantic.com/ideas/archive/2020/06/police-academies-paramilitary/612859/?utm_source=facebook&utm_medium=social&utm_campaign=share&fbclid=IwAR02KvsVWxDxLe5x—BOS3MsAw-wfoNnuJiPQKUy2xyd17dTJUq54OCLwPg.

Bibliography

Addison, James Thayer. *War, Peace, and the Christian Mind: A Review of Recent Thought.* Greenwich: Seabury, 1953.

Alexis-Baker, Andy. "Community, Policing, and Violence." *Conrad Grebel Review* 26.2 (2008) 102–16.

———. "The Gospel or a Glock? Mennonites and the Police." *Conrad Grebel Review* 25.2 (2007) 23–49.

Allman, Mark, and Tobias Winright. *After the Smoke Clears: The Just War Tradition and Post-War Justice.* Maryknoll: Orbis, 2010.

Anonymous. "In This World: By a Policeman." *Student World* 56.3 (1963) 247–53.

Ansari, Talal. "Dayton Police Provide Minute-by-Minute Timeline of Shooting." *The Wall Street Journal,* August 13, 2019. https://www.wsj.com/articles/dayton-police-provide-minute-by-minute-timeline-of-shooting-11565731906.

Ascoli, David. *The Queen's Peace: The Origins and Development of the Metropolitan Police 1829–1979.* London: Hamish Hamilton, 1979.

Asfaw, Semegnish, et al., eds. *The Responsibility to Protect: Ethical and Theological Reflections.* Geneva: World Council of Churches, 2005.

Atack, Iain. *The Ethics of Peace and War: From State Security to World Community.* New York: Palgrave Macmillan, 2005.

Augustine. *Augustine: Political Writings.* Edited by E. M. Atkins and R. J. Dodaro. New York: Cambridge University Press, 2001.

———. "Reply to Faustus the Manichean." In *War and Christian Ethics: Classic Readings on the Morality of War,* edited by Arthur F. Holmes, 63–68. Grand Rapids: Baker Academic, 2005.

Baer, H. David. *Recovering Christian Realism: Just War Theory as a Political Ethic.* Lanham: Lexington, 2015.

Bainton, Roland H. *Christian Attitudes Toward War and Peace: A Historical Survey and Critical Re-evaluation.* New York: Abingdon, 1960.

———. "War and the Christian Ethic." In *The Church and Social Responsibility,* edited by J. Richard Spann, 201–19. Nashville: Abingdon-Cokesbury, 1953.

Baker, Al. "U.S. Police Leaders, Visiting Scotland, Get Lessons on Avoiding Deadly Force." *The New York Times,* December 11, 2015. https://www.nytimes.com/2015/12/12/nyregion/us-police-leaders-visiting-scotland-get-lessons-on-avoiding-deadly-force.html.

Balko, Radley. *Rise of the Warrior Cop: The Militarization of America's Police Forces*. New York: PublicAffairs, 2013.

Barbash, Fred, and Abby Phillip. "Fatal Shooting of 18-year-old by Off-Duty Police Officer Ignites Protests in St. Louis." *Washington Post*, October 9, 2014. https://www.washingtonpost.com/news/morning-mix/wp/2014/10/09/crowds-in-streets-of-st-louis-after-fatal-shooting-by-off-duty-police-officer/?utm_term=.525fe7c20838.

Barclay, Oliver R., ed. *Pacifism and War: When Christians Disagree*. Leicester: Inter-Varsity, 1984.

Barker, Tom, and David Carter. eds. *Police Deviance*. Cincinnati: Anderson, 1986.

Bayley, David H. "Police Brutality Abroad." In *Police Violence: Understanding and Controlling Police Abuse of Force*, edited by William A. Geller and Hans Toch, 273–91. New Haven: Yale University Press, 1996.

Bayley, David H., and Robert M. Perito. *The Police in War: Fighting Insurgency, Terrorism, and Violent Crime*. Boulder: Rienner, 2010.

Bell, Daniel M., Jr. *Just War as Christian Discipleship: Recentering the Tradition in the Church Rather than the State*. Grand Rapids: Brazos, 2009.

Bellamy, Alex J. "The Responsibility to Protect—Five Years On." *Ethics and International Affairs* 24.2 (2010) 143–69.

Benedict XVI, Pope. "Address of His Holiness Benedict XVI: Meeting with the Members of the General Assembly of the United Nations Organization." http://www.vatican.va/content/benedict-xvi/en/speeches/2008/april/documents/hf_ben-xvi_spe_20080418_un-visit.html.

———. *Caritas in Veritate*. Vatican City: Libreria Editrice Vaticana, 2009.

Benne, Robert. "The Paradoxical Vision: A Lutheran Nudge for Public Theology." *Pro Ecclesia: A Journal of Catholic and Evangelical Theology* 4.2 (1995) 212–23.

Berkley, George E. *The Democratic Policeman*. Boston: Beacon, 1969.

———. *Policing Liberal Society*. New York: Oxford University Press, 1988.

Betz, Joseph. "Police Violence." In *Moral Issues in Police Work*, edited by Frederick A. Elliston and Michael Feldberg, 177–96. Totowa: Rowman & Allanheld, 1985.

Bittner, Egon. *The Functions of the Police in Modern Society*. Cambridge: Oelgeschlager, Gunn & Hain, 1980.

Bluffon, Deborah, ed. *Religion, War and Peace: Proceedings of the Conference at Ripon College*. Stevens Point: The Wisconsin Institute for Peace and Conflict Studies, 1996.

Boatwright, H. Lee. "Legalized Murder of a Fleeing Felon." *Virginia Law Review* 15, no. 6 (1929) 582–86.

Brady, James B. "The Justifiability of Hollow-Point Bullets." *Criminal Justice Ethics* 2.2 (1983) 9–19.

Burke, Francis V., Jr. "Lying During Crisis Negotiations: A Costly Means to Expedient Resolution." *Criminal Justice Ethics* 14.1 (1995) 49–62.

Cadoux, Cecil John. *Christian Pacifism Re-examined*. Oxford: Basil Blackwell, 1940.

Cady, Duane L. *From Warism to Pacifism: A Moral Continuum*. Philadelphia: Temple University Press, 1992.

Cahill, Lisa Sowle. "Abortion and Argument by Analogy." *Horizons* 9.2 (1982) 271–87.

———. *Love Your Enemies: Discipleship, Pacifism, and Just War Thinking*. Minneapolis: Fortress, 1994.

———. "Theological Contexts of Just War Theory and Pacifism: A Response to J. Bryan Hehir." *Journal of Religious Ethics* 20.2 (1992) 259–65.

Cahill, Lisa Sowle, and Michael Baxter. "Is This Just War?" In *Moral Issues and Christian Responses*, edited by Patricia Beattie Jung and Shannon Jung, 355–61. 7th ed. Belmont: Wadsworth, 2003.

Calhoun, Robert Lowry. *God and the Common Life*. New York: Scribner's, 1954.

Callahan, Sidney Cornelia. "Killing Kills the Spirit: The Need for Nonviolent Discipline." *Commonweal* 121.14 (1994) 7–8.

Capizzi, Joseph. "Against: The Problems Associated with the Complementarity Thesis." In *Religion, War and Peace: Proceedings of the Conference at Ripon College*, edited by Deborah Bluffon, 221–26. Stevens Point, WI: The Wisconsin Institute for Peace and Conflict Studies, 1996.

———. "War Remains Church Dividing." In *Just Policing: Mennonite-Catholic Theological Colloquium, 2002*, edited by Ivan J. Kauffman, 76–88. Kitchener, Ontario: Pandora, 2004.

Casey, Shaun. "Face to Face: Just War and Iraq? Ethical Theory Says No." *Word & World* 23.1 (2003) 94.

Central Committee of the World Council of Churches. "The Protection of Endangered Populations in Situations of Armed Violence: Toward an Ecumenical Ethical Approach." Presented at the World Council of Churches Central Committee, Potsdam, Germany, February 6, 2001.

Charles, J. Daryl. *Between Pacifism and Jihad: Just War and Christian Tradition*. Downers Grove: InterVarsity, 2005.

Chevigny, Paul. *Edge of the Knife: Police Violence in the Americas*. New York: New Press, 1995.

Child, James W., and Donald Scherer. *Two Paths Toward Peace*. Philadelphia: Temple University Press, 1992.

Childress, James F. "'Answering that of God in Every Man': An Interpretation of George Fox's Ethics." *Quaker Religious Thought* 15.3 (1974) 2–41.

———. "Just-War Theories: The Bases, Interrelations, Priorities, and Functions of Their Criteria." *Theological Studies* 39.3 (1978) 427–45.

———. "The Just-War Tradition and the Invasion of Iraq." Conference on Ethical Issues Raised by Pre-Emptive War, Churches' Center for Theology and Public Policy, Wesley Theological Seminary, Washington, DC, May 1, 2003.

———. "Moral Discourse about War." In *Peace, Politics, and the People of God*, edited by Paul Peachey, 117–34. Philadelphia: Fortress, 1986.

———. "Moral Discourse about War in the Early Church." *Journal of Religious Ethics* 12.1 (1984) 1–18.

———. "Nonviolent Resistance: Trust and Risk-Taking Twenty-Five Years Later." *Journal of Religious Ethics* 25.2 (1997) 213–20.

———. *Practical Reasoning in Bioethics*. Bloomington: Indiana University Press, 1997.

Christiansen, Drew. "Whither the 'Just War'?" *America* 188.10 (2003) 7–11.

Clark, Robert. "Case for All-Out Pacifism." In *Pacifism and War: When Christians Disagree*, edited by Oliver R. Barclay, 85–113. Leicester: Inter-Varsity, 1984.

Close, Daryl, and Nicholas Meier, eds. *Morality in Criminal Justice: An Introduction to Ethics*. Belmont: Wadsworth, 1995.

Colwell, Jack. "Ex-POW Kernan Backs Objector." *South Bend Tribune*, December 2, 1996.

Conway, Trudy D., et al., eds. *Redemption and Restoration: A Catholic Perspective on Restorative Justice*. Collegeville: Liturgical, 2017.

Curran, Charles E. *Critical Concerns in Moral Theology*. Notre Dame: University of Notre Dame Press, 1984.

Curran, Charles E., ed. *Moral Theology Challenges for the Future*. New York: Paulist, 1990.

Daskalos, Christopher. "Current Issues in Policing." In *The Past, Present, and Future of Criminal Justice*, Maguire and Radosh, 57–76. New York: General Hall, 1996.

Davis, Angela Y. "From Michael Brown to Assata Shakur, the Racist State of America Persists." *The Guardian*, November 1, 2014. https://www.theguardian.com/commentisfree/2014/nov/01/michael-brown-assata-shakur-racist-state-of-america.

Davis, Michael. "Do Cops Really Need a Code of Ethics?" *Criminal Justice Ethics* 2.10 (1991) 14–28.

Delattre, Edwin J. *Character and Cops: Ethics in Policing*. Washington, DC: American Enterprise Institute for Public Policy Research, 1989.

Dennis, Marie, and Eli McCarthy. "Jesus and 'Just War?' Time to Focus on Just Peace and Gospel Nonviolence." *Huffington Post*, October 1, 2016. https://www.huffingtonpost.com/entry/jesus-and-just-war-time-to-focus-on-just-peace-and_us_57ec6282e4b0972364deab50.

de Waal, Alex, ed. *War in Darfur and the Search for Peace*. Studies in Global Equity. London: Global Equity Initiative, 2007.

Dombrowski, Daniel A. *Christian Pacifism*. Philadelphia: Temple University Press, 1991.

Dougherty, James E. *The Bishops and Nuclear Weapons: The Catholic Pastoral Letter on War and Peace*. Hamden: Archon/Institute for Foreign Policy Analysis, 1984.

Edmonds, Martin. *Armed Services and Society*. Boulder: Westview, 1990.

Elias, Robert. "A Peace Movement against Crime." *Peace Review* 2.6 (1994) 209–20.

———. "Taking Crime Seriously." *Peace Review* 2.6 (1994) 131–38.

Elliston, Frederick, and Norman Bowie, eds. *Ethics, Public Policy, and Criminal Justice*. Cambridge: Oelgeschlager, Gunn & Hain, 1982.

Elliston, Frederick A., and Michael Feldberg, eds. *Moral Issues in Police Work*. Totowa: Rowman & Allanheld, 1985.

Erdahl, Lowell. *Pro-Life/Pro-Choice: Life-Affirming Alternatives to Abortion, War, Mercy Killing, and the Death Penalty*. Minneapolis: Augsburg, 1986.

Evans, Gareth. "Responsibility to Protect." In *The Responsibility to Protect: Ethical and Theological Reflections*, edited by Semegnish Asfaw et al., 3–9. Geneva: World Council of Churches, 2005.

Fahey, Joseph J. *War and the Christian Conscience: Where Do You Stand?* Maryknoll: Orbis, 2005.

"Fatal Force." *The Washington Post*. https://www.washingtonpost.com/graphics/2019/national/police-shootings-2019/.

Fehr, James Jakob. "The Responsibility to Confront Evil: A Pacifist Critique of R2P from the Historic Peace Churches." Unpublished manuscript.

Fiala, Andrew G. "Citizenship, Epistemology, and the Just War Theory." *Logos* 7.2 (2004) 100–117.

Fogelson, Robert. *Big-City Police*. Cambridge: Harvard University Press, 1977.

Forster, Greg. *"To Live Good": The Police and the Community*. Bramcote: Grove, 1982.

Fosdick, Raymond B. *American Police Systems*. New York: The Century Company, 1920.

Foster, Gregory D. "Just-War Doctrine: Lessons from Iraq." *Commonweal* 130.14 (2003) 11–12.

Francis, Leah Gunning. *Ferguson & Faith: Sparking Leadership & Awakening Community*. St. Louis: Chalice, 2015.

Francis, Pope. "*Misericordiae Vultus*: Bull of Indiction of the Extraordinary Jubilee of Mercy." http://www.iubilaeummisericordiae.va/content/gdm/en/giubileo/bolla.html.

Friedmann, Robert R. *Community Policing: Comparative Perspectives and Prospects*. New York: St. Martin's, 1992.

Friedrichs, David O. "Crime Wars and Peacemaking Criminology." *Peace Review* 2.6 (1994) 159–64.

Fyfe, James J. "Training to Reduce Police-civilian Violence." In *Police Violence: Understanding and Controlling Police Abuse of Force*, edited by W. A. Geller and H. Toch, 65–179. New Haven: Yale University Press, 1996.

Geller, William A. "Officer Restraint in the Use of Deadly Force: The Next Frontier in Police Shooting Research." *Journal of Police Science* 13 (1985) 153–71.

———. "Police and Deadly Force." In *Moral Issues in Police Work*, edited by Frederick A. Elliston and Michael Feldberg, 197–235. Totowa: Rowman & Allanheld, 1985.

Geller, William A., and Hans Toch. "Understanding and Controlling Police Abuse of Force." In *Moral Issues in Police Work*, edited by Frederick A. Elliston and Michael Feldberg, 292–328. Totowa: Rowman & Allanheld, 1985.

Geller, William A., and Hans Toch, eds. *Police Violence: Understanding and Controlling Police Abuse of Force*. New Haven: Yale University Press, 1996.

Global Centre for the Responsibility to Protect. "Resolution 63/308 (The Responsibility to Protect) A/RES/63/308." https://www.globalr2p.org/resources/resolution-63-308-the-responsibility-to-protect-a-res-63-308/.

Goodman, Amy. "Angela Davis on Abolition, Calls to Defund Police, Toppled Racist Statues & Voting in 2020 Election." *Democracy Now!* June 12, 2020, https://www.democracynow.org/2020/6/12/angela_davis_on_abolition_calls_to?fbclid=IwAR3HrnkByfYv_Rh78yXrmYSgczX9ZG5P6joGNIJx1iOppv3baYWA-sR5jig.

Graham v. Connor, 490 U.S. 396, 109 S. Ct. 1865, 104 L. Ed. 2d 443 (1989).

Guyot, Dorothy. *Policing as though People Matter*. Philadelphia: Temple University, 1991.

Haberfeld, M. R., and Ibrahim Cerrah, eds. *Comparative Policing: The Struggle for Democratization*. Los Angeles: Sage, 2008.

Hall, John C. "Deadly Force, the Common Law and the Constitution." *FBI Law Enforcement Bulletin* 53.4 (1984) 26–31.

Hamann, Eduarda P., and Robert Muggah. "Implementing the Responsibility to Protect: New Directions for International Peace and Security?" https://igarape.org.br/pdf/r2p.pdf.

Hansen, David A. *Police Ethics*. Springfield: Thomas, 1973.

Hanson, William L. "Police Power for Peace." *Friends Journal* (August 2004) 6–7.

Hauerwas, Stanley. *Dispatches from the Front: Theological Engagements with the Secular*. Durham: Duke University Press, 1994.

———. *The Peaceable Kingdom: A Primer in Christian Ethics*. Notre Dame: University of Notre Dame Press, 1983.

———. "Reflections on the 'Appeal to Abolish War.'" In *Between Poetry and Politics: Essays in Honour of Enda McDonagh*, edited by Linda Hogan and Barbara FitzGerald, 135–47. Dublin: Columba, 2003.

———. "Who Is 'We'?" *Sojourners* 22 (1993) 15.

Hauerwas, Stanley, and Enda McDonagh. "Abolishing War? An Appeal to Christian Leaders and Theologians." *Quaker Theology* 7 (2002). http://quakertheology.org/issue7-1-hauerwas.htm.

Hauerwas, Stanley, et al. "The Case for Abolition of War in the Twenty-First Century." *Journal of the Society of Christian Ethics* 25.2 (2005) 17–35.

Hauerwas, Stanley, et al., eds. *Theology Without Foundations*. Nashville: Abingdon, 1994.

Hauerwas, Stanley, et al., eds. *The Wisdom of the Cross: Essays in Honor of John Howard Yoder*. Grand Rapids: Eerdmans, 1999.

Hedges, Chris. *War Is a Force That Gives Us Meaning*. New York: Anchor, 2002.

Hehir, J. Bryan. *Catholic Teaching on War and Peace the Decade 1979-1989*. Mahwah: Paulist, 1990.

———. "Just War Theory in a Post-Cold War World." *Journal of Religious Ethics* 20.2 (1992) 237–57.

———. "What Can Be Done? What Should Be Done?" *America* 185.10 (2001) 9–12.

Hershberger, Guy Franklin. *War, Peace, and Nonresistance*. Scottdale: Herald, 1946.

———. *The Way of the Cross in Human Relations*. Scottdale: Herald, 1958.

Himes, Kenneth R. "Catholic Social Thought and Humanitarian Intervention." In *Peacemaking: Moral and Policy Challenges for a New World*, edited by Gerard F. Powers et al., 215–28. Washington, DC: US Catholic Conference, 1994.

———. "Intervention, Just War, and US National Security." *Theological Studies* 65.1 (2004) 141–57.

Hoekema, David A. "Punishment, the Criminal Law, and Christian Social Ethics." *Criminal Justice Ethics* 2.5 (1986) 31–54.

Hogan, Linda, and Barbara Fitzgerald, eds. *Between Poetry and Politics: Essays in Honor of Enda McDonagh*. Dublin: Columba, 2003.

Holdaway, Simon. "Policing and Consent." *Modern Churchman* 25.3 (1983) 30–39.

Holleman, Joe, and Lisa Brown. "St. Louis Police Fatally Shoot Man Who Brandished Knife." *St. Louis Post-Dispatch*, August 20, 2014. https://www.stltoday.com/news/local/crime-and-courts/st-louis-police-fatally-shoot-man-who-brandished-knife/article_85d27316-a17a-5e0a-b1d6-8a6753e2fcb2.html.

Hollenbach, David. "Humanitarian Intervention: Why, When and How." *Commonweal* 137.19 (2010) 9–11.

———. *Nuclear Ethics: A Christian Moral Argument*. New York: Paulist, 1983.

———. "War and Peace in American Catholic Thought: A Heritage Abandoned?" *Theological Studies* 48.4 (1987) 722–23.

Holmes, Arthur F., ed. *War and Christian Ethics: Classic Readings on the Morality of War*. Grand Rapids: Baker Academic, 2005.

Hoover, Dennis R. "Pacifism on the Record." *Religion in the News* 4.3 (2001) 9–11.

Hunter, David. "The Christian Church and the Roman Army in the First Three Centuries." In *The Church's Peace Witness*, edited by Marlin E. Miller and Barbara Nelson Gingerich, 161–81. Grand Rapids: Eerdmans, 1994.

International Commission on Intervention and State Sovereignty. "The Responsibility to Protect." http://responsibilitytoprotect.org/ICISS%20Report.pdf.

Jackson, Dave. *Dial 911: Peaceful Christians and Urban Violence*. Scottdale: Herald, 1981.

Jaycox, Michael. "Black Lives Matter and Catholic Whiteness: A Tale of Two Performances." *Horizons* 44.2 (December 2017) 306–41.

———. "A Catholic Case for Police Defunding and Abolition." https://catholicethics.com/forum/police-abolition/.

John Paul II, Pope. *Evangelium Vitae*. Vatican City: Libreria Editrice Vaticana, 1995.

Johnson, James Turner. "The Broken Tradition." *The National Interest* 45 (1996) 27–36.

———. *Ideology, Reason, and the Limitation of War*. Princeton: Princeton University Press, 1975.

———. *The Just War Idea and the Ethics of Intervention*. The Joseph A. Reich, Sr., Distinguished Lecture on War, Morality and the Military Profession, no. 6. Colorado: US Air Force Academy, 1993.

———. "Just War Tradition and the American Military." In *Just War and the Gulf War*, edited by James Turner Johnson and George Weigel, 3–42. Washington, DC: Ethics and Public Policy Center, 1991.

———. *Just War Tradition and the Restraint of War: A Moral and Historical Inquiry*. Princeton: Princeton University Press, 1981.

———. Review of *Love Your Enemies*, by Lisa Sowle Cahill. *Horizons* 22 (1995) 284.

Johnson, James Turner, and George Weigel, eds. *Just War and the Gulf War*. Washington, DC: Ethics and Public Policy Center, 1991.

Jung, Patricia Beattie, and Shannon Jung, eds. *Moral Issues and Christian Responses*. 7th ed. Belmont: Wadsworth, 2003.

Juvenal, Decio Junio. *Sixteen Satires*. Translated by Steven Robinson. Manchester: Carcanet New Press, 1983.

Kappeler, Victor, et al. *The Mythology of Crime and Criminal Justice*. Prospect Heights: Waveland, 1993.

Kaufman, Gordon. *The Context of Decision*. New York: Abingdon, 1961.

Kauffman, Ivan J., ed. *Just Policing: Mennonite-Catholic Theological Colloquium, 2002*. Kitchener: Pandora, 2004.

Kelling, George L., and James Q. Wilson. "Broken Windows: The Police and Neighborhood Safety." *The Atlantic*, March 1982. https://www.theatlantic.com/magazine/archive/1982/03/broken-windows/304465/.

Kerber, Guillermo. "Responsibility to Protect." In *The Responsibility to Protect: Ethical and Theological Reflections*, edited by Semegnish Asfaw et al., 114–20. Geneva: World Council of Churches, 2005.

Kleinig, John. *The Ethics of Policing*. New York: Cambridge University Press, 1996.

Kleinig, John, and Yurong Zhang, ed. *Professional Law Enforcement: A Documentary Collection*. Westport: Greenwood, 1993.

Klimas, Jacqueline. "Sen. Claire McCaskill: Police are the Problem, not the Solution, in Ferguson, Missouri." *The Washington Times*, August 14, 2014. https://www.washingtontimes.com/news/2014/aug/14/sen-claire-mccaskill-police-are-problem-not-soluti/.

Kowalski, Judith A., and Dean J. Collins, eds. *To Serve and Protect: Law Enforcement Officers Reflect on Their Faith and Work*. Minneapolis: Augsburg, 1992.

Kumanyika, Chenjerai. "Ruth Wilson Gilmore Makes the Case for Abolition." *The Intercept*, June 10, 2020. https://theintercept.com/2020/06/10/ruth-wilson-gilmore-makes-the-case-for-abolition.

Kushner, Rachel. "Is Prison Necessary? Ruth Wilson Gilmore Might Change Your Mind." *The New York Times Magazine*, April 17, 2019. https://www.nytimes.com/2019/04/17/magazine/prison-abolition-ruth-wilson-gilmore.html.

Lane, Roger. *Policing the City: Boston 1822–1885*. Cambridge: Harvard University Press, 1967.

Langan, John. "Should We Attack Iraq?" *America* 187.6 (2002) 7–8, 10–11.

Lango, John W. "Preventive Wars, Just War Principles, and the United Nations." *Journal of Ethics* 9.2 (2005) 247–68.

Loftus, Irene Prior, et al. "The 'Reasonable' Approach to Excessive Force Cases Under Section 1983." *Notre Dame Law Review* 64 (1989) 136–56.

Long, Edward LeRoy, Jr. *Academic Bonding and Social Concern: The Society of Christian Ethics 1959–1983.* Notre Dame: Religious Ethics Incorporated, 1985.

———. *Facing Terrorism: Responding as Christians.* Louisville: Westminster John Knox, 2004.

Long, Michael G., ed. *Christian Peace and Nonviolence: A Documentary History.* Maryknoll: Orbis, 2011.

Mackey, Virginia. "Mixed Motives, Mixed Messages." *Peace Review* 2.6 (1994) 183–85.

Maguire, Brendan, and Polly Radosh, eds. *The Past, Present, and Future of Criminal Justice.* New York: General Hall, 1996.

Malloy, Edward A. *The Ethics of Law Enforcement and Criminal Punishment.* Washington, DC: University Press of America, 1982.

Mann, Jeffrey K. *May I Kill? Just War, Non-Violence, and Civilian Self-Defense.* Eugene, OR: Wipf & Stock, 2018.

Marrin, Albert, ed. *War and the Christian Conscience: From Augustine to Martin Luther King Jr.* Chicago: Regnery, 1971.

Martineau, James. "Rights of War." In *War and the Christian Conscience: From Augustine to Martin Luther King Jr,* edited by Albert Marrin, 212–15. Chicago: Regnery, 1971.

McCormick, Richard A. "Theology and Bioethics." *Hastings Center Report* 2.9 (1989) 5–10.

McCormick, Richard A., and Paul Ramsey, eds. *Doing Evil to Achieve Good: Moral Choice in Conflict Situations.* Chicago: Loyola University Press, 1978.

McDonagh, Enda. *Church and Politics: From Theology to a Case History of Zimbabwe.* Notre Dame: University of Notre Dame Press, 1980.

McElwee, Timothy A. "Instead of War: The Urgency and Promise of a Global Peace System." *Cross Currents* 53.2 (2003) 148–70.

McLaughlin, Vance. *Police and the Use of Force: The Savannah Study.* Westport: Praeger, 1992.

Michaels, Samantha. "The Infuriating History of Why Police Unions Have So Much Power." *Mother Jones,* September/October 2020. https://www.motherjones.com/crime-justice/2020/08/police-unions-minneapolis.

Miller, Marlin E., and Barbara Nelson Gingerich, eds. *The Church's Peace Witness.* Grand Rapids: Eerdmans, 1994.

Miller, Richard B. "Casuistry, Pacifism, and the Just-War Tradition." In *Peacemaking: Moral and Policy Challenges for a New World,* edited by Gerard F. Powers et al., 199–213. Washington, DC: US Catholic Conference, 1994.

———. *Interpretations of Conflict: Ethics, Pacifism, and the Just War Tradition.* Chicago: University of Chicago, 1991.

———. "Pacifism and Just War Tenets: How Do They Diverge?" *Theological Studies* 47.3 (1986) 448–72.

Miller, William R. *Nonviolence: A Christian Interpretation.* New York: Association Press, 1964.

Murnion, Philip J., ed. *Catholics and Nuclear War: A Commentary on the Challenge of Peace, The US Catholic Bishops' Pastoral Letter on War and Peace.* New York: Crossroad, 1983.

Nagourney, Adam. "Police Armored Vehicle Is Unwelcome in California College Town." *New York Times,* September 13, 2014. https://www.nytimes.com/2014/09/14/us/police-armored-vehicle-is-unwelcome-in-california-college-town.html.

Nation, Mark Thiessen. *John Howard Yoder: Mennonite Patience, Evangelical Witness, Catholic Convictions.* Grand Rapids: Eerdmans, 2006.

National Conference of Catholic Bishops. *The Challenge of Peace: God's Promise, Our Response.* Washington, DC: United States Catholic Conference, 1983.

Nelson-Pallmeyer, Jack. "Wise as Serpents, Gentle as Doves?" *Sojourners* 22 (April 22, 1993) 10–13.

Neufeldt-Fast, Arnold. "Christianity and War." In *The Responsibility to Protect: Ethical and Theological Reflections,* edited by Semegnish Asfaw et al., 114–20. Geneva: World Council of Churches, 2005.

Niebuhr, Reinhold. *Christianity and Power Politics.* New York: Scribner's, 1940.

———. *Moral Man and Immoral Society.* New York: Scribner's, 1932.

———. "Why the Christian Church Is Not Pacifist." In *War in the Twentieth Century: Sources in Theological Ethics,* edited by Richard B. Miller, 31–36. Louisville: Westminster/John Knox, 1992.

Ninth Assembly of the World Council of Churches. "Vulnerable Populations at Risk: Statement on the Responsibility to Protect." Adopted by the Ninth Assembly, meeting in Porto Alegre, Brazil, February 14–23, 2006. https://www.oikoumene.org/en/resources/documents/assembly/2006-porto-alegre/1-statements-documents-adopted/international-affairs/report-from-the-public-issues-committee/responsibility-to-protect.

Novak, Michael. "An Argument that War against Iraq Is Just." *Origins* 32.36 (2003) 593, 595–98.

Nozick, Robert. "Moral Complications and Moral Structures." *Natural Law Forum* 13 (1968) 1–50.

Orsi, Michael P. "Expand 'Just War' Theory to Probable Cause Standard." *Social Justice Review* 94 (2003) 107.

Patterson, Margot. "Experts Say Bombing Is Risky Strategy: Terrorism—Its Roots and Realities—Resistant to Violent Response." *National Catholic Reporter* 38.2 (2001) 3–4.

Paul VI, Pope. "Gaudium et Spes." http://www.vatican.va/archive/hist_councils/ii_vatican_council/documents/vat-ii_const_19651207_gaudium-et-spes_en.html.

———. "If You Want Peace, Work for Justice." http://www.vatican.va/content/paul-vi/en/messages/peace/documents/hf_p-vi_mes_19711208_v-world-day-for-peace.html.

Peachey, Paul, ed. *Peace, Politics, and the People of God.* Philadelphia: Fortress, 1986.

Pepinsky, Harold E., and Richard Quinney, eds. *Criminology as Peacemaking.* Bloomington: Indiana University Press, 1991.

Petrowski, Thomas D. "Use-of-Force Policies and Training: A Reasoned Approach." *FBI Law Enforcement Bulletin* 71.10 (2002) 25–32.

———. "Use-of-Force Policies and Training: A Reasoned Approach (Part Two)." *FBI Law Enforcement Bulletin* 71.11 (2002) 24–34.

Phillips, Robert L., and Duane L. Cady, eds. *Humanitarian Intervention: Just War vs. Pacifism.* Lanham: Rowman & Littlefield, 1996.

Pollock-Byrne, Joycelyn. *Ethics in Crime and Justice: Dilemmas and Decisions.* Pacific Grove: Brooks, 1989.

Pontifical Council for Justice and Peace. *Compendium of the Social Doctrine of the Church.* Washington, DC: United States Conference of Catholic Bishops, 2004.

Potter, Ralph B. *War and Moral Discourse.* Richmond: John Knox, 1973.

Powers, Gerard F., et al., eds. *Peacemaking: Moral and Policy Challenges for a New World.* Washington, DC: US Catholic Conference, 1994.

"A Pre-emptive War?" *America* 187.7 (September 6, 2002) 3.

Raiser, Konrad. "Ethics of Protection." In *The Responsibility to Protect: Ethical and Theological Reflections*, edited by Semegnish Asfaw et al., 10–16. Geneva: World Council of Churches, 2005.

Ralph, Laurence. "To Protect and Serve: Global Lessons in Police Reform." *Foreign Affairs*, September/October 2020. https://www.foreignaffairs.com/articles/united-states/2020-07-30/police-reform-global-lessons?utm_medium=newsletters&utm_source=fatoday&utm_campaign=To+Protect+and+to+Serve&utm_content=20200730&utm_term=FA+Today+-+112017&fbclid=IwAR3bj3ZniDUY63-9Lg12Nwo6xnc1z2h5B-S1ok8l5NVGdtMzvnvlMToNxLE.

Ramsey, Paul. *Basic Christian Ethics*. Louisville: Westminster/John Knox, 1993.

———. *The Just War: Force and Political Responsibility*. New York: Scribner's, 1968.

———. *The Patient as Person: Explorations in Medical Ethics*. New Haven: Yale University Press, 1970.

———. *Speak Up for Just War or Pacifism: A Critique of the United Methodist Bishops' Letter "In Defense of Creation."* University Park: The Pennsylvania State University Press, 1988.

———. *War and the Christian Conscience: How Shall Modern War Be Conducted Justly?* Durham: Duke University, 1961.

Raven, Charles E. *War and the Christian*. New York: Macmillan, 1938.

Ray, Rashawn. "What Does 'Defund the Police' Mean and Does It Have Merit?" *Brookings* (blog), June 19, 2020. https://www.brookings.edu/blog/fixgov/2020/06/19/what-does-defund-the-police-mean-and-does-it-have-merit/.

Regehr, Ernie. "Comments from Ernie Regehr." In *The Responsibility to Protect: Ethical and Theological Reflections*, edited by Semegnish Asfaw et al., 105–7. Geneva: World Council of Churches, 2005.

Reiman, Jeffrey. "The Scope and Limits of Police Ethics." Review of *The Ethics of Policing*, by John Kleinig. *Criminal Justice Ethics* 16.2 (1997) 45.

———. "Social Contract and the Police Use of Deadly Force." In *Moral Issues in Police Work*, edited by Frederick A. Elliston and Michael Feldberg, 237–49. Totowa: Rowman & Allanheld, 1985.

Reiner, Robert. *The Politics of the Police*. 2nd ed. Toronto: University of Toronto, 1992.

Reith, Charles. *Police Principles and the Problem of War*. London: Oxford University Press, 1940.

Rochin v. California, 342 U.S. 165, 72 S. Ct. 205, 96 L. Ed. 183 (1952).

Rock, Judith. "Voices of My Selves." *Cross Currents* 43.3 (1993) 390–96.

Ross, William D. *Foundation of Ethics*. Oxford: Clarendon, 1939.

———. *The Right and the Good*. Oxford: Clarendon, 1930.

Roth, Kenneth. "The Law of War in the War on Terror." *Foreign Affairs* 83.1 (2004) 2–7.

Ruether, Rosemary Radford. "The Wrong Response to Terrorism." *National Catholic Reporter* 41.36 (2005) 21.

Ryan, Edward A. "The Rejection of Military Service by the Early Christians." *Theological Studies* 13.1 (1952) 1–32.

Ryan, John A., and Francis J. Boland. *Catholic Principles of Politics*. Revised edition of *The State and the Church*. New York: Macmillan, 1958.

Sasser, Charles W. *Shoot to Kill: Cops Who Have Used Deadly Force*. New York: Pocket, 1994.

Schaff, Philip, ed. *The Confessions and Letters of St. Augustine*. Vol. 1 of *Nicene and Post-Nicene Fathers, First Series*. Peabody: Hendrickson, 1994.

Scharf, Peter, and Arnold Binder. *The Badge and the Bullet: Police Use of Deadly Force*. New York: Praeger, 1983.

Scheingold, Stuart. *The Politics of Law and Order: Street Crime and Public Policy*. New York: Longman, 1984.

Schlabach, Gerald W. "Just Policing: How War Could Cease to Be a Church-Dividing Issue." In *Just Policing: Mennonite-Catholic Theological Colloquium, 2002*, edited by Ivan J. Kauffman, 19–75. Kitchener, Ontario: Pandora, 2004.

———. "Just Policing, Not War." *America* 189.1 (2003) 19–21.

———. "Just Policing: Response to the Responses." In *Just Policing: Mennonite-Catholic Theological Colloquium, 2002*, edited by Ivan J. Kauffman, 112–26. Kitchener, Ontario: Pandora, 2004.

———. *A Pilgrim People: Becoming a Catholic Peace Church*. Collegeville: Liturgical, 2019.

Schlabach, Gerald W., ed. *Just Policing, Not War: An Alternative Approach to World Violence*. Collegeville: Liturgical, 2007.

Sewell, James D., ed. *Controversial Issues in Policing*. Needham Heights: Allyn & Bacon, 1999.

Shannon, Thomas A., ed. *War or Peace? The Search for New Answers*. Maryknoll: Orbis, 1980.

Sharp, Gene. *The Politics of Nonviolent Action*. Boston: Porter Sargent, 1973.

Sherman, Lawrence W. *Ethics in Criminal Justice Education*. Hastings-on-Hudson: Hastings Center, 1982.

———. "Execution without Trial." In *Police Deviance*, edited by Tom Barker and David Carter, 188–221. Cincinnati: Anderson, 1986.

———. "Learning Police Ethics." *Criminal Law Justice Ethics* 1.1 (1982) 10–19.

Sider, Ronald J. *Non-violence: The Invincible Weapon?* Dallas: Word, 1989.

Sider, Ronald J., and Richard R. Taylor. *Nuclear Holocaust and Christian Hope: A Book for Christian Peacemakers*. Downers Grove: InterVarsity, 1982.

Simmons, Ernest J. *Leo Tolstoy*. Boston: Little, Brown, 1946.

Simon, Yves R. *Philosophy of Democratic Government*. 4th ed. Chicago: University of Chicago Press, 1993.

Sizemore, Russell. "Just Cause and New World Order: Sovereignty, Rights, and International Community." *Annual of the Society of Christian Ethics* 12 (1992) 173–99.

Skolnick, Jerome H., and James J. Fyfe. *Above the Law: Police and the Excessive Use of Force*. New York: Free Press, 1993.

Slim, Hugo. *Killing Civilians: Method, Madness, and Morality in War*. New York: Columbia University Press, 2008.

Smith, Gregory A., et al. "In US, Decline of Christianity Continues at Rapid Pace." https://www.pewforum.org/2019/10/17/in-u-s-decline-of-christianity-continues-at-rapid-pace/.

Smith, Michael Joseph. "Strengthen the United Nations and International Efforts." In *Just Peacemaking: The New Paradigm for the Ethics of Peace and War*, edited by Glen H. Stassen, 166–76. Cleveland: Pilgrim, 2008.

Sofaer, Abraham D. "On the Necessity of Pre-emption." *European Journal of International Law* 14.2 (2003) 209–26.

Spann, J. Richard, ed. *The Church and Social Responsibility*. Nashville: Abingdon-Cokesbury, 1953.

Stålsett, Sturia J. "Notes on the Just War Tradition." In *The Responsibility to Protect: Ethical and Theological Reflections*, edited by Semegnish Asfaw et al., 28–30. Geneva: World Council of Churches, 2005.

Stassen, Glen H., ed. *Just Peacemaking: The New Paradigm for the Ethics of Peace and War*. Cleveland: Pilgrim, 2008.

Steidle, Brian, and Gretchen Steidle Wallace. *The Devil Came on Horseback: Bearing Witness to the Genocide in Darfur*. New York: PublicAffairs, 2007.

Steinfels, Peter, et al. "What Kind of 'War': Four Responses." *Commonweal* 128.16 (2001) 8–10.

Stephens, Gene. "Future of Policing." In *The Past, Present, and Future of Criminal Justice*, edited by Brendan Maguire and Polly Radosh, 77–93. New York: General Hall, 1996.

Stephens, Gene, and William Doerner. "Peace in the 'Hood.'" In *Controversial Issues in Policing*, edited by James D. Sewell, 189–205. Needham Heights: Allyn & Bacon, 1999.

Surlis, Paul. "The War in Iraq." *The Furrow* 54.11 (2003) 597–608.

Swartley, Willard, and Alan Krieder. "Pacifist Christianity: The Kingdom Way." In *Pacifism and War: When Christians Disagree*, edited by Oliver R. Barclay, 38–60. Leicester: Inter-Varsity, 1984.

Teichman, Jenny. *Pacifism and the Just War: A Study in Applied Philosophy*. Oxford: Basil Blackwell, 1986.

Tennessee v. Garner, 471 U.S. 1, 105 S. Ct. 1694, 85 L. Ed. 2d 1 (1985).

Toch, Hans. *Peacekeeping: Police, Prisons, and Violence*. Lexington: Lexington, 1976.

Tolstoy, Leo. "Advice to a Draftee." In *War and the Christian Conscience: From Augustine to Martin Luther King Jr*, edited by Albert Marrin, 212–15. Chicago: Regnery, 1971.

Trollinger, William Vance, Jr. "Nonviolent Voices: Peace Churches Make a Witness." *Christian Century* 118.34 (2001) 18–22.

Uglow, Steve. *Policing Liberal Society*. Oxford: Oxford University Press, 1988.

United Methodist Council of Bishops. *In Defense of Creation: The Nuclear Crisis and a Just Peace: Foundation Document*. Nashville: Graded, 1986.

United Nations. "The United Nations and Darfur." http://www.unis.unvienna.org/pdf/UN-Darfur_fact_sheet.pdf.

United Nations General Assembly. "2005 World Summit Outcome." http://www.who.int/hiv/universalaccess2010/worldsummit.pdf.

———. "United Nations: Code of Conduct for Law Enforcement Officials." https://www.un.org/ruleoflaw/files/CODEOF~1.PDF.

United States Conference of Catholic Bishops. *Catechism of the Catholic Church*. 2nd ed. Vatican City: Libreria Editrice Vaticana, 2000.

———. *The Harvest of Peace is Sown in Justice*. Washington, DC: US Catholic Conference, 1994.

———. "Statement on Iraq." *Origins* 32.24 (2002) 407.

Wagner-Pacifici, Robin. *Discourse and Destruction: The City of Philadelphia v. MOVE*. Chicago: University of Chicago Press, 1994.

Walker, Samuel. *Popular Justice: A History of American Criminal Justice*. New York: Oxford University Press, 1980.

Wallis, Jim. "Hard Questions for Peacemakers: Theologians of Nonviolence Wrestle with How to Resist Terrorism." *Sojourners Magazine* 31.1 (2002) 29–34.

———. "Interview with Stanley Hauerwas." *Sojonet: Faith, Politics, and Culture*, November 8, 2001.

———. "Renewing the Heart of Faith." *Sojourners* 22 (February-March 1993) 10–14.

Walzer, Michael. *Arguing about War*. New Haven: Yale University Press, 2004.

———. *Just and Unjust Wars: A Moral Argument with Historical Illustrations*. 2nd ed. New York: Basic Books, 1992.

Weiderud, Peter. "Foreword." In *The Responsibility to Protect: Ethical and Theological Reflections*, edited by Semegnish Asfaw et al., vii. Geneva: World Council of Churches, 2005.

Weigel, George. "Back to Basics: Moral Reasoning and Foreign Policy 'After Containment.'" In *Peacemaking: Moral and Policy Challenges for a New World*, edited by Gerard F. Powers et al., 57–69. Washington, DC: US Catholic Conference, 1994.

———. "The Just War Case for the War." *America* 188.11 (2003) 7–10.

———. "Moral Clarity in a Time of War." *First Things* 129 (2003) 20–27.

———. *Tranquillitas Ordinis: The Present Failure and Future Promise of American Catholic Thought on War and Peace*. New York: Oxford, 1987.

———. "War, Peace, and the Christian Conscience." In *Just War and the Gulf War*, edited by James Turner Johnson and George Weigel, 45–92. Washington, DC: Ethics and Public Policy Center, 1991.

Wertheimer, Roger. "Regulating Police Use of Deadly Force." In, *Ethics, Public Policy, and Criminal Justice*, edited by Frederick Elliston and Norman Bowie, 93–109. Cambridge: Oelgeschlager, Gunn & Hain, 1982.

Wester, Franklin Eric. "Preemption and Just War: Considering the Case of Iraq." *Parameters* 34.4 (2004) 20–39.

Williamson, Roger. "Further Developing the Criteria for Intervention." In *The Responsibility to Protect: Ethical and Theological Reflections*, edited by Semegnish Asfaw et al., 59–69. Geneva: World Council of Churches, 2005.

Wink, Walter. *Engaging the Powers*. Minneapolis: Fortress, 1992.

Winright, Tobias. "Bowling Alone But Not Patrolling Alone." *FBI Law Enforcement Bulletin* 70.4 (April 2001) 11–12.

———. "The Challenge of Policing: An Analysis in Christian Social Ethics." PhD diss., University of Notre Dame, 2002.

———. "Community Policing as a Paradigm for International Relations." In *Just Policing, Not War: An Alternative Response to World Violence*, edited by Gerald W. Schlabach, 130–52. Collegeville: Liturgical, 2007.

———. "The Complementarity of Just War Theory and Pacifism." In *Religion, War and Peace: Proceedings of the Conference at Ripon College*, edited by Deborah Bluffon, 216–20. Stevens Point, WI: The Wisconsin Institute for Peace and Conflict Studies, 1996.

———. "Demilitarize the Police!" *Sojourners* 43.11 (December 2014) 10–11.

———. "Faith, Justice, and Ferguson: Insights for Religious Educators." *Religious Education* 113.3 (May-June 2018) 244–52.

———. "The Force of Law—and Ethics—Rather than the Law of Force." *St. Louis Post-Dispatch*, September 21, 2017. http://www.stltoday.com/opinion/columnists/the-force-of-law-and-ethics-rather-than-the-law/article_9db64f19-0d5c-5f24-b70b-7d387666e49a.html.

———. "From Police Officers to Peace Officers." In *The Wisdom of the Cross: Essays in Honor of John Howard Yoder*, edited by Stanley Hauerwas et al., 84–114. Grand Rapids: Eerdmans, 1999.

———. "How Long?" *US Catholic*, July 8, 2016. https://www.uscatholic.org/articles/201607/how-long-30697.

———. "I Was John Howard Yoder's Graduate Assistant: Should I Still Use His Work?" *Sojourners*, October 23, 2015. https://sojo.net/articles/i-was-john-howard-yoders-graduate-assistant-should-i-still-use-his-work.

———. "Just Cause and Preemptive Strikes in the War on Terrorism: Insights from a Just-Policing Perspective." *Journal of the Society of Christian Ethics* 26.2 (2006) 157–81.

———. "Just Policing and the Responsibility to Protect." *Ecumenical Review* 63.1 (March 2011) 84–95.

———. "Keeping the Peace." *US Catholic* 80.4 (April 2015) 18–22.

———. "A Matter of Degrees." *Sojourners* 44.6 (June 2015) 24–27.

———. "Militarized Policing: The History of the Warrior Cop." *Christian Century* 131.19 (September 17, 2014) 10–12.

———. "An Open Letter to ICE from a Former Law Enforcement Officer." *America*, June 21, 2018. https://www.americamagazine.org/politics-society/2018/06/21/open-letter-ice-former-law-enforcement-officer.

———. "Peace Cops? Christian Peacemaking and the Implications of a Global Police Force." *Sojourners* 35.3 (March 2006) 20–24.

———. "The Perpetrator as Person: Theological Reflections on the Just War Tradition and the Use of Force by Police." *Criminal Justice Ethics* 14.2 (1995) 37–56.

———. "The Police and the Community." *New York Times*, November 10, 2014. https://www.nytimes.com/2014/11/11/opinion/the-police-and-the-community.html.

———. "Pope Francis on Capital Punishment: A Closer Look." *America*, August 17, 2018. https://www.americamagazine.org/faith/2018/08/17/pope-francis-capital-punishment-closer-look.

———. "St. Louis Should Look at Examples to Change Culture of Policing." *St. Louis Post-Dispatch*, April 27, 2017. https://www.stltoday.com/opinion/mailbag/st-louis-should-look-at-examples-to-change-culture-of-policing/article_a1cfdb30-07f1-5889-82ea-3d56e301e9dd.html.

———. "Two Rival Versions of Just War Theory and the Presumption Against Harm in Policing." *Annual of the Society of Christian Ethics* 18 (1998) 221–239.

———. "Undertaking an Evaluation of War with an Entirely New Attitude? Just-War Theory & Global Policing." In *Political Ethics and International Order*, edited by Stefan Heuser and Hans G. Ulrich, 357–69. Münster: Lit-Verlag, 2007.

———. "A Vocation to Serve and Protect." *St. Louis Review: The Publication of the Archdiocese of St. Louis*, October 11, 2017. http://stlouisreview.com/article/2017-10-12/guest-columnist.

———. "The Walter Scott Shooting and Use of Police Force." *US Catholic*, April 2015. https://www.uscatholic.org/articles/201504/walter-scott-shooting-and-use-police-force-29989.

———. "What Might a Policing Approach Contribute to the Pacifist/Just-War Debate on Dealing with Terrorism?" In *Conflict and Conciliation: Faith and Politics in an Age of Global Dissonance*, edited by Jason Daverth, 39–69. Dublin: Columba, 2007.

Winright, Tobias, and M. T. Dávila. "The Police Are Highly Militarized." *Sojourners* 46.2 (February 2017) 21.

The White House. *The National Security Strategy of the United States*. Washington, DC: US Government Printing Office, 2002.

Wogaman, J. Philip. *Christian Ethics: A Historical Introduction*. Louisville: Westminster John Knox, 1993.

The Workshop for Peace Theology of "Church and Peace" and of the "International Fellowship of Reconciliation" (German Branch). "S4C—Suffer for Christ: A Response to the WCC Paper Concerning the Responsibility to Protect (R2P)." November 17, 2007, unpublished manuscript.

World Council of Churches Executive Committee. "Document no. 12." https://www. oikoumene.org/en/resources/documents/executive-committee/2009-02/statement-on-the-gaza-war.

World Synod of Catholic Bishops. "Justice in the World." https://www.cctwincities.org/wp-content/uploads/2015/10/Justicia-in-Mundo.pdf.

Yoder, John H. *Christian Attitudes to War, Peace, and Revolution: A Companion to Bainton*. Elkhart: Co-Op Bookstore, 1983.

———. *The Christian Witness to the State*. Newton: Faith and Life, 1964.

———. "Gordon Zahn Is Right." Unpublished draft of a paper, dated January 1997.

———. "How Many Ways Are There to Think Morally about War?" *The Journal of Law and Religion* 11.1 (1994) 83–108.

———. *Nevertheless: The Varieties and Shortcomings of Religious Pacifism*. Scottdale: Herald, 1976.

———. "On Not Being Ashamed of the Gospel: Particularity, Pluralism, and Validation." *Faith and Philosophy* 9.3 (1992) 285–300.

———. *The Original Revolution: Essays on Christian Pacifism*. Scottdale: Herald, 1971.

———. *The Politics of Jesus: Vicit Agnus Noster*. 2nd ed. Grand Rapids: Eerdmans, 1994.

———. *The Priestly Kingdom: Social Ethics as Gospel*. Notre Dame: University of Notre Dame, 1984.

———. "Reinhold Niebuhr and Christian Pacifism." *Mennonite Quarterly Review* 29.2 (1955) 101–17.

———. Review of *Tranquillitas Ordinis*, by George Weigel. *The Journal of Law and Religion* 6.2 (1988) 501–8.

———. "Walk and Word: The Alternatives to Methodologism." In *Theology without Foundations: Religious Practice and the Future of Theological Truth*, edited by Stanley Hauerwas et al., 77–88. Nashville: Abingdon, 1994.

———. "War as a Moral Problem in the Early Church." Unpublished paper. Dated June 4, 1991.

———. "'What Would You Do . . . ?' Revisited." Unpublished memo "for interested ethics students." December 1996.

———. *When War Is Unjust: Being Honest in Just-War Thinking*. Minneapolis: Augsburg, 1984.

———. *When War Is Unjust: Being Honest in Just-War Thinking*. Rev. ed. Maryknoll: Orbis, 1996.

Zehr, Howard. *The Christian as Victim*. Akron: Office of Criminal Justice, Mennonite Central Committee, 1982.

Zimbelman, Joel Andrew. "The Contribution of John Howard Yoder to Recent Discussions in Christian Social Ethics." *Scottish Journal of Theology* 45.3 (1992) 367–400.

Index

Made in the USA
Middletown, DE
25 August 2022

72279858R00118